The University
of Winchester

Tom Beaumont James

The University of Winchester

175 Years of Values-Driven Higher Education

Third Millennium
Publishing

Time Table. 1879.

Leet A.

Time	Monday	Tuesday	Wednesday	Thursday	Friday	Saturday
6.45 am / 7.45	1. Reading Mr Searle / 2. Reading Mr Haworth	1. Euclid Mr Haworth / 2. Method Mr Coombes	1. Grammar Mr Bright / 2. Algebra Mr Haworth	1. Algebra Mr Haworth / 2. Geography Mr Searle	1. French Mr Bright / 2. Algebra Mr Haworth	1. Euclid Mr Haworth / 2. French Mr Bright
7.45	Prayers. Breakfast. and Leisure.					
9–	1. Algebra Mr Haworth / 2. French Mr Bright	1. French Mr Bright / 2. Bacon Mr Martin	1. Arithmetic Mr Bright / 2. Euclid Mr Haworth	1. Private Study / 2. Private Study	1. Grammar Mr Bright / 2. Private Study	1. Drawing and / 2. Garden Mr Bright
10–11	1. Old Test: Mr Martin / 2. History Mr Searle	1. History Mr Searle / 2. Private Study	1. Cæsar Mr Haworth / 2. Pol: Econ: Mr Martin	1. Acoustics Mr Haworth / 2. and Private Study	1. Arithmetic Mr Bright / 2. Euclid Mr Haworth	1. Electricity Mr Searle / 2. Private Study
11–12	1. Drawing Mr Bright / 2. Private Study	1. Latin Ex: Mr Searle / 2. Acts Mr Martin	1. Electricity Mr Bright / 2. and Private Study	1. Prayer Bk: Mr Martin / 2. French Mr Bright	1. Geography Mr Searle / 2. Prayer Bk: Mr Martin	1. Examination
12–1 pm	1. Private Study / 2. Epistles Mr Martin	1. Acoustics Mr Haworth / 2. Private Study	1. New Test: Mr Martin / 2. Music/Theory Mr Searle	1. French Mr Bright / 2. Trigonometry Mr Haworth	1. Latin Ex: Mr Searle / 2. Shakespeare Mr Martin	1. Drill
1–4	Dinner and Leisure					
4–5	1. / 2. Lessons	1. Mensuration / 2. Mensuration Mr Haworth	*Holiday*	1. Drawing Mr Bright / 2. Private Study	1. Cæsar Mr Haworth / 2. Physiography Mr Searle	*Holiday*
5–6	1. Cæsar Mr Bright / 2. Private Study	1. Music Mr Searle / 2. Physiography Mr Bright		1. Arithmetic Mr Bright / 2. Arithmetic Mr Bright	1. Method Mr Coombes / 2. Vocal Music Mr Searle	
6–7	Tea and Leisure					
7.15 / 8 / 9.20	1. / 2. Private		Study.			1. Composition Mr Searle / 2. Composition Mr Bright / 1. Vocal Music Mr Searle / 2. Vocal Music Mr Searle

Time devoted to each Subject per Week.

First Year.

Reading – 1 hour.
Algebra – 3 hours.
Euclid – 3 hours.

Drawing – 2 hours.
Method – 1 hour.
Electricity – 2 hours.

New Test. – 1 hour.
Prayer Book – 1 hour.
Composition – 1 hour.

Second Year.

Reading – 1 hour.
Algebra – 2 hours.
Euclid – 1 hour.

Drawing – 3 hours.
Method – 1 hour.
Electricity – 2 hours.

Corinthians – 1 hour.
Acts – 1 hour.
Prayer Bk – 1 hour.

Above: Timetable as Principal Martin arrived in 1879.
Note his and Mr Searle's teaching contributions.

Previous pages: University Centre from the north-west.

First published in Great Britain in 2015 by Third Millennium
Publishing, an imprint of Profile Books Ltd

3 Holford Yard
Bevin Way
London WC1X 9HD
United Kingdom
www.tmiltd.com

A CIP catalogue record for this book is available
from The British Library.

ISBN (*hardback*): 978 1 908990 37 2
ISBN (*paperback*): 978 1 908990 38 9

Editor and project manager: Neil Titman
Design: Matthew Wilson and Susan Pugsley
Production: Debbie Wayment
Picture research: Patrick Taylor
Proofreading: Margaret Histed
Indexing: Neil Burkey

Reprographics by Tag Publishing, London
Printed by DZS Grafik on behalf of Latitude Press
on acid-free paper from sustainable forestry

THE UNIVERSITY OF
WINCHESTER

Contents

King Alfred in stained glass, formerly in St Peter's Church, Southampton, now at Winchester.

Foreword

The University of Winchester is an institution with a long and distinguished history. As we reach our 175th year this is a time to pause and reflect, to celebrate our successes, to look forward to the future, and to affirm the constants running through our story. One of these constants is our commitment to our history, our heritage and our values, which is as strong now as it was in 1840. We celebrate our Christian foundation, welcoming people of all faiths and none. Together we aim to explore the mystery of life and to grow in wisdom and love. Our foundation and our values among other things, drive our commitment to widening participation in Higher Education, our ties to our local and global communities, and our passion for student engagement.

This book is a fascinating account of our history – with all its highs and lows – and it is also a tribute to the generations of people, staff, students and supporters who have made the University the unique place it is today.

Today we have a bright future. We are renowned for our specialisation in the arts, humanities and social sciences and our values-led approach to all that we undertake. We look forward to the coming years with confidence.

Professor Joy Carter DL, Vice-Chancellor

Above: Interior of the Chapel, *c.*1913.

Right: University Centre.

Left: The Stripe, 2015.

Below: One of many carved heads decorating the Chapel, built in 1881.

Author's Note

This work was commissioned by Vice-Chancellor Professor Joy Carter DL. Its text and illustrations celebrate 175 years of endeavour in Higher Education in Winchester. The book recalls the Diocesan Training School founded in 1840 to train male school teachers for the dioceses of Winchester and Salisbury and its development as King Alfred's College from 1928. Its University Title was endorsed by the Privy Council in 2005, with Research Degree Awarding Powers from August 2008. Underlying the narrative of the individual institution the swirling tides of changing government policy, always the key game-changers, fashioned the community of staff and students that survives today.

Martial Rose's *A History of King Alfred's College, Winchester 1840–1980* (1981) and his *1980–1990 King Alfred's College, Winchester: A Decade of Change* (1990) remain fundamental to understanding the origins and development of the institution, its curriculum and the government policies that so often led to changes in direction and focus. Having led the institution from a mono-technic teacher-training institution into the world of diversified Higher Education, his major work was completed within a decade of the start of course diversification.

This work is an individual perspective on the development of the institution. After a visual essay on the University today and discussion of the circumstances that led to the foundation in 1840 and the first two decades, the central material star of the book appears: the Gothic 'Main Building' of 1862. While students and staff of different regimes did not all know one another, all have known that great building at different times, and it engenders much affection. The addition of a separate chapel in 1881 provided a second focus on the site. Since 1919 the Chapel also served as a war memorial.

What follows is undoubtedly an 'insider' history. Treatment of the built environment as a theme of continuity – encapsulating the academic, domestic, learning and sporting environment for staff and students – necessarily starts with decision-making at the top of the institution, coupled with reaction to intellectual, governmental and social change. That the institution in Winchester has survived, where many did not, is remarkable in itself. But this is not history from below, although we meet staff and students, examiners and visitors, along the way.

This account has been written with Gary McCulloch's criticisms of 'house histories' in *Researching Education from the Inside* (2008) in mind. McCulloch insists they must avoid focusing on growth and successes in an account viewed from the top down, simply eulogising the central institution as a 'symbol of growth and progress, finally dissolving into a mass of lists and statistics', 'uncritical accounts devoid of candour'. While the perspective chosen here does not answer all of McCulloch's criticisms, and certainly shows 'growth and progress', it does not, I hope, lack candour. In the pages that follow, alongside successes we encounter bankruptcy, bullying, death, dismissal, various kinds of failure, hierarchies and a great deal of struggle – even a Vice-Principal resorting to shooting at students! It is to be hoped that this account will prove a 'house' history that is not mere panegyric.

Tom James, 1981.

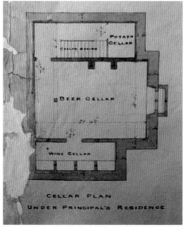

Census return — Principal Martin's household, 1881.

Right: Principal Martin's household, 1881.

Below: Dancing in The Vault.

Below right: The design for the Principal's wine and beer cellars, c.1860.

It is further hoped that this account will commend itself not only to alumni (staff and students), but also to current and future staff and students at Winchester. It may also help the people of the city to understand the cuckoo in the nest that has come to the fore in Winchester – what Steve Brine, the current MP for Winchester, in his maiden speech in Parliament in June 2010 called 'the self-confident University of Winchester'. Few in Winchester, even if they knew of the existence of King Alfred's, ever grasped what a 'College of Higher Education' was or did. Among others who may find this text of value are those who have an interest in the development of Higher Education, especially in the turbulent last half-century, and those with an interest in the development of government policy and the history of education since the mid-nineteenth century.

The sources used in this account include materials on aspects of the development of the institution not previously seen by Martial Rose and earlier writers. Some, such as the nineteenth- and early twentieth-century census returns, provide useful snapshots of the College community between 1841 and 1911. Rose's use of the returns to the National Society for Promoting the Education of the Poor in the Principles of the Established Church in England and Wales has rendered it unnecessary to revisit them; however, the materials in the College archive, deposited since 1991 at the Hampshire Archives and Local Studies, have been extensively re-examined. Materials from the University not found in the Hampshire Archives, such as the Principals' reports to the governors from 1948 to 1991, have proved most useful, as have more recent archival materials stored in the basement of the Main Building, the former Principals' wine and beer cellars. For the most recent period oral testimony from specially commissioned conversations and interviews with current and former staff and supporters of the institution have enlivened the written sources.

Above all, alumni of all varieties recall with affection the fun, jollity and (not entirely uninterrupted) pleasure during their associations with Winchester.

Timeline from 1840

1840
Diocesan Training College opens in St Swithun Street 'under the roof' of Principal David Waugh for male teachers in Winchester and Salisbury dioceses

1874
Foundation of the Re-union Club

1846
Principal John Smith appointed

1859–62
West Hill building designed and built for 56 students

1840 · · · · · · 1850 · · · · · · 1860 · · · · · · 1870

1841
Salisbury College opens for schoolmistresses

1847–58
College at Wolvesey Palace

1870
'Forster'
Education Act

1838
Church of England Training Colleges planned to train teachers for the Church's National Schools

1875
College Volunteer battalion formed. Included cyclists

1881
First Chapel built

Refoundation of
Re-union Club

1895
Hardy's *Jude the Obscure*
highlights students from
Winchester and Salisbury
training colleges

1901
Census: 81 men

King Alfred
statue erected in
Winchester

1902
The Balfour Act empowered
LEAs to support training

1904
Foundation of College
masonic lodge

1880   1890   1900   1910

1880
Elementary Education Act makes
School attendance compulsory

1912–33
Principal Ernest
Wainwright

1879–1912
Principal Henry Martin

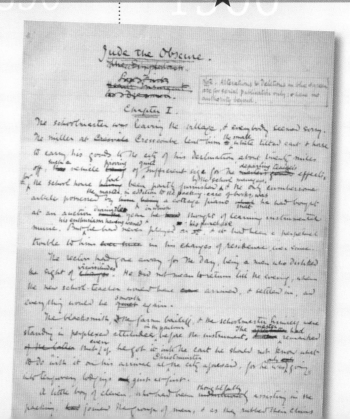

1940
Centenary expedition from
Culham by evacuees to King
Alfred statue in Wantage

1919
Reopened for 72 students,
electric lighting installed.
Winton Memorial in
Chapel established

1926
Winchester students work
at Southampton docks

1935
Bar End fields
purchased

1914
104 students at
summer camp on
Salisbury Plain.
College closes

*c.*1925
Proposed expansion to
200: Nonconformists and
Roman Catholics admitted

*c.*1929
Linked with Bristol University
in regional grouping

1939–45
Second World War

1926
General strike

1928
King Alfred's
Diocesan Training
College

1939
Within 9 months
College closes

1927
Chapel extended, followed by
additional glazing schemes

1933–45
Principal R. C. White.
Suggests mixed 'rural' college

1914
First World War

1962
New Dining Room
finished in January

Alwyn Hall opens

1964–5
New Chapel and Herbert
Jarman science and craft
buildings opened. Largest
Church of England mixed
college at 566 students

1946–58
William Dickinson, first layman
Principal. Reopens 'desolate'
college. Austerity. Values
communal dining and chapel

1960s
Students from pre-1900
attend reunions

1967–84
Principal Martial
Rose: mono-
technic becomes
'diversified'

1944
McNair Report addressed regionalisation
of training and suggested every university
should have an Institute of Education

1958–67
Principal John Stripe
presides over expansion in
students and facilities

1968
Student Union Building
opened. Establishment of the
'Basingtoke Outpost'

Intelligence Corps, ATS women use the buildings

1969
John Stripe
Theatre opened

Women exceed
men numerically

1960
First women governors,
staff and students

St Elizabeth's residence
opened for women

Course extended from two
years to three

1962–3
Old Dining Hall and kitchen
converted to Libraries

New pavilion at Bar End

1982
Link with Shoei brings
20 Japanese women
and building finance

1974
Approach to Council for
Academic Awards validation

1976
First BA
degrees started

1978
New Library opened

First CNAA graduation

1970   1980

1975
Total students exceeds 1,000

1977
'Basingstoke Outpost' closes

1979
First cathedral graduation (1982 seen here)

1994
West Downs purchased

1991
Christopher Ball Report
'Seeking the Common Good'

1983
Staff student ratio 1:10

1996
Governors no
longer chaired
by the Bishop
of Winchester.
Research
Assessment
Exercise: a new
income stream

1992
*Further and Higher
Education Act*

*Polytechnics become
universities*

Colleges left out

1990
Sesquicentenary: celebrations of 150 years

New Articles of Government replaced
Staff Conference and College Council with
Academic Board

1984
Principal John
Cranmer, to 1992

1990

1988
*Education Reform
Act. National
Curriculum
introduced.
Brought more
students into HE*

1990
*Student loans
introduced: numbers
burgeoned*

1993
'A View of the Next
Five Years' paper
by John Dickinson:
local press reports
University aspirations

1987
*'Marginal fees' open
the door to expansion*

1992
John Dickinson Principal to 2000

Strategic Plan produced by Vice-
Principal Drey: looked to the future

CNAA abolished

Validation by
Southampton University

1995
Governors received
plan for University
title in 2005

1997
1960s Chapel houses a
computer suite centre

Total students exceed 5,000

1881 Chapel reopened

1996
'University for Winchester'
campaign grows, Lord
Lieutenant joins

2000
Library extension opened

Paul Light Principal, then
Vice-Chancellor to 2006

Staff student ratio 1:18

2005
Privy Council sealed
University of Winchester
Vice-Chancellor Joy
Carter appointed

2000

1998
Official opening of West
Downs Student Village by
Duke of Gloucester

2003–11
Chute House outpost
opened in Basingstoke

2001
Refurbished West Downs Arts Centre
opened by Lord Puttnam

1997
Quality Assessment Agency
established overseeing 87
universities and 47 other HEIs

Student grants turned to loans.
50% participation in Higher
Education proposed

2004
University College
Winchester under Paul Light

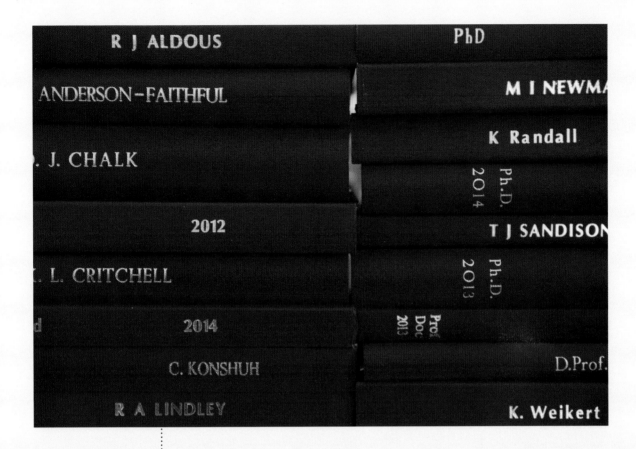

2008
Research Degree Awarding Powers
bring full university status

2012–13
Completion of St
Alphege teaching and
Burma Road student
accommodation

2007
University Centre and Sports
Stadium at Bar End opened

2011
Winchester Business School
opened at West Downs

2015
University celebrates 175 years of Higher Education.
Honorary graduation for former teaching certificate
students attracts 600 graduands, some from the 1930s. Over
7,000 students, 175 doctoral and MPhil completions

2006
The Stripe completed

Prologue: The Evolving University

The institution has evolved dramatically since its foundation in 1840 as a Christian, Anglican diocesan college for the training of male teachers, but one thing remains constant: the provision of high-quality, values-driven Higher Education. The University of Winchester was delivered into existence by Privy Council endorsement on 30 June 2005, following the achievement of Taught Degree Awarding Powers in 2004.

For the last decade Winchester has been led by Vice-Chancellor Professor Joy Carter, appointed in November 2005. Professor Carter brought with her a number of key passions: teaching quality, research and knowledge exchange, continuous improvement, volunteering within a local and international framework, sustainable development and ethical catering, internationalisation and widening participation to name but a few. She founded the Winchester Business School. Over and above all these key elements lies an absolute commitment to the Christian Foundation and an inclusive institution with a strong and distinct ethos.

Winchester's mission is clear: 'To educate, to advance knowledge and to serve the common good.' Likewise the University's foundation values encapsulate intellectual freedom, social justice, diversity, spirituality and creativity.

WINCHESTER VALUES ....

We value freedom, justice, truth, human rights and collective effort for the common good. The plans and actions of the University of Winchester are founded on these ideals together with the following values:

Intellectual freedom – Intellectual freedom and its appropriate expression are at the heart of our business.

Social justice – We seek to embody social justice and develop our students as effective and fulfilled global citizens. They will be prepared to challenge the status quo and will have the strength to stand up for what they believe to be true.

Diversity – Diversity enriches our community, learning experience and global outlook.

Spirituality – The University celebrates its Christian foundation, and welcomes people of all faiths and none. Together, we aim to explore the mystery of life and to grow in wisdom and love.

Individuals matter – The wellbeing of individuals is important, as are their opinions and views.

Creativity – Permeability, agility and imagination are central to our thinking: we endeavour to act as a crucible for the generation and exchange of knowledge.

Gay Pride march, February 2015.

The University of Winchester campus with student accommodation, the King Alfred site, Queens Road, Burma Road and West Downs.

While there has been this focus on mission and values over the last decade and during Professor Carter's stewardship, there have also been significant, practical building programmes in all areas of the University's main foci – accommodation for students, teaching accommodation and sporting facilities. Student-centred building developments have included the extension to the University's prime auditorium, The Stripe (2005), used as the major lecture hall for teaching and for public lectures, and for conferences such as University of Winchester Writers' Festival. On 17 September 2007 the University Centre was completed (£9 million), housing facilities from the Learning Café and University Reception and the Boardroom on the top floor, through bars and the Food Hall – the major catering provision – to the basement Vault, buried deep in the chalk of the hillside, for students' entertainments and dancing. Student Services was moved to the Main Building in 2009 into a space known as The Zone which occupies the original 1862 teaching areas, latterly successively student and staff common rooms, and which open on to the south-facing, sunny Terrace.

Student accommodation burgeoned to add to what had been created on the West Downs area of the campus, where a student village was built in the 1990s. Two major developments have occurred: the Queens Road Student village (2010) replaced former hospital nurses' accommodation and contains 400 study bedrooms with spectacular views down the Itchen Valley, beyond which the Isle of Wight may be glimpsed to the south. On the Burma Road, north of the 1862 building, also on former hospital land, a further series of hostel 'pavilions' were completed in 2012– 13, providing a further 500 rooms including dedicated space for disabled students and a state-of-the-art gymnasium. Meanwhile, sporting facilities were improved with the transformation of the Bar End playing field to all-weather sports facilities and with a new sports pavilion, replacing the 1960s building where the College had instituted its first bar facility in 1963.

For the first time in a generation teaching and learning areas were adapted, created and enhanced by major works, especially the St Alphege building (£9.2 million), completed in 2012 on the site of the former pre-war Great Hall and Gymnasium. This is

Right: The Writers' Festival in The Stripe.

Below: University Centre from Sparkford Road.

Bottom: University Centre Terrace Bar.

These building projects have been supported by a careful programme of landscaping and by the development of the long-running campus sculptural displays to improve the environment for all.

The University campus has developed in a logical and practical fashion. The original King Alfred's site – incorporating the first purpose-built college structure, the venerable Main Building – is now linked by residential accommodation to adjacent West Downs, developed from the mid-1990s. At the King Alfred's site are also found the Chapel (1881), and more recent buildings of which the main survivor of those from between the wars is St Grimbald's Court (1932), the former Exam Hall and Gymnasium buildings of the late 1930s having been demolished recently. Post-war expansion reflected in buildings began c.1960, when women were admitted and overall numbers started to rise, a trend ever since. A new Dining Room (1961–2) was a striking neo-Gothic structure. In the same year new residences were opened: a separate residence for the women students, St Elizabeth's Hall, and new accommodation for men at Alwyn Hall.

In 1964 a new chapel was completed as well as the Science and Craft Block (later named after Herbert Jarman, who served 1911–51, latterly as Vice-Principal), and in the following year Medecroft, a grand, part-panelled 1868 suburban villa built with an orangery to the south-east of the King Alfred's Campus across Sparkford Road, was purchased as a practical Art Department to include pottery and textile work, as well as painting and sculpture instruction for intending teachers.

The Tom Atkinson Building and adjoining Wessex Closed Circuit Television Centre both opened in 1968. In the

a thoroughly green creation, employing by coincidence, and in modern electronic form, a ventilation system that echoes the ground-breaking system of stale air (!) extraction from teaching areas in the Victorian Main Building.

Specialist teaching areas have been enhanced, including the provision of major Performing Arts accommodation in 2010 (£2.4 million), in addition to the 'Black Box' – a flexible-space, fully-equipped small performance and teaching facility created in 2003. Extended accommodation for the archaeology department was provided in 2011. Specialist work in this department led to the identification of skeletal fragments arguably of King Alfred (d. 899) found in a ruined abbey in the city and reported in January 2014 (see p37). An extension was added to the Centre for Sport in 2011. Nor were staff forgotten, with a new Staff Common Room as part of the Atrium development opened Christmas 2013, in an area originally part of the 1862 Exercising Court. Meanwhile adaptations such as the conversion of the former Student Union building to a teaching area were begun in 2010, and a third floor added in 2013 at a total cost of just under £1 million.

Performing Arts Studios.

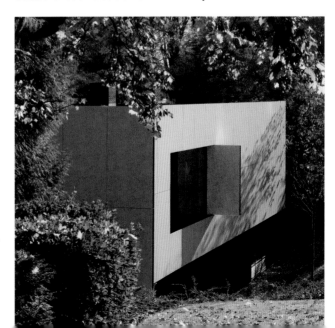

Below: West Downs and the Student Village on former playing fields.

Bottom: University Library, extended 2000.

same year, the year of international student revolution and unrest, the new King Alfred's Student Union building (now St Edburga's), on a terrace below the Main Building, was provided with impeccable timing should the students have felt rebellious or under-valued in that turbulent era. The John Stripe Theatre opened in October 1969, a stone's throw away from the SU. On-site accommodation was enhanced by the purchase of various large houses in the city, in Christchurch Road, adjacent to the King Alfred campus, just across the railway towards the city, and on St Giles's Hill, across Winchester to the east and elsewhere. These were the last major projects in the mono-technic era.

As the institution diversified into arts degrees in the mid-1970s, new facilities on, and associated with, the King Alfred's campus included student accommodation at Chilbolton Court (from 1976, now largely demolished) and a new Library (1978) with an ambitious roof garden. A new Sports Hall appeared west of the Dytche, below the Main Building, from 1971 to 1974, with squash courts added in 1976. A joint venture with the Shoei College of Tokyo led to the arrival of 20 young Japanese women in 1982 *(see pp124–5)*, when accommodation was provided for them on the Chilbolton Court site and an upper floor on the 1976 Medecroft Opportunity Centre. The pre-war Gymnasium remained of value as an examination hall, but new facilities were needed beyond the Sports Hall, and in 1984 a new Gymnasium and Human Movement Studio were opened. Space on the campus was limited: In the late 1950s Principal Dickinson estimated no more than 250 students could effectively be taught on-site. In the early 1980s there were already four times that number, and further growth was envisaged. The 1960s Herbert Jarman and Tom Atkinson buildings had shown that the way forward was upwards into multi-storey buildings. Thus in 1984 another multi-storey building appeared over the TV studio, to house Computing, Geography and the Diploma in Environmental Studies. Three years on, a Design and Technology building was created behind the Herbert Jarman, 'changing the College's skyline', as Principal Cranmer put it.

By the early 1990s the long-hoped-for expansion in numbers was achieved by genuinely creative management thinking, and a student body of around 1,000 in the early 1980s had reached nearly 4,500 by 1995. To meet this demand a bold purchase was made, that of the redundant preparatory school building at West

Downs, just beyond the hospital to the west of King Alfred's. This brought 12.5 acres of land, the former gardens and playing fields, on which student accommodation could be built. Between 1996 and the opening by the Duke of Gloucester in 1998, an award-winning student village was created for some 450 students. With this consolidation of accommodation, the focus shifted

Above: West Downs, flying the University flag.

Below: Interior of The Stripe after refurbishment.

to extending the learning facilities, with a new Library in 2000, another startling and award-winning creation.

In the new millennium growth continued, surpassing 5,000 students in 2000. The all-male college of the 1950s had become a community of some 4,000 women and 1,200 men. The focus turned to an idea floated in the mid-1990s that Winchester should seek to be a university by 2005, an apparently impossible dream at the time. Arriving in 2000, Principal Light poured cold water on any such scheme, concentrating instead on gaining independent Taught Degree Awarding Powers, which were achieved in 2004, with the title University College Winchester accorded in the same year. On 30 June of the following year the Privy Council endorsed Winchester as a university in its own right. Now a Vice-Chancellor, Professor Light retired in 2005.

For 175 years there has been a centre of Higher Education in Winchester: the Diocesan Training School (1840), King Alfred's Diocesan Training College (1928), King Alfred's College of Higher Education (1976) and the University of Winchester from 2005. From the panorama provided by this visual snapshot, we will now take a closer look at the origins of the institution.

Carved head of a king from the main building.

Origins 1840–1914

THE DIOCESAN TRAINING SCHOOL: CONTEXT AND FOUNDATION

The Diocesan Training School for Anglican schoolmasters was opened by the Diocese of Winchester on 15 August 1840, making it one of the oldest institutions of Higher Education in the country. In the neighbouring Diocese of Salisbury a similar training school, for schoolmistresses, opened the following year, planned like Winchester to supply both dioceses. Fictionalised early students from both these colleges appear in Thomas Hardy's *Jude the Obscure*. Other institutions that began at that time included St John's,

Battersea, the first training college in London; Chester in the north; and Chichester in Sussex, driven forward by Bishop Otter, who had been the first Principal of the Anglican King's College London, which had opened in 1831 offering university education. A further ten Anglican training colleges were founded between 1841 and 1962, when St Martin's, Lancaster, was instigated and opened soon afterwards in a former barracks of the King's Own Royal Regiment.

Medieval collegiate universities such as Oxford, Cambridge and St Andrews and the Tudor foundation of Trinity College, Dublin (1592), which was to furnish two of the first three Principals at Winchester, were the

SOUTH ELEVATION

models for the Winchester Training School, both in their religious foundation and their collegiate structure. Provincial English university colleges came later, for example Bristol (1876), Reading (1892) and Southampton (1902). It has been argued that training colleges developed in very different ways from universities. However, what is clear in the history of this college is that there was always a strong academic underpinning of the training, with a special emphasis on English and History, which have remained key elements of the curriculum ever since. From the earliest days and throughout its association with teacher training, Mathematics was also fundamental. For much of its existence until the Second World War students at Winchester included those studying for

Right: Charles Sumner, Bishop of Winchester 1827–69.

Below: Rev. John Keble (1792–1866), Vicar of Hursley, Professor of Poetry at Oxford and an early examiner in English at the Training School.

degrees, a tradition revived around 1970 with the emergence of teaching as a graduate profession, and from 1976 with the diversified degree courses in the arts and in nursing, then later business, law, psychology and sport. With this widening of degree work the mono-technic past was abandoned.

The period in the late 1830s, when the Winchester Diocesan Board of Education was established and settled upon providing a training school for schoolmasters, was the era of the Oxford Movement and of the emergence of muscular Christianity, with its twin foci of a strong body and an educated mind. Indeed, among the sponsors of the original institutions was the inspirational John Keble, Vicar of Hursley, near Winchester and inaugurator of the Tractarians. This was also the period of the re-emergence of Roman Catholicism, following the Emancipation Act of 1829, while the Church of England was being revitalised by bishops such as Charles Sumner (Bishop of Winchester 1827–69). Sumner, a favourite of George IV and an enthusiast for education, was a prime mover in the foundation of the Training School.

Although some teacher training in Winchester under the monitorial system in the early nineteenth century preceded the founding of the Diocesan Training School, it was the establishment of the Diocesan Board of Education by Bishop Sumner in 1838, amid fears about the quality of teacher training and the outreach

of the teaching profession at that time, that led to the founding of the Diocesan Training School. The establishment of the Board of the great and the good in the Winchester Diocese shows significant intent. The Diocesan Board of Education was a formidable body, drawing for its permanent members on worthies from both Hampshire and Surrey, the core of the diocese, stretching from Hampshire north-east to the south bank of the Thames in London and southwards across the Isle of Wight to include the Channel Islands. Not only the two counties (lords lieutenant, high sheriffs, nobles, privy councillors, etc), but also the city of Winchester (mayor, recorder, 'wardens, fellows and masters of Winchester College', including the Headmaster as Treasurer) were strongly represented. The diocese and its supporters clearly took this venture to their hearts. The elected members comprised a baronet, a naval captain, six armigerous lay people (including W. C. Yonge, father of Charlotte Yonge who wrote so charmingly, in thin disguise, about the Winchester Diocese), and four clergy including Samuel Wilberforce and the exceptional talent of Keble. The support of such an august body ensured that the institution got off to a sound start. Unlike Chester or Chichester, for example, no grand buildings were planned at the outset.

The Chichester Training College, unlike Winchester, began in the 1840s with purpose-built accommodation.

Left: William of Wykeham, Bishop of Winchester 1367–1404, founder of New College, Oxford, and Winchester College which has supported the Training College and its successors staunchly throughout 175 years.

Below: The Winchester Training School began in Principal Waugh's household in St Swithun Street where, as prescribed, they 'boarded and lodged' under the Principal's roof.

The original location in Winchester was at 26/27 St Swithun Street, a grand terraced house only a short walk south-west of the cathedral that was the bishop's residence at Wolvesey and Winchester College, a school founded by Bishop Wykeham. Thus the University at Winchester, in all its manifestations, has always been closely allied to the bishops of Winchester who, since Wine, the first bishop, was appointed c.660, have watched over spiritual life and championed many developments in the city, including the economy and educational provision. Bishop Wykeham founded Winchester College in 1382 after having founded New College, Oxford, in 1379. Bishop Waynflete, who was Headmaster of Winchester College c.1440, was another founder of a school, and also Magdalen College, Oxford, in the fifteenth century. He was the only schoolmaster to become Chancellor (first minister) of England. Not surprisingly, these foundations had many influences on the Diocesan Training School, the new educational institution

opened by their successor, Bishop Sumner, in 1840. Bishops chaired the Governing Body from the early days of the nineteenth century until 1996, when the incoming bishop declined the chair but remained a governor. The Governing Body, formerly packed with clergy, diocesan nominees and representatives of Winchester College, was changing as the new structures and responsibilities emerged. The chair passed to the Rev. Jim Hale and then to Daniel Hodson *(see p169)*. A third of the governors are currently nominated by the diocese.

THE FIRST INTAKE

In the 1841 census we have our first snapshot of the resident community at St Swithun Street, taken shortly after the Training School had opened under the leadership of the Rev. David Waugh. The rules for the institution at its foundation decreed

Below: George Monk, recommended by his parish priest at nearby Wonston, was the first student entered in the Register, in August 1840.

Bottom: Stratton Park, at East Stratton, home of Sir Thomas Baring (1772–1848) of the banking family, a philanthropist and magistrate who took an interest in the education of his estate workers.

| Name— *George Monk (1.)* | REGISTER No. *1.* |
| | Period of Admission. *Aug.ᵗ 20.ᵗᵒ 1840* |

Age.

Former Occupation.

Station in Life, and Residence of Parents or Friends. — *Wonston.*

By whom recommended, and on what terms admitted. — *Rev.ᵈ Alex.ʳ Dallas — Exhibitioner*

What Schools previously attended, and for what periods. — *Attended the Wonston National School for*

State of Acquirement on Admission. — *Possessed a tolerable acquaintance with Arithmetic*

that the students should 'board and lodge' in the Principal's house, a rule which more or less pertained under different roofs and circumstances until the purchase in the 1920s of a separate residence, Holm Lodge, to which the Principal migrated (and where students also lodged). In 1841 Waugh was resident in St Swithun Street with his wife Letitia (both were aged 30) and their three children all under five, and all except the youngest, who was less than a year old and born in Winchester, born in Ireland. The choice of a top scholar from Trinity College, Dublin, with its Protestant ethos, provides an insight into Sumner's wish to promote the Church of England with vigour. Waugh's experience in largely Catholic Ireland might, to Sumner's mind, have added impetus to Anglican teaching during Catholic and nonconformist resurgence in England. There were also Irish servants, notably Patience Oxley, who was still there in 1851.

Occupations of these early students' fathers ranged from butcher, carpenter and labourer to farmer, schoolmaster and smith. The students themselves gave a variety of previous occupations including cabinet-maker, coach-builder, linen draper and shepherd. The fourth student to be enrolled was Henry Potter. He came recommended by Sir Thomas Baring of the family bank, a generous benefactor of the foundation

and a major Hampshire landowner. Potter's father was the schoolmaster at Baring's Estate School at East Stratton, where Henry had been a student 'for many years'. The Barings' estates had been a focus of the notorious Swing Riots of 1830, to which the Potters would have been witnesses: Henry Cooke had been sentenced to death for a hammer attack on Bingham Baring during the riots. The catchment of the Winchester

Diocese was largely rural, and Thomas Baring was perhaps atypical in promoting education among his tenantry and workers. Many Hampshire (and other) landowners feared an educated proletariat.

In 1841 there were ten 'pupils' in the Training School, one aged 13, five aged 15, the eldest (another native of Ireland) aged 25. Fewer than half were born in Hampshire, but as the census only required information as to whether an individual was born in Hampshire or not, others may also have come from the diocese as well as from the Salisbury Diocese. In the original plan the trainee teachers were provided with the choristers from the cathedral and the quiristers from Winchester College on whom to practise their skills. These arrangements did not survive the first five years. The complexities of arranging teaching of the trainees and the choir boys' requirements to both attend

services and practise proved too complex to organise. Among those present in 1841 was the 15-year-old William Whiting, who had just arrived on 25 March from his Clapham home. He was recommended by the Rev. William Dealtry, Vicar of Holy Trinity, Clapham Common and a leader of the Clapham sect, Anglican evangelicals who lived round Clapham Common in the London part of the Winchester Diocese. Dealtry was also a distinguished mathematician and had been appointed a prebendary of Winchester Cathedral in 1830. These Clapham people exemplify the links of the evangelical Bishop Sumner's Winchester Diocese and its Training School with the strong evangelical tradition of the Clapham sect in the diocese. Among the shared attributes of the evangelicals was their high regard for the authority of the Bible, and so they were natural supporters of education and the development of literacy based around Bible-reading. Whiting, whose accomplishments listed on admission included 'an excellent mathematician', was employed in 1843 at age 17 to be master of the Winchester College quiristers, when they removed in that year to 5, College Street. He remained in that post for 36 years, during which time he became a noted hymn-writer, remembered especially for the text of 'Eternal Father, Strong to Save', which became very popular with seafarers. When this lame, classical schoolmaster and poet died on 3 May 1878 he was buried on the steep south-facing slope of the West Hill cemetery, opposite the Training College. Those at the graveside, and many others of his acquaintance, lamented his passing as 'a catastrophe' for the Quiristers' School classical education.

A CHANGE OF PRINCIPAL

Principal Waugh, already unwell in 1845, died the following year still in his mid-30s, one historian claiming 'he often lectured fourteen hours *per diem*, which contributed to his untimely demise'. Within a month he was succeeded by the Rev. John Smith MA of Magdalen College, Oxford, 'a gentleman long engaged in tuition' in his early 30s and a 'fanatical scientist' – although he also

How and where disposed of.   If as Schoolmaster or Assistant.   Amount of Salary obtained.

Left: Wolvesey Palace, home of
The Training College 1847–58.

Below: St John's Training College,
Battersea, housed in a non-Gothic
building. From a lithograph by
E. H. Hurdle. *c.* 1845.

Bottom: Magdalen College,
Oxford, Principal Smith's
alma mater.

taught all the arts subjects from classical languages and history
to scripture and Shakespeare. The appellation 'gentleman' was
a characteristic of Magdalen men at that time. Among the first
duties for John Smith, a bachelor, was to move the institution
from St Swithun Street, where the lease had come to an end, to
Wolvesey, the bishop's Winchester residence. This was facilitated
by Bishop Sumner, who made his Wolvesey Palace in Winchester
available in 1847 for this 'missionary' enterprise in schools. The
young teachers were expected to evangelise the children – for
boosting education on Anglican principles was part of the Church
of England's mission. The existence at Wolvesey of a chapel
would have been a bonus for Principal Smith, with his previous
experience of an Oxford college. Thus Sumner put the 'Palace of
Wolvesey at the disposal of the Board free of rates and taxes for
the Training School … for the term of his episcopacy'. The bishop,
like his predecessors and his successors down to the division of
the diocese in 1927, did not live in Winchester. As his immediate
predecessors had done, Sumner lived in style at Farnham Castle
in Surrey. Wolvesey had been recreated by Bishop Morley after
1662, so was getting on for 200 years old by the mid-nineteenth
century. The Baroque palace alongside the ruins of the bishops'
huge medieval palace was very dilapidated.

   To gain perspective for his fledgling institution, Smith visited
both Battersea and St Mark's colleges in London to view two
different visions of training. Prompting these visits there is much
in the early records of the Diocesan Board about the necessity to
provide education for the children of the middle classes which,
it was noted with regret, had become the territory of dissenters

Rev. George Moberly, Headmaster of Winchester College 1835–66, Treasurer to the Diocesan Board of Education when the Training School was founded, an examiner and good neighbour when the students were billeted at Wolvesey.

was founded in 1458 by Bishop Waynflete of Winchester and remained under the eye of successive bishops of Winchester as 'Visitors'. The purpose of Waynflete's College was to promote religion and provide education, and for the furtherance of learning, although academic research was a low priority until the twentieth century. These fundamentals ebbed and flowed: when Edward Gibbon was there *c.*1750 the fellows had 'absolved their consciences' from 'the toil of reading, or thinking, or writing'. Reform, looming since 1837, did not come until after Smith's time, in 1854, with Magdalen long remaining 'monastic', maintaining a strong clerical tradition of worshipping and dining together. It was these characteristics that Smith brought south with him to Winchester, and which became for a century the foundation principles of successive institutions that developed from the Diocesan Training School. This is not at all surprising, as there were virtually no other models to follow. One of these rare models was just across the road: Winchester College, the boys' school founded before 1400, whose headmaster, the Rev. George Moberly, was the Treasurer to the Diocesan Board of Education. Smith, like the fellows of his Oxford College, was a clerk in holy orders, and had been allowed an opportunity to set his own course at Winchester in a budding institution that also enjoyed an ecclesiastical basis and oversight.

Such 'missionary' aspirations as Smith encountered at Battersea were fine and perfectly acceptable to him, but practicalities loomed. One was the necessity of securing funding for students under the terms of the Privy Council Minutes of 1846. To this end, and to meet the requirement for funding, in 1847 Smith encouraged an inspection (perhaps Kay's greatest innovative contribution) of the Training School, which led to the appointment of additional staff to assist him. These staff included two former students of Battersea, so perhaps at that point he was tending toward the Battersea rather than the St Mark's model by choosing students from Kay's foundation and by showing respect for inspection. Conditions at Wolvesey were indeed spartan, but also grand in an old-fashioned way. Much building work was essential to make the rooms less 'rat-infested' and more habitable. Government funding helped in that respect.

There was nonetheless significant sickness. The location of Wolvesey, like its neighbour Winchester College, was downstream of the city, washed through by 'The Brooks', which acted as drains and sewers, flowing out there on the south side of the city. Recent

– not, it was conceded, that those people necessarily provided an inadequate education, but the established Church should be doing better in this regard. Some felt that the working classes were getting a better primary education than their counterparts in the middle classes. Battersea was founded by Dr Kay (who from 1842, on his marriage, became Kay-Shuttleworth) and taken over by the Church of England's National Society in 1843. This supremely bureaucratic, enigmatic, powerful and self-centred man had been brought up as a dissenter, as a result of which the established Church had in 1839 opposed his appointment as Secretary to the government's committee for dispensing funding for education. Around this time, always seeking preferment, Kay changed his allegiance to the Church of England. As founder of Battersea College, which had also opened in 1840, he believed that 'elementary schoolteachers should be first and foremost Christian missionaries'. At Battersea, based on Kay's own puritanical upbringing, there was a Spartan inculcation of its 'Christian aims'. At St Mark's, under Derwent Coleridge, by contrast, the mission was to 'nurture educated and cultured persons' amidst buildings which 'might foster gracious living'. Smith returned to Winchester to reflect on what he had seen.

A third element drawn from Smith's own experience contributed to the fundamental ethos of the Training School. This was his experience at Magdalen College, Oxford. Magdalen

Map to show the proximity of Wolvesey Palace to the poor eastern suburb where life expectancy in the mid-19th century was very low. Student sickness caused Wolvesey to be abandoned in the late 1850s.

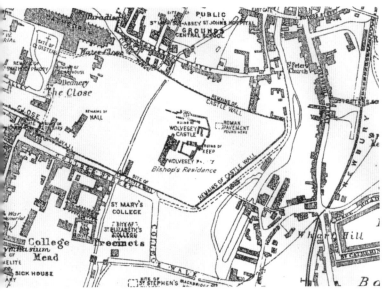

work has shown how the early boys at Winchester College in the first centuries after its foundation in 1389 suffered fatal epidemics: as well as deaths from plague, danger came from diseases carried downstream in the monastic and town drains. This situation for the staff and students at Wolvesey was little different in the 1840s, when there was a fierce debate in the city about public health and drainage in which the ratepayers (in the city) and the institutions (such as Winchester College, which did not pay rates) were locked in conflict – the 'muckabite' controversy – over (lack of) improvement of the drains after a sanitary inspector's report in 1844. Average age at death for most of those in the city was 58, but it fell to 42 at that time in St Peter Chesil, adjacent to Wolvesey and the water-courses to the east of the city. Against this background mortality among the residents at Wolvesey was not uncommon and sickness rife: cholera in 1849 carried off students, despite the best efforts of John Smith and his mother in nursing and typhus broke out in 1857–8. At that date Smith himself became ill, and all students had to move out of Wolvesey to other accommodation in the city.

Right: Samuel Sebastian Wesley, organist and choirmaster, was at Winchester Cathedral 1849–65 when he also taught at the Training College, was organist and ran the choir at Winchester College.

Far right: The Meads, or Water Meadows, which had inspired Keats to write his ode 'To Autumn', and where the students from Wolvesey 'exercised'.

ACADEMIC LIFE IN THE 1850s

If healthcare provision at Wolvesey was primitive and circumscribed by location, on the academic side there was exceptional talent available. Students were required to work long hours, starting at 6.15am and finishing at 9.30pm following a session learning verses and a Bible lecture (twenty-first-century students take note!). There was a two-hour break between 1pm and 3pm for 'dinner and walking', no doubt through the adjacent water meadows. Among the lecturers whose skills were engaged by John Smith was the cathedral organist, the celebrated (and at times savage) S. S. Wesley, who had a fixed slot in the timetable from 7pm to 8pm to teach music, including singing, which was such a key part of the mission. In the lecture room the main emphasis of the teaching in Smith's time was on Mathematics, which occupied some 14 hours a week; next came Scripture and Liturgy (eight and a half hours), History, Grammar, etc. and Milton (seven hours), music (six and a half), Latin and Physical Science (four), and so on.

Who were the students and other members of the Training School community at this time? In the 1851 census we catch a glimpse of Smith's students and the staff, and find a very

	Parish or Township of Extra Parochial	Ecclesiastical District of	City or Borough of Winchester	Town of	Village of

No.	Name of Street, Place, or Road, and Name or No. of House	Name and Surname of each Person who abode in the house, on the Night of the 30th March, 1851	Relation to Head of Family	Condition	Age of Males	Age of Females	Rank, Profession, or Occupation	Where Born
133	Wolvesey Training School	John Smith	Head	U	38		Master, Principal of Training School & Chaplain	Bucks Beaconsfield
		Nicholas Smith	Father	Married	88		Gent	Northumberland Chatton
		Lucy Do	Mother	Mar		70	Mistress of Family	Bucks Beaconsfield
		Edwin Gyles		U	22		Vice Principal of Training School	Surrey Camberwell
		Albert Smith	Student	U	17		Student	Kent Rochester
		John Tanswell	"	U	18		do	Dorset Monkton
		Nehemiah Boswell	"	U	19		do	Surrey G Bookham
		Francis W Dunkerton	"	U	17		"	Somerset Pilton
		William F Kelley	"	U	19		"	at Sea
		Henry Target	"	U	19		"	Hants Winchester
		Charles A Page	"	U	16		"	Do Do
		John H Ruffell	"	U	17		"	Dorset Shaftesbury
		William Prescott	"	U	21		"	Wilts Aldbury
		Edwin Young	"	U	19		"	Do Salisbury
		Thomas W Jones	"	U	19		"	Middlesex Bayswater
		Henry W Nutley	"	U	18		"	Wilts Burbage
		Edward T Kellow	"	U	15		"	Hants Hurstbourne
		John H Edwards	"	U	32		"	West Indies Barbadoes
		John Richardson	"	U	18		"	Wilts Heewil
		Edwin Biddick	"	U	20		"	at Sea

Total of Persons...

The 1851 census showing Principal Smith, his parents and some of the students at Wolvesey.

different Training School from that recorded in 1841. Now in more spacious accommodation at Wolvesey, the institution was effectively a tenant of the bishop, whose interests were overseen on site by an octogenarian 'Housekeeper by Patent of Wolvesey', with her 48-year-old niece as a charwoman.

The only continuity from 1841 was Patience Oxley, born in Ireland, now 29 and the only remnant of the Irish community of a decade earlier. Compared with the ten 'pupils' resident in 1841, the majority aged 15 or under, there were now 20 'students', of whom the youngest was 16 years old, with 13 being teenagers aged 17–19. The remainder were in their 20s, with the exception of John Edwards, 32, a British Subject born in 'Barbadoes', West Indies. Bachelor John Smith's parents were living with him: his father (88) a 'Gent', Northumbrian by birth, and his mother (70), described as 'Mistress of Family' who, like her son, was a native of Beaconsfield, Bucks. Edwin Gyles, a Battersea College man aged 22, was the Vice-Principal, and his entire teaching programme appears to have been in Mathematics, in which he was highly proficient. He left by the end of 1851, en route to Cambridge University. The evidence of these early years shows unequivocally the importance of Maths then as now in the school and training college curricula.

Apart from Maths, teaching of English is a noteworthy and unusual feature of this early period of the curriculum. Those involved represented the cream of scholars available at the

> **Monday.**—Before Breakfast—six to eight o'clock, Washing, Clean Shoes. Preparation of Lessons, Prayers, Scripture Lecture. Forenoon.—nine to ten, Writing; ten to eleven, Church; eleven to twelve, Spelling, Latin, Grammar, English Grammar and Parsing—2d class. Afternoon—English History, Delectus—2d class; Caesar, Euclid—1st class.
>
> **Tuesday.**—Before Breakfast—same as on Monday. Forenoon—nine to ten, Arithmetic; ten to eleven Church; eleven to twelve, Spelling, Latin Grammar, and Mensuration—2d class. Afternoon—Geography, English Parsing—1st class; delectus—2d class. Exercises, (Latin and English).
>
> **Wednesday.**—Before Breakfast—Same. Forenoon—nine to ten, Ecclesiastical History, ten to eleven, Church, eleven to twelve, Prepare Music. Afternoon—Half Holiday.
>
> **Thursday.**—Before Breakfast—Same. Forenoon—nine to ten, Writing; ten to eleven, Church; Eleven to twelve, Spelling, Chronology, and Latin Grammar—2d class. Afternoon—English History, Euclid, Caesar—1st class. Delectus and Dictation.
>
> **Friday.**—Before Breakfast—Same. Forenoon—nine to ten, Arithmetic; ten to eleven, Church; eleven to twelve, English Grammar and Parsing, Latin Grammar—2nd class. Afternoon—Geography, Delectus, Caesar—1st class. Exercises, (Latin and English).
>
> **Saturday.**—Before Breakfast—Same. Forenoon—nine to ten, Scripture, Catechism; ten to eleven, Church; eleven to twelve, Prepare Music. Afternoon—Half Holiday.
>
> This is the table employed for the winter quarter of the present year:—
>
> Dinner is served at one o'clock
>
> The afternoon school hours are from two to four, or half-past four in winter; till five in summer. From five to six, voluntary study, or recreation. Six to half-past six, supper. Half-past six to eight, prepare lesson. Eight to quarter before nine, music (practice), or read in the books of the Library of the School. Quarter to nine, prayers and scripture lecture.

Scheme of Instruction at the Winchester Training School, 1844.

time. The Rev. John Keble, for example, had been Professor of Poetry at Oxford until 1841. The youthful Dr Moberly, since 1835 Headmaster of Winchester College across the road, and involved in the plans for the Training School from the outset, questioned the Wolvesey students on Shakespeare's *Henry V*, requiring them to explain the grammatical and historical context. Moberly had a professional interest in education: he was later to publish a biography of William of Wykeham (d. 1404), founder of Winchester College. When Moberly moved on from Winchester College in 1866 (he became Bishop of Salisbury in 1869), the Winchester Training School was firmly established in its Wykehamical, quasi-medieval building on West Hill. A further long-term element of the curriculum was established at this time: the teaching of horticulture, which was carried out by Mr Weaver, the Warden of Winchester College's gardener, whose main responsibility was again just across the road behind the high wall of Winchester College.

Closer scrutiny of the timetable and knowledge of the wider educational context of this period suggests that, alongside established Maths and History, English was emerging as a key element of work at the Training School. The timetable in census year 1851, for example, includes two sessions of Grammar on Tuesdays and English Grammar (before breakfast) and English Literature (three quarters of an hour in the evening) on Wednesdays, with two further sessions of Grammar on Fridays.

The focus on English rather than Latin, important though that was, suggests that the authorities were aware of the growing need for literacy in schools beyond the Public Schools. As much as classical languages were important to the understanding and administering by Public School men of an Empire based on Graeco-Roman models, a good grasp of English grammar and literature was necessary to developing the lower classes for the home economy. Thus it is exciting to note that Richard Chenevix-Trench, Rector of Itchenstoke, Hampshire and Professor of Divinity at King's College, London (opened in 1831 by Anglican churchmen in competition with 'the godless college in Gower Street' – later University College, London), came in 1851 to deliver a series of five lectures to the students called 'On the Study of Words'. The Diocesan Board, in emphasising their thanks to Trench, noted that, 'not content with delivering the lectures, he has generously presented a copy of them to each of the pupils in training'. The wider community was also involved at Winchester: the *Winchester Quarterly Record* discussed the importance of English, bemoaning the lack of such study in the wider educational establishment. The *Hampshire Chronicle* wrote at length about the lectures, placing Trench's work in the wider field of language studies of the time, where etymology and philology were coming to the fore. Thus the link with theology was teased out, the contemporary maxim *'res, non verba'* was questioned, and the importance of showing 'not only how

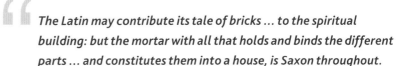

> *The Latin may contribute its tale of bricks ... to the spiritual building: but the mortar with all that holds and binds the different parts ... and constitutes them into a house, is Saxon throughout.*
>
> R. Chenevix-Trench, 1855

much history, but how much morality, there is in words, to be a most important acquisition'. Under the title *Trench on Words* the lectures gained much wider currency, with 19 editions appearing in the following 35 years.

Trench returned in 1855 to proffer a further series of lectures entitled 'English, Past and Present', praising the quality of Smith's students – 'a body of young Englishmen, all with a fair amount of classical knowledge (in my explanations I have some-times had others with less than theirs in my eye)' – and stressing Englishness, as these 'young Englishmen' have 'as yet marked out to them the duty in general of living lives worthy of those who have England for their native country, and English as their native tongue'. In 1855 theology still suffuses Trench's lectures, but the social and political significance of language is more to the fore. This tradition of theology and morality through the study of English, and its contribution to society, has continued through the history of the College. Whereas Trench was lecturing from a Christian theological standpoint, Friedrich Nietzsche was to take up similar themes in his 1873 *On Truth and Lie in an Extra-Moral Sense*, 'serving a different morality and very different politics' by the rejection of Christian morality as that of the slave; and by rejection of eternity in favour of Superman on

earth. When John Simons was writing about Trench in 1991, the teaching of undergraduate English at King Alfred's was focused on 'linguistically based literary theories' fashionable at that time. In the new millennium the same department has reintroduced the study of the Old English language: the kind of work that would have been equally familiar to Trench in the evaluation of the Germanic origins of the language in an Anglo-Saxon world that was changing from pagan to Christian. In 1845 Trench had been Hulsean lecturer at Cambridge, and was also examining chaplain to the Bishop of Oxford. This was Bishop Samuel Wilberforce, who became bishop there in 1845, having formerly been Archdeacon in the Winchester Diocese. Wilberforce was another of the luminaries who supported the foundation of the Training College, recommended early students to its authorities, and contributed to the education of the students at Wolvesey. These early links with the hierarchy of the Church of England and with Oxford and Cambridge university graduates and teachers were important.

The Rev. John Smith of Magdalen College was Oxford-educated and, like Moberly across at Winchester College, a Christ Church man. Smith was first of several Oxbridge Principals who Martial Rose (Principal 1967–84, a Cambridge

Far left: Rev. Richard Chenevix-Trench, Wordsworthian poet, Rector of Itchenstoke, chaplain to Bishop Samuel Wilberforce, philologist supporter of the Oxford English Dictionary project, and enthusiast for the students at the Training College.

Left: Bishop Samuel Wilberforce, 'Soapy Sam', challenger of Darwin and supporter of the Training School foundation, was involved in teaching there.

1st Committee. Winchester Reunion Club

Coombes Street Smith Tuck Flux Brunn

Initiating Committee of the Winchester Re-union Club, 1874.

Kingsman) characterised as the men who hardened the division between the 'academic' and the 'professional' – 'academic' being the learning and teaching conducted in the College, and 'professional' the practical teaching carried out from the 1840s in a school fitted out with a special extra classroom in which the trainee teachers could practise, in St Michael's parish in the city. Rose also conceded that the distinction between academic and professional training within the institution had 'not yet disappeared' in 1981. The sustained focus on academic content undoubtedly contributed in Rose's own days (he retired in 1984) and later to the ability of the College to survive through diversification of its curriculum from teacher training. Indeed, the separation probably did not effectively occur until the arrival on the scene of the National Curriculum in the 1990s, introduced under the terms of the Thatcher government's Education Reform Act (1988). The National Curriculum was deemed to provide sufficient content for professional teachers, so that the subject teaching within the institution migrated from the hands of subject departments to reside within what was to become the Faculty of Education. By that time, however, the 'academic' side of the institution had burgeoned in many and various directions – undergraduate American Studies, Archaeology, Drama, English, History, etc. – at the same time reducing the role of teacher training at Winchester and broadening its subject-specialist base.

A second inspection was encouraged by Principal Smith five years after the 1847 inspection. It was conducted on 6 October 1852 by H. M. I. Wandsworth, who noted that at that date the Training School had sent out 115 masters since 1840, including 13 in the previous year. In a note on remuneration it was recorded that none was paid over £50 with a house, and one was noted as paid an annual salary of only £35 without a house. Smith achieved a great deal in his term as Principal, not least being the fact that the inspection had shown the quality of what was being offered at Winchester, and had therefore

gained students who could claim government funding as 'Queen's Scholars' (like Sue Bridehead in Hardy's *Jude the Obscure*; see pp162–3) an essential income-stream for the Training School. The sickness at Wolvesey, which had meant that ten of the 38 students were too ill to be examined that year, along with the sickness of the Principal, were real problems, and had focused minds on planning for a purpose-built college on a more sanitary site. When Smith left in 1858 during the planning stages of the creation of the new buildings he did not lose touch, returning in 1874 to contribute an 'excellent address' at the inaugural meeting of the alumni club at the Old Market Inn. This would have been an especially joyful occasion for John Smith, as he would have been very aware that the sickness and migration of staff and students in the late 1850s had led the Diocesan authorities to delay the appointment of a successor and consider closure and extinction of the College.

Principal Smith was replaced the following year, 1859, by the Rev. Charles Collier. A Yorkshireman born in 1819 at Sheffield, Collier was a graduate of Trinity College, Dublin, where he took his MA in 1850 before being ordained priest in 1854. Collier moved in to Wolvesey, where he was living with his wife and young family of three children under ten at the time of the 1861 census, supported by five servants. The students, meanwhile, had moved away from the challenging environment at Wolvesey to live in St Peter's Street within the walls of the city. Collier and his wife produced more children in the 1860s, but at least two died young, burial being recorded in the West Hill cemetery opposite the College. One way in which Collier encouraged community among the students was through military affiliation and camps. A College company called 'The Winchester Diocesan Training College Corps' was founded in 1875, there being sufficient demand in the wake of the 1859 instigation of the county-based volunteer force. Principal Collier entered wholeheartedly into the scheme, becoming Chaplain to the Corps, a post he retained long after his departure from the College.

Principal Collier, the Alfred bones and Archaeology ....

The apparent discovery of King Alfred's bones, among other skulls and skeletal fragments, was announced by the 'romantic antiquarian' John Mellor in 1866. The claim that these bones had come from Hyde Abbey, where Alfred had been reburied after 1110, was investigated by a local committee in 1870, who agreed that they were likely to have come from the site of the long-demolished abbey. However, despite Mellor's production of a spurious lead label which, he asserted, identified remains of Alfred among the finds, his claims were disputed. The Reverend Charles Collier was among those who doubted the authenticity of Mellor's discoveries – scepticism which at the time included the comment 'It is surprising he didn't find the burnt cakes' – and on 7 March 1870 Collier delivered a report on the committee of inquiry into Mellor to the Winchester and Hampshire Scientific and Literary Society. Collier examined Mellor's lead plates, identifying one as tea lead and one as plumber's lead – both modern types of the metal. Collier has since been vindicated by scientific examination in 2013 confirming the misidentification of the bones.

Collier had a serious interest in antiquarianism, and was elected a Fellow of the Society of Antiquaries in 1860, well before the foundation of the Hampshire Field Club c.1885. Indeed, a paper was presented on the Roman villa at Itchen Abbas to a meeting at which the formation of such a local archaeological and antiquarian society was discussed. Working with the owner of the Avington Park estate, near Winchester, Collier obtained permission from the tenant to excavate a villa at Itchen Abbas in the Itchen Valley. Drawing on his military interests, also shown at the College, he noted 'the fine

look out over the neighbouring country. The inhabitants … would have ample opportunity of knowing the approach of an enemy from any quarter.' The excavation in March 1878 produced discoveries of tessellated pavements, and fine plans and colour-coded drawings of the pavements of these black, red and white *tesserae* were drawn up by his son, Ernest, a budding architect, and swiftly published in the national *Proceedings of the Archaeological Association*, prompting the chairman to note 'how little we know of the plans and arrangements of Roman villas in this country…'.

Archaeology remained among the interests of Collier's successors, and a century on from the excavation at Itchen Abbas (and two centuries after the alleged rifling of the royal tombs at Hyde Abbey), an Archaeology Department was established at Winchester c.1978 under Principal Martial Rose, who had himself sat the Archaeological and Anthropological Tripos at Cambridge 30 years previously.

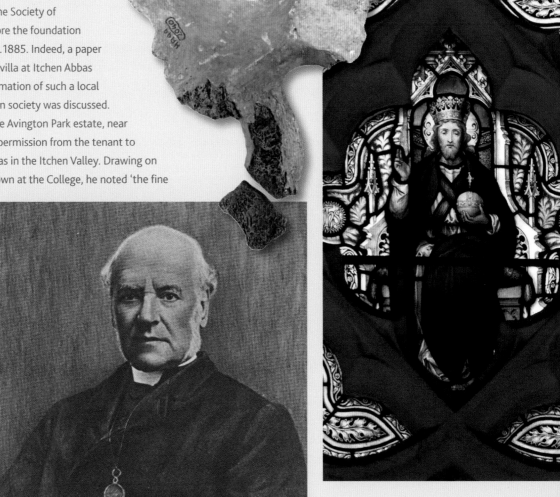

Right: Rev. Charles Collier, Principal of the Training College 1859–79.

Inset: A pelvic bone, likely from King Alfred, identified at the University of Winchester in 2013.

Far right: King Alfred in stained glass in the rose window at the west end of the Chapel of 1881.

The architect John Colson Sr's vision of the Training College Gothic building of 1862 from the south-east. Colson was noted for his enthusiasm for small carved heads which are found all around the building, and the later Chapel.

A NEW BEGINNING: THE WEST HILL SITE

1861 was the last year before the new buildings on West Hill were occupied. Work had begun on purpose-built accommodation in 1860, and the foundation stone was laid in the spring of 1861 by the Rt Hon. Lord Viscount Eversley, Charles Shaw-Lefevre of Heckfield (b. 1794), the former Whig Speaker of the House of Commons. It had been hoped that HRH Prince Albert – one of whose servants had previously attended the College for training – would perform either the foundation ceremony or even, perhaps, the official opening, but his illness and premature death in December 1861 prevented that. In the event the opening ceremony and service took place on Monday 13 October 1862, some six weeks later than planned due to the sudden bankruptcy of the original builders. Bishop Wilberforce of Oxford, who returned to preach the sermon, was embroiled at the time in the aftermath of his dispute of the previous year with Darwin and Huxley, in which he famously asked Huxley whether he was descended from a monkey on his grandfather's or grandmother's side. Wilberforce was acknowledged as one of the great preachers of his generation. Among the guests present at the opening was the Prime Minister, Lord Palmerston, who lived nearby at Romsey. The *Hampshire Chronicle* reported the opening in great detail – as it had the foundation-stone ceremony – and also with great pride, referring to the opening day as:

Replete with interest for the ancient City of Winchester. The merry ringing of Church bells, the 'City Standard' waving above the battlements of the West Gate and numerous banners of a gay and diversified manner … signified the proceedings of the day were of great local importance… The day had been appointed for the singularly interesting and gratifying ceremony of the inauguration of the New Diocesan Training School building by the Lord Bishop of Winchester, and the occasion was rendered still more attractive by the announcement that the Lord Viscount Palmerston was to be present to take part in the celebration arrangements.

This great Gothic Revival building in 'true-Christian' pointed architecture reinforced the message that here was a Christian foundation in a world where the Church of England was beset by intellectual and religious challenges even at its centre, notwithstanding the comfortable evangelicalism of the long-serving Bishop Sumner at Winchester. Many of Wilberforce's immediate family, and his brother-in-law Manning (later Cardinal), had been received into the Roman Catholic Church. The building on West Hill addressed Derwent Coleridge's tenet of fostering 'gracious living', although many students found the regime tough and demanding, both physically and mentally.

Not only were students now released from the disease-ridden south-east quarter of the city, they were also freed from the cramped accommodation of their family homes, each being provided with 'a separate stall in the dormitories and each stall will have a window, water, basin and tap' (although for many years only with cold water), such was the ecclesiastical terminology of the time. The site is attractive: high and airy, with wonderful panoramic views to the south and south-east, while to the south west is the wooded Sleeper's Hill, with its echo of Arthurian folk tradition. By 1840, the year of the foundation of the Training School, the West Hill had been cut off from the city by the arrival of the London and South-Western Railway running

north–south in a deep cutting excavated outside the walled area of the Roman and medieval city to the west, emerging on a high embankment south-east of the new College building. Thus it was that when the Training School was relocated to the West Hill in 1862, it added to provision in this area west of the city, which had been developed in the previous two decades as quasi-social service organisation for the people of Winchester from cradle to grave. Here were sited, alongside the long-established Roman Catholic cemetery and near the site of the medieval Jewish cemetery, the new West Hill Cemetery for Anglicans and Dissenters (1840), the hospital (1849), gasworks, police headquarters, prison, and, from 1862, the Training School in a Gothic building in a permanent home on a five-acre site. Here were to be trained the male Anglican teachers who would undertake the education of the children of the Winchester Diocese, picking up the baton from the staff at the hospital, where their Winchester charges were born, and setting them on the right path of life, children who might in the fullness of time be buried in the adjacent cemetery.

The building of 1862 became known as the 'Main Building', a term that is still common currency today. The building contract had been signed for £7,450 excluding land, to which Queen Victoria donated a generous £100 and which was matched by the local and more distant aristocracy, Lord Ashburton, the Duke of Buccleuch,

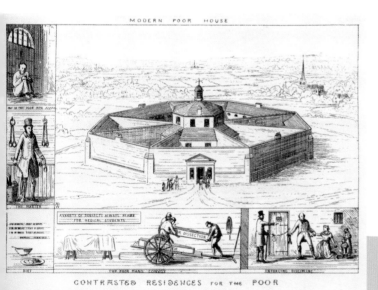

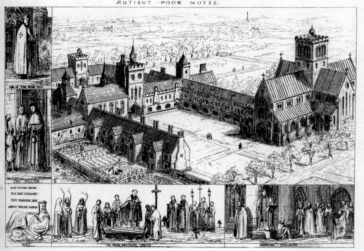

Right: The True Christian architecture of the Training College, photograph *c.* 1865.

Far right: Colson's apprentice master Owen Carter's Classical 'pagan' Corn Exchange for Winchester, completed in 1838. Carter died in 1859, just as Colson was making plans for the neo-Gothic Training College.

Below: Selection of Colson's plans for the Training College, *c.*1860.

Lord Carnarvon (of Highclere), Sir William Heathcote (of Hursley), and others such as 'the late' Rev. Dr Williams, Warden of New College, Oxford, and Lord Chief Justice Erle. Larger sums came from the Rev. Morgan Tritton (£105), Lord Calthorpe (£200), and the Warden and Fellows of Winchester College (£300). Thus from the outset the Diocesan Training College was closely associated with the University of Oxford, where New College was founded by William of Wykeham, and its feeder school, Winchester College *(see p27)*. These links remained strong for over a century, and continue today. The next tier of donors was the Church in its various manifestations: the National Society (£500), the Bishop of Winchester (£585) and the Dean and Chapter (£500, in addition to the land). Top of the list was £2,000 from the Education Department, established in 1856 as the administrative arm of the Government's Committee of Council. This was an excellent start, although ominously for the future the government by its grant gained a significant say over the development of the institution, which it was to exercise in due course with vigour.

Unfortunately the contractor, Mr Watts of Southampton, had underestimated the financial viability of the project for his company, and went bankrupt before completion of the work, which was carried out by another Southampton builder, Mr Briton. The bankruptcy was a distant precursor of events during the building programme at West Downs over 150 years later. The plans of the 1862 building show an arrangement around an 'Exercising Court' to the north of the Main Building. This central structure spanned the south side of the courtyard, following the contour of the hillside, with two classrooms towards the west and a Lecture Room – mirroring the chancel of a church? – to the east. Thus we see learning and exercise in equal proportions, the footprint of the 'Exercising Court' matching that of the teaching spaces. The plans for the teaching accommodation show the tiered desks in the lecture room. In the basement there were two cellars: one for the students, divided into areas labelled 'Potatoes' and 'Beer'; these two areas were echoed in the other, the Principal's cellar, where a third division for 'Wine' was also marked on the plans *(see p9)*. East of the Lecture Room was accommodation for the Principal, with five bedrooms, and for the Vice-Principal to the west of the classrooms, as well as accommodation for a Matron. The west

PLAN OF FIRST FLOOR

Nº II
DIOCESAN TRAINING SCHOOL
WINCHESTER HANTS.

NºVIII
DIOCESAN TRAINING SCHOOL
WINCHESTER HANTS.

SECTION ON LINE C.D.

SECTION ON LINE A.B.

PLAN OF GROUND FLOOR

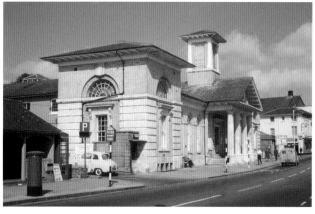

wing included a Teachers' Private Room and a Students' Sitting Room. The central accommodation was to house 56 students. Land was donated by the Diocese, originally two acres, but before the building scheme was completed this was raised to five.

The architectural style of the Diocesan Training School was Gothic, embodying the 'moral superiority' which A. W. N. Pugin attributed to Gothic as true Christian architecture in stark and striking contrast to 'pagan' Romanesque styles such as that of the Corn Exchange (now the Discovery Centre) on Jewry Street in Winchester, the work of Colson's mentor Owen Browne Carter. This Gothic style at the Training School tells us much about the Christian aspirations of its founders. It was the work of local architect John Colson, who had served as drawing master to the Training School students when they were taught at Wolvesey, and so knew their requirements from the inside. Colson had been appointed cathedral architect in 1857, was elected fellow of the Royal Institute of British Architects in 1858 and won the competition for the design of the Training School in 1859, with a design he called *Spes* (Hope). His main output was focused on churches, parsonages and schools in Hampshire.

It is instructive to dwell on the detail of this key building in the history of the institution. On 5 April 1861 the foundation stone was laid by Viscount Eversley, the Lord Lieutenant of Hampshire, amidst civic and ecclesiastical rejoicing and feasting, with music provided by a military band and a Benediction by Bishop Sumner. A trust deed and the dedication were placed in a glass bottle and incorporated into a 'cell' in the foundation. A new era of teaching prowess was hailed by Eversley, as compared to a recent time when teachers had been selected because of their 'infirmity' or 'deformity'. The *Hampshire Chronicle* report of 18 October 1862 is full and highly informative, opening with a comment that the building forms 'a striking object when seen from the railway', which lay some 400 yards to the east. The late-fourteenth-century style provided 'accommodation of a very superior kind'. This in itself is a noteworthy choice of period architecture. Comparisons would have been lost neither on the planners of the institution nor the architect nor many of those present, for the 'late 14th century' was precisely the date of the buildings of Winchester College. In some respects there were congruities, such as the proximity of the teaching spaces to the Dining Hall and kitchens found at both sites, and the similarity in proposed size of initial intake, 70 at Winchester College, 56 at the Training School in purpose-built accommodation. The Training School was finished to a high specification:

> over the students entrance on the Terrace is a tower 78 feet high
> with ornamental ironwork coloured by gilt … the whole of the
> building is faced with Swanage Stone, and that on the south
> and west set in cement, to exclude the wet [within a decade
> or so the buildings were beset by damp which required
> ongoing maintenance] … *doorways and copings are of
> boxground Bath Stone.*

John Colson Sr, who designed the College.

Right: An early 19th-century print showing the cathedral (right) and the former royal palace (barracks) dominating the skyline with the canal in the foreground.

Below: The modern St Alphege building employs a similar design of clean air-management to the 1862 building.

There was a grey-and-red-banded tiled roof, with the tower, turrets and gables surmounted by gilt vanes while the window arches of grey and red bricks 'add much to their effect by their colour'. All very grand.

Such a large mass of a building in a prominent position was undoubtedly the Church of England placing itself in the public eye: the building was intended to be seen. In addition to the aesthetic effect and the dominating presence of the structure, it was noted that it was proposed to lower the terrace in front to the south 'when funds allow' to form two terraces to 'give the effect of heightening the appearance of the building and being seen better from below'. This plan was, no doubt, to impress and maybe even intimidate students and visitors as they puffed up the hill from the lower entrance, today near The Stripe *(see pp40–1)*.

The Principal, by contrast, could approach his house on level ground. At the time of the opening ceremony, however, the area in front of the building remained incomplete, and 'will improve when grass [is] added on the terraces'. A report to the Board of Education in 1864–5, soon after the opening, noted with pleasure the work carried out by students subsequent to the opening in levelling the site and thereby, no doubt, contributing to the desired visual improvement arising from the creation of the terraces.

The throng on 13 October 1862 was so large that the corridors to the lecture hall where the ceremony took place were crammed with Winchester people and 'an unusually large influx of people from all parts of the County and from Surrey and other distant districts'(!). This parish-pump observation by the local reporter reminds us of the intensely local nature of life and work even over 20 years after the railway arrived at Winchester (there was no train from Winchester that arrived in London before nine in the morning until the electrified service in the 1960s). But it also reminds us of the extent and remaining resources of the diocese of Winchester, which (while no longer the wealthiest diocese north of the Alps, as it was in the Middle Ages) retained religious dominance over a great and wealthy swathe of largely agricultural land from the Channel to the Thames – an undoubted advantage for the founders of the institution. The crowding of the building by interested parties during the opening ceremony necessitated using larger spaces elsewhere in the city when the official opening had occurred at the West Hill site at 2.30pm. Allowing reasonable time for passage down the hill, there was 'Divine Service' at the cathedral at 4pm, followed by an address from the Mayor and

Corporation of the city to Lord Palmerston, at the Chapter House. The day concluded 'with a grand banquet, at half-past six in the evening, at St John's House, Lord Palmerston presiding'.

Indeed, everyone wanted to see the new building outside and in when it was thrown open that day. As people toured the building and the site in high spirits after the opening ceremony, which had concluded after 3pm with 'an enthusiastic rendering of the National Anthem', the 'students and others showing themselves quite proficient in vocal ability', frequent 'terms of approbation [were] heard expressed as to the salubrity and convenience of the site'. Those present were, it appears, overwhelmingly impressed on a number of fronts, displaying 'perceptible and universal admiration of the elegant design of the architect and the completeness of the fitting and arrangements of the interior, every portion of it being provided with the most modern and approved appliances'. Among these last, special

Below: Modern light 'wells' over the new Senior Common Room echo the lost Victorian airvents on the Main Building.

note was made of the ventilation provided – the memories of the health hazards in the valley bottom at Wolvesey fresh in everyone's minds. The ground-floor lecture rooms were served by tubes under the floor, with valves for 'the admission of pure air' and valves near the ceiling 'for the exit of foul air'. Rooms were warmed with Hyde Stoves, 'which warm and at the same time ventilate'. Dormitories and sick rooms were similarly ventilated, 'except that the valves in the ceilings are connected with the turrets which are under zinc cowls, turned by the vanes, so there is no possibility of the wind blowing down'. Ventilation for an estimated 56 students, staff and the Principal's family was clearly at the forefront of the architect and patrons' minds. The most modern structure on the site today, the St Alphege 'Learning and Teaching' building, employs a comparable, if more

sophisticated, scheme of ventilation employing grilles and towers for a university population of some 7,300, though fortunately not all taught together.

Elsewhere, for example at the women's college at Fishponds, Bristol, the initial plan was earlier and more ambitious: to build and equip *c.*1850 a training school of 80 women to teach in Bristol with Gloucester and Oxford dioceses. However, it was a struggle to find funds to build the Fishponds college on a site which was a former quarry – and looked as much to the first arrivals – and to recruit local students. There were additional expenses as the land had to be purchased, unlike at Winchester. However, after a shaky start there were the planned-for 80 recruits by 1860. Fishponds followed hard on the heels of Bishop Wilberforce's college at Culham for men of the two dioceses, foundation stones being laid a year to the day in succession in 1852 and 1853. Wilberforce was a key figure in the foundation and early history at Winchester. The buildings of the Dioccesan Training Colleges at Culham, and at Fishponds, Bristol, as at Winchester, Cheltenham, Chester, Chichester and elsewhere of this date are all Gothic in character, built of local stone, and proclaim the Christian mission of the Church of England *(see p26, pp74–5 and p114)*.

THE IMPACT OF EDUCATIONAL REFORM

It was hugely to the credit of those who had planned and implemented the Training School scheme at Winchester that their proactive work had reached a conclusion when it did. All this proud building occurred just in time, for a cold wind then blew through the development of teacher training. These events are dealt with in detail by Martial Rose, whose account of the opening of the College on 13 October 1862 ends with the observation that 'on the morning of 14 October the Principal, staff and students of Winchester Training College knew they were facing a winter that would blow bleakly on educational endeavour'. The source of this chill blast was a government report on 'popular' education (the Royal Commission of 1858 under the Duke of Newcastle, popularly known as the Newcastle Commission), and the Revised Code of 1862, which reduced public expenditure by 25 per cent, from £800,000 to £600,000. These were changes of national significance, and the ramifications of these changes were tough on Principal Collier

Above: Bishop G. H. Sumner and his family. Sumner's tenure as diocesan Treasurer involved overseeing difficult financial times for the Training College *(see p44)*.

and his Training College: reduction in the grants augmenting teachers' salaries ended grants to pupil teachers and, in the words of the Principal of the Cheltenham Training College, 'dealt the training colleges a deadly blow'. A key section of the code relating to colleges and their cash-flow laid down that no payment should be made until students had 'completed two years' training and had remained in post in the same elementary school for a further two years'.

Charles Sumner was still Bishop of Winchester at this date and had ensured that his family sustained a close interest in the School. His son, Canon George Henry Sumner (1826–1909), served as treasurer and secretary to the School, then the College, for 17 years from the start of work on the West Hill site in 1861 until he resigned in 1878. Thus it was that G. H. Sumner, in his role as treasurer of the Training School at Winchester, wrote to Canon Lonsdale, the Secretary of the National Society, that such arrangements were 'objectionable'. There were anxieties among the Principals that students could hold the colleges to ransom, knowing that each was 'worth £100' to the College in his second year. Recruitment faltered despite the new buildings: totals of 21 students in 1862, 40 in 1863 and 34 in 1864 according to Collier's returns to the National Society. Borough Road College, built for 100, was only populated by 68 in 1866. In 1869 Chichester, despite its splendid new building less than 20 years old *(see p26)*, and Highbury colleges were forced to close. The quality of intake also declined, and in the 1860s many of the early supporters of the Training School moved, or passed, on: Keble died in 1866, Bishop Charles Sumner retired in 1869, and in the same year George Moberly, who had

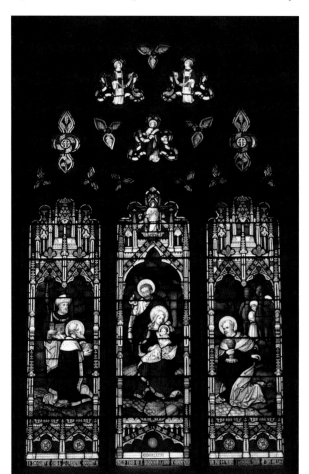

left Winchester College, became Bishop of Salisbury. Samuel Wilberforce replaced Sumner until he fell from his horse and died in 1873.

The 1870 Education Act established a state system of elementary education. Church colleges, which exclusively trained teachers for elementary schools, were threatened by these proposed state elementary school teacher-training colleges. This situation had been anticipated by those involved at Winchester. Canon Jacob, faithful servant to the Training School, recorded wearily that 'each new bill was pregnant with consequences'. The 1870 Act allowed the right of withdrawal on the grounds of conscience, and was thus a threat to Church of England schools. Again, the Winchester Diocese was ahead of the game, with Church schools already built so that they were in a state of preparedness when the six-month period of grace was allowed before school provision was surveyed: no 'feverish' building occurred. The diocese was therefore prepared for any challenges that might occur.

By 1871, when the decennial census came round again, nine years after the new accommodation opened, the Training School was settled on the West Hill. In the census

The 'grateful memorial' window to Archdeacon Jacob (1803–84), erected in 1886.

PHILIP JACOB O

Above: Early picture of the Dining Hall, as described by Attwood with the staff table, here decorated with a vase of flowers *(see p56)*. Note the hatch, and a mountain scene – Principal Martin *(see p46)* was a keen mountaineer.

Left: Plan of Colson's kitchen hatch, designed to mask kitchen staff from the students as food was passed through.

'School' has given way to 'College', with the 'Principle' (*sic*) being classed by the census checker in London as 'Instr'[uctor], as distinct from 'Schoolmaster'. On census night there were 32 students, although in 1862 the intention had been that there should be 56. The reason for this discrepancy is not known, and may indicate continuing troubles with recruitment. The Principal in post at that date was Charles Collier, 52, with his 42-year-old wife, two sons and two daughters ranging in age from 18 to nine: all born in Sheffield except the youngest, born in Winchester after Collier had arrived in 1859. The five servants were all local women: two were widows aged 37 and 44, and another was a nursemaid. The somewhat 'monastic' design of the men's college included features aimed to render females invisible to the men. Colson's drawings of the 1862 building included a marginal representation of the complex hatch between the dining hall and the kitchen. This was observed by the curious *Hampshire Chronicle* reporter in October 1862, who wrote that the dining hall hatch consisted of 'a zinc cylinder turning on a pivot' that 'turned round without people on either side seeing one another'. The 32 students consisted of five aged 18, 15 aged 19, nine aged 20 and three aged 21. These ages are significantly older than the early students in the 'school', and contributed to their greater authority in the classroom and society. Surveys of teachers during this difficult period showed conclusively that those who were trained justified beyond doubt the expenditure on their training.

Their birthplaces were diverse, with a majority from the designated dioceses of Winchester and Salisbury: some ten were born in Hampshire and a further six from the islands in the diocese (four from the Isle of Wight, and one each from Guernsey and Jersey). From the west there were six natives of Wiltshire, three of Dorset and another of Devon. From north and east of Winchester there were a couple from Surrey, two from London, one from Birmingham and one Yorkshire native. Already there are signs that the institution was attracting students from a broad area of the country, and that traditions were being established that have been sustained: the islands, for example, remain a fruitful recruiting base to this day. The Christian names of the students were overwhelmingly traditional – Albert, Alfred, George, Henry, James, John, William, etc. – while the surnames include many which have reappeared in the annals of the institution – Bundy, Fowler, Richardson, Rose, Ward, etc. Finally, there was a 29-year-old couple, a clergyman, Parker Fennear (who doubled as Chaplain to the Winchester Union, i.e. Workhouse), who was the Vice-Principal, living at the west end of the Main Building, and his wife Clara (like the Colliers a native of Sheffield), with a single servant. A clear photograph taken *c.*1865 *(see pp40–1)* shows the original building: its new stonework starkly white on the hillside and the upstairs windows on its central, students' section, showing clearly against the dark, banded, French-Gothic-style roof tiling.

Right: The memorial plaque to Richard Wheeler, erected in the Entrance Hall as there was no Chapel in 1875.

Far right: The entrance to the Principal's house, with carved heads and the decorative brickwork over, a feature of the 1862 building.

In memory of
Richard Wheeler
of this College 1874-5 drowned at
the burning of the Goliath Training Ship
in which he was Schoolmaster.
Dec. 1875.
His fellow students desire by this tablet
to perpetuate his memory.

COLLIER'S ACHIEVEMENTS

Among Collier's contributions to the development of the College, and with the firm support of students, a Re-union Club was founded, which first met – and was photographed – in August 1874 at the Old Market Inn in The Square near the cathedral (see p36). Here they indulged in time-honoured student activities: drinking, feasting, reminiscing, singing together and proposing toasts to the Principal and their 'Masters', among others. The best attended of the early meetings of the Re-union Club was in 1878, when Principal Collier, who was moving on to the living of Andover, was presented with a fine retirement gift of a 'handsome centre piece of solid silver' at a gathering characterised by Martial Rose as 'private and domestic'. Collier was some 60 years old when he left. During his 20-year Principalship the College had recovered from the threat of extinction and had taken up residence in the splendid new buildings on West Hill. It had weathered the storm of the Revised Code and the foundation of state schools from 1870 and was in good shape overall.

A survival of Collier's time in the fabric today is a plaque erected following a former student's untimely death: Richard Wheeler had sadly drowned when fire broke out on HMS *Goliath*; he was serving there as schoolmaster in December 1875, within months of leaving College. Richard Wheeler was still well known to the College community, and his death led to subscriptions to a commemorative tablet recounting the circumstances of his death. This plaque was placed in the Entrance Hall, now the south-eastern entrance to the Main Building from the Terrace, at the foot of the former Students' Staircase up to their sleeping quarters. The inscription reads 'His fellow students desire by this tablet to perpetuate his memory'. Later, such a memorial would have found a place in the Chapel, but in 1875 there was no separate chapel.

Henry Martin, Principal 1878–1912, as a Major in the uniform of the Hampshire Volunteers in 1900.

HENRY MARTIN TAKES OVER

The Rev. Henry Martin replaced Collier. A graduate of St Edmund Hall, Oxford, he had taught in Guernsey, and had been a Vice-Principal at Cheltenham before appointment to Winchester. His interests and achievements suggest he was very well suited to leading a college inhabited by young men: he was a keen soldier, a crack shot representing Winchester in annual competitions at Bisley, and a keen skier and mountaineer who had climbed to the top of the Matterhorn. He was, as his predecessors, a clerk in holy orders, having undertaken parish work in Guernsey when he taught there.

Martin would immediately have been aware that there was no separate chapel at Winchester, and prioritised remedying that deficiency. In 1880 a tender for the Training College Chapel by a local builder named Macklin was accepted for £1,038. This rose to £1,250, including internal fittings, with a completion date of Christmas 1880 agreed. So it was that the Chapel, west of the Main Building, was consecrated in February 1881, following a subscription campaign led by Bishop Harold Browne and

EARLY SPORTING HEROES ....

Both staff and students were among the leading lights in late nineteenth-century sport at the Training College. They included George Muir (1869–1939), a native of Southampton and a student at the Diocesan Training College (c.1888–90). By 1891 he was recorded as a Schoolmaster and remained teaching in Southampton Elementary Schools for many years. G. H. Muir (right) was a fine sportsman. Among his claims to fame was that he featured in the *first ever* game, in November 1885, involving what is now the Premier League's Southampton Football Club who play at the St Mary's Stadium, then the St Mary's Young Men's Association Football Club. He was on the 'Saints' Board from 1915 to 1936. He became a top referee, overseeing the 1913 Charity Shield Match, now contested by the winner of the FA Cup and the winner of the Premier League, but in that year uniquely between a team of 'Professionals' (who scored seven goals) and 'Amateurs' (who scored two goals). He was President of the Hampshire Football Association 1911–13 and again 1934–7. C. A. Whatmore was another early footballer of note at the College, playing for Wolverhampton Wanderers while pursuing a career in teaching.

On the staff side Muir would have known Humphrey Searle (c.1856–1934). Searle's obituary in the *Hampshire Chronicle* (10 November 1934) reminds us that he had trained at the College in 1876, and soon afterwards returned in 1879. 'He himself excelled as a footballer, and he played for the Winchester team back in the days when Mr Arnold Tebbutt and Mr C. S. Wooldridge were prominent as players. He was smart, too, at cricket, though football was especially his game.' At the College Searle was Assistant Chaplain as well as teaching Music – in which he had considerable talent – and also Science. He was especially interested in retaining links with his contemporaries and with other former Wintonians. His obituarist commented: 'He was practically the founder of the Winchester Training College Club (for former students); he was its secretary for many years, and was in every way conducive to its progress.' This was the Club renamed in 1881, taking over the Re-union Club founded in 1874. He left in 1903.

The College football team of 1900–1, with Humphrey Searle (circled), sportsman, master, musician and scientist.

The Chapel of 1881, before extension in 1927.

advertised in the *Hampshire Chronicle* in 1880. It was designed by the architects Colson and Son and bears further evidence of John Colson Sr's 'passion for small carved heads': a pair may still be seen either side of the main entrance to the Principal's residence, the East Wing of the Main Building, and higher round the whole building at eaves level. The original chapel was also decorated with a fine series of heads *(see p7, p24 and p62)*. A picture of this chapel before extension shows the door at the West End and four windows down the south side. The east window carries a 'grateful memorial' of 1886 to Canon Archdeacon Philip Jacob (1803–84). Jacob had been a member of the founding group from the diocese and had remained 'for 44 years a generous friend of this College' – in other words for the rest of his life. He was responsible in the early days for recording the achievements of the students in their work in schools. In his time the College had very much been part of the local community: famous lecturers such as Chenevix-Trench *(see pp34–5)* lectured to audiences including townspeople as well as students. There was much oral examination in which, twice a year, students were tested before their peers and a

Bernard Richard Goddard.

gathering of outsiders from the city and elsewhere. During these public spectacles, Jacob's task was to read out the reports on the students' performance in their teaching practice as reported by school managers. Through these early years such friends and supporters were essential to the survival of the College, and the subsequent establishment of the Chapel – to which it is very likely he contributed – enabled erection of a permanent memorial to Canon Jacob *(see p44–5)*.

An early glimpse of the institution under Principal Martin is found in the 1881 census. At this date the figure of 56 students intended for the 1862 building is found in residence. There were 19 aged 19 (and one 18-year-old), with a further 36 in their early 20s, making up 56. Three further 'boarders' appear in the census: James Haworth (a servant), William Bright and Humphrey Searle (taught 1879–1903), lecturers.

Searle went on to be Vice-Principal of the Home and Colonial College, London, for women, run on Pestalozzi lines, and was a founder member of the Wintonian Lodge of masons in London in 1904 *(see p50)*, through which he no doubt kept up with former students. He was also a member of a Hampshire lodge of masons. Principal Martin, his wife and their two young children, had a single female servant, and there were a further seven female servants for the resident students. The birthplaces of the students in 1881 were only half in Winchester and the associated diocese of Salisbury, with many born further afield in Edinburgh, Lancashire, Middlesex, Norfolk and Suffolk. Students in the census who attended the new chapel became Wintonians, as the former students chose to be called when they left the College.

In the 1891 census, styled 'The Training College', the students were away for Easter, leaving the Principal in residence with his Welsh-born wife Constance, their three younger children, his mother-in-law, a governess (native of Winterthur, Switzerland) and seven servants, including a Kentish cook and a nurse (all the others being Hampshire-born). Ten years on, in the

REFORMING THE RE-UNION ....

Another early change enacted by Principal Martin was to reform the Re-union Club of 1874, later the Winton Club. In 1881, in his presence in the chair, the organisation was re-founded, with new rules:

– to unite together in sympathy
– to provide prizes and exhibitions
– to alleviate distress
– to further the interests of the College generally

The surviving early minute books show that he attended almost every meeting, his bold signature of 'H. Martin' appearing at the foot of the minutes. He kept an eye on activities and encouraged collegiality not only among students in college, but also among their predecessors who had joined the alumni Winton Club

A firescreen from Henry Martin's time, 1902–4, embroidered with the College arms – those of the Bishops of Winchester – and the motto. In 1904 the College Masonic Lodge was founded.

Bernard Goddard's letter to V. S. Manley, ten years after the end of the Great War, preserved in Manley's albums (see pp58–61).

and the lavatories and baths. He taught History, was loved by the students and fought in the First World War. Also a linguist, he learnt Pathan while stationed in India, using it to good effect when working with Indian troops at the siege of Jerusalem in 1918. His lectures on his Palestine and India experiences were very popular, but he also captured attention with his lectures on diverse topics such as 'English Folk Songs'. On occasions when he was able to lecture outside Winchester, he was also received with respect and praise. Speaking at a national musical congress at Reading University in 1927 – the year after that institution received its royal charter – he chose the (rather unlikely) title 'The Mediaeval Craft Guild, its ideals and duties with an excursus on the place music ought to fill in any scheme of life worth living'. A reporter to *The Musical Times*, clearly sceptical of this 'history lecturer at Winchester Training College', was obliged to concede that 'The lecture was highly interesting, perhaps unexpectedly so, and those present felt that their knowledge was increased and their vision enlarged about things in history which really mattered'. Goddard was everything a Principal and a student could wish for in a member of staff.

In the 1901 census the 75 students are entered in orderly fashion, alphabetically in three groups (14, 31, 30), perhaps representing year groups, followed by seven female servants ranging in age from a 40-year-old widowed housemaid born in Bath to a 17-year-old kitchen maid born in Winchester, who was one of six single women there. Compared with 1871 there is a marked shift away from a small, almost familial atmosphere with ten women to 36 men, compared with ten women to 81 men, including family members and the three single, live-in male academic staff: a change in ratio of some 4:1 men to women to 8:1 in the 30-year period. The tutors' origins were diverse: London and Wales for Principal Martin and his wife; Cornwall, Jersey and Berkshire for the academics. Of the students 37 were natives of Hampshire plus two Isle of Wight men and two Jerseymen, comprising some 50 per cent; 12 were from neighbouring counties – Dorset (one), Wiltshire (three), Berkshire (two), Surrey (three) and Sussex (two); seven were from further West – Devon (three), Gloucestershire (one) and Somerset (three); and 13 were from London and other Home Counties –

census of 1901, the institution was still under the leadership of the Rev. Henry Martin (56). Also listed are his two younger sons, one born 18 years previously in Winchester, after the Principal had arrived from Cheltenham, where he had been Vice-Principal and where his eldest child had been born. Martin was the longest-serving Principal at Winchester, 1879–1912. They are followed in turn by a second clergyman, Henry Edmund Gill (34), Vice-Principal 1897–1902, and two resident tutors, John Robert Brown (27) and Bernard Richard Goddard (26). Goddard, a student from 1897 to 1900, was appointed junior tutor soon after completing his studies as one of the earliest candidates to stay on for a three-year BA degree.

B. R. Goddard is a towering figure in the history of the institution. The announcement that he had been awarded an MA in 1902 was met with 'uproarious cheers' and celebrations until midnight. He remained connected with the College for some 60 years, even today over a third of its existence, despite having had to bow to the governors who refused him permission to marry and move out of the unmarried tutors' accommodation in 1913, an echo of the rules for fellows of Oxbridge colleges. His 'crude' office, lacking in privacy, was sited between the common room

William Smoker in the historic uniform of the Volunteers.

Mottos for life...............................

The motto '*Qualis vita finis ita*' was associated with the saintly Winchester bishop Lancelot Andrewes (d. 1626), and so with the diocese. It is encapsulated in a small book Principal Martin gave a young student, William Smoker, in 1903. In the volume, entitled 'Companionship', he had inscribed, 'Be thou faithful unto death.' Smoker recalled many years later that he had discarded many of his College papers, but that he had preserved that small book with its challenging inscription ever since.

Buckinghamshire (one), Essex (two), Hertfordshire (one), 'London' (one) and Kent (eight). Four were from further afield – Leicester (one), Lancashire (two) and Dublin (one), with a British Subject born in Austria making up the total.

A further example of the developing community spirit that the students carried forward into later life came in July 1904, when a masonic lodge, called 'Winton Lodge', was 'consecrated' at Frascati's Restaurant in London by Sir Edward Letchworth. Letchworth, a former royal official, was closely associated with the Volunteer Movement and consecrated over 500 masonic lodges in a long association with the craft. A masonic lodge could not have been initiated without the support of Principal Martin, who no doubt saw it as an element in sustaining links between students of the kind he had supported through the introduction of sports and his involvement in the military Volunteers. Winton Lodge, No. 3048, was formed as a Masonic home for Old Wintonians – i.e. ex-students of the Training College.

The founder's jewel (badge) of the lodge is inscribed with a Latin motto 'from the arms of the See of Winchester': '*Qualis vita finis ita*', which translates as 'the style of life determines its outcome', as the masons put it. Thus the lodge brought together the Christian foundation and the Volunteers, aspects of the development of the Training College close to Henry Martin's heart as he neared the end of his long term as Principal. Among the 11 founder members was Charles J. Mitchell, a Middlesex mason from Lodge Unity No. 1637, who was involved in the College Company of the 1st Volunteer Battalion of the Hampshire Regiment. A history of the first 50 years of the lodge was prepared by Alan Older some years ago, and he wrote up the centenary in 2004. Apart from the general lodge, there was also an inner

P.S. a day or two before Certif. conducted under arduous circumstances.

Wishing you all success

R. Gorman 03-05

Revising while shaving, from a 'Farewell Scrapbook' compiled in c.1904 for a leaver. It contains a wonderful series of images, some by men such as Bogie who were later to die in the First World War.

chapter. The lodge, although now less populated with Wintonians, still meets at Freemasons' Hall.

The final glimpse of the Training College in the census is in 1911, still under Henry Martin aged 66, but with a different, young wife and a one-year-old baby, his first wife having died in 1905. He was to retire the following year after a most distinguished and popular term of nearly 35 years as Principal. Comparison of the 1881 census soon after he arrived with that for 1911, when he was about to retire, shows that the number of students had risen from 56 in 1871 to some 80 at the end of his service, an impressive achievement. When he departed, on medical advice, he was described by the Archbishops' Inspector as 'one of the best Principals it has been my pleasure to be associated with'.

Several staff members he had appointed were to serve periods of over 30 years, as he himself had done. Goddard has already been mentioned. The 1911 census also records the 32-year-old William Lockton, who stayed on at the College until 1935 and was a much loved, and gently teased, clergyman. One student recorded that he was able to shave in the allegedly short-sighted Lockton's lectures without being observed!

Martin could look back on a period which had seen not only the service of loyal staff, including his appointees who had passed to other colleges in senior positions, but also Winchester students taking up posts in the diocese and further afield, many in London and other towns as well as at country positions. One student, William Smoker, recalls the personal interest taken by Principal Martin in bringing him up to speed on the catechism and rewarding him with a book on 'Companionship' inscribed 'Be thou faithful unto death'. Smoker had served an apprenticeship at an east London dockland school before entering the College aged 21 soon after 1900. Predictably, the overwhelming majority like Smoker were drawn from the pupil teacher regime, trained and entered the teaching profession. Some, however, branched out from schools to become clergy, were promoted in the prison service or worked with the forces. G. B. Lowndes (1910), for example, was on the training ship HMS *Exmouth* off Essex in 1913–14. Others took degrees, and others again joined the forces. Some of these anxieties about whether students who trained were committed to the profession had been behind the Revised Code of 1862, and the question of funding of training for candidates who did not enter or sustain a career in teaching has remained a weapon of assault

Left: John Stainer, Professor of Music at Oxford, examiner at the College.

Far left: I Company of the Volunteers on the Terrace in 1907 (note the Sphinx).

on training since. A few emigrated or took posts abroad: in 'America', Canada (several), Australia, Egypt, New Zealand, West Africa (Benin) and South Africa, and some died abroad, such as John Browne in Mauritius in 1883.

During Principal Martin's time, a music block was added north-west of the Main Building. The appearance of the Chapel consecrated in 1881, the addition of a music block and the close proximity of the cathedral remind us of the importance of music in both church and college and its importance therefore in the classroom, led by the evangelising schoolmasters from the Training College. Music was flourishing in Winchester in the middle and latter part of the nineteenth century; the singing of hymns and of the National Anthem by the students had been

noted at the opening on the new site in 1862. Music education at Winchester was under the eye of the best-known musicians in the land. Sir John Stainer, organist of St Paul's Cathedral 1872–88, had joined Her Majesty's inspectorate of music in training colleges and schools. One candidate recalled encountering Stainer (a one-eyed, genial son of a schoolmaster, but by then a noted music educationist and Professor of Music at Oxford) face to face in the music exam room in 1894.

The musical tradition continues down to the present, and the Winton Summer Reunion always includes the annual chapel service, which features hearty singing. The original music block, sited north of the courtyard, which itself lies north of and parallel to the Main Building, has been much altered and extended, both

John Colson Jr (right) and Mr Hill, the overseer of the work to support the cathedral between 1907 and 1912. Colson had designed the Training College's chemical laboratory in 1890, submitting the design to the Royal Institute of British Architects (RIBA).

The class of 1914 in the Main Building lecture hall with George Barker (seated in the aisle, left).

upwards and outwards. The Arts and Crafts superstructure over an ashlar-work south face, north of the Chapel, with knapped flint on the rear lower elevations and known to later generations at the music centre, lies west of the original music block site. Additional buildings indicate a broadening and deepening of the curriculum. College spirituality was strengthened by the addition of the Chapel, underpinned by music and the extension of the curriculum by a building programme described above in the 1880s providing the first additional teaching accommodation: a Music Room and a Laboratory, which passed building regulations in May 1885. This was the domain of Humphrey Searle. The architect John Colson Jr's application for membership of the RIBA in 1890 included the design for the chemical laboratory. With these changes and with the provision of teaching facilities for physical education, Principal Martin brought the institution into the twentieth century enlarged and firmly established.

In addition to academic and religious foundations Principal Martin had linked the institution to the army. He was at least as enthusiastic about the Volunteers as Collier, his predecessor. Both Principal Martin and some of his deputies were officers in the Volunteers and the Territorials in the College. One of his sons, Lionel, died serving in West Africa in 1905. Principal Martin's first wife also died in 1905, and as part of a

refurbishment of the Chapel the eastern wall of the chancel was decorated with *opus sectile* work in memory of mother and son. The Rev. R. A. Thomas, Vice-Principal of the College 1904–10, wrote a history of the Volunteer Company. Ten years after he left there was a very different story to tell, for the military training that the Territorials and the Volunteers received in College was to be called upon all too soon, in a world war the horrors of which they could never have imagined.

Masters and students in 1913. Many would not return.

2

The memorial window to G. H. Barker (left) in the Chapel.

The Era of the World Wars.......

PRINCIPAL WAINWRIGHT AND THE COMING OF WAR

Principal Ernest George Wainwright, like his two predecessors, became a Canon of Winchester Cathedral; he succeeded Martin in 1912 and served until 1933.

One under-recorded area of College life is that of the servants, who have always played a significant and valuable role. Fortunately, Albert Attwood wrote a memoir in the 1970s in which he briefly describes his perspective of working at the College before 1914, serving in the First World War and leaving the College afterwards.

Attwood was a Winchester boy relishing the 'joy of living near home' – his family lived at 10 Staple Garden, just inside the Westgate of the city, although he slept in the College, which 'did not concern me one bit'. As one of the kitchen staff, he 'learnt to carve a joint which proved invaluable to me in later years'. The text reproduced here has never appeared in print, and is a charming coda (written in 1980) to his published memoirs *(see p56)*.

Wainwright's tenure was soon to be interrupted by the outbreak of war. An inspection dated 31 July 1914 provides a snapshot of aspects of the College on the eve of the war. It highlights the success of Wainwright in his early years,

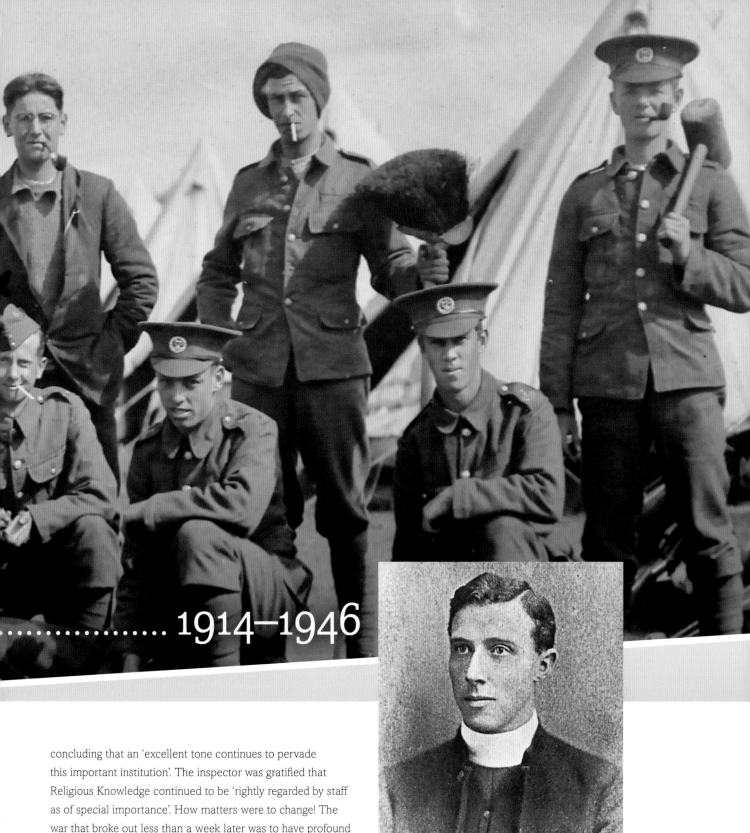

1914–1946

concluding that an 'excellent tone continues to pervade this important institution'. The inspector was gratified that Religious Knowledge continued to be 'rightly regarded by staff as of special importance'. How matters were to change! The war that broke out less than a week later was to have profound effects on the religious commitment of the country at large. In 1916, when the Archbishop of Canterbury's Religious Knowledge Certificate Inspector retired, he was not replaced. Over 20 years later, in 1938, Principal White lamented that there had been no inspection of Religious Knowledge in the institution for all that time, and reflected that the Church appeared to have lost interest in the College.

Above: George Wainwright, Principal 1912–33.

Centre: College Volunteers were at Summer Camp on Salisbury Plain when war broke out in August 1914, from V. S. Manley's albums.

Both staff and students were involved in the two world wars, and the College was twice closed to be put to military use. It is clear that skills fostered at Winchester, including leadership, Christian fortitude and sporting acumen, contributed to their efforts in the war. Especially under Principals Collier, Martin and Wainwright, the work of the Volunteers and the emphasis on physical education both contributed strongly to the sense of community at Winchester and, as demonstrated by students' attendance, at the Winton Club reunions.

WINTONIANS IN THE FIRST WORLD WAR

When the First World War broke out on 4 August 1914, the 104 students of the College Company (B Company of the 4th Hampshire Battalion) were at summer camp on Salisbury Plain. These were the successors of the Volunteer Company originally founded in 1875 and which had included an elite cyclist corps. Some pre-war students, such as H. A. Alexander (in Hungary) and A. E. Beaumont (in Germany), found themselves in enemy territory at the outbreak of war. Beaumont, who had left the College in 1904, returned home, fought as a Rifleman and was killed on 2 July 1915 on the Western Front. Sixteen of the Company volunteered 'for Irak' and so served in Mesopotamia, where some, such as H. W. Rose (Ongar, Essex), A. Warne (Brighstone, Isle of Wight) and A. Tarrant (Wroughton, Wilts), were among many from the battalion who did not return *(see p60)*.

In all some 60 Wintonians lost their lives during the war. These servicemen were almost all soldiers: one sailor drowned

THE DIOCESAN TRAINING COLLEGE: A VIEW FROM THE KITCHEN ....

- Previous to the outbreak of The First World war the above named college was known as the Diocesan Training College.
- Only male students were accepted, and the number in training at that time was approximately one hundred and fifty, most of whom were in residence.
- The students at all times were seen to be well dressed, all conforming to the same style.
- Strict discipline for students and staff alike prevailed throughout the college.
- The Principle *[sic]* at all times held fast his given authority, and when decisions had to be made, he made them, sometimes contrary to the many opinions which were adverse to his.
- A hand bell ringing was the method used for calling all students to assemble together at a given locality, which could be for church, dinning hall *[sic]*, or lectures.
- Silence throughout the whole college at times presented an uncanny atmosphere.

- At mealtimes the students would make their way to the Dinning Hall in an orderly manner, and then sit quietly until the arrival of the three masters, namely Reverend Lockton, Mr Goddard, Mr Jarman. A table was provided for them at the far end of the dinning hall.
- Great respect was always shown to the masters except on one occasion the fifth of November when late at night a terrible bang went off outside Reverend Lockton's door. The date may have excused the culprit or culprits as nothing came of it.
- The college was based upon Ecclesiastical ruling, thus providing a firm and essential foundation upon which to build.
- The training was hard, and often a student would be sent home for a rest, due to overstudy, known as brain fag.
- The staff, excluding the masters numbered nine, this included Reverend Wainwright's personal staff, Parlourmaid and Housemaid.
- The Principles' *[sic]* residence at the east end of the college looked toward the main entrance.
- The little church at the west end stood detached from the college.
- This historical college and the little church before the first world war stood alone amid lovely country, which presented a most beautiful panoramic picture.

Albert E. Attwood

'... a most beautiful panoramic picture'.

Captain George H. Barker, MC of the
Hampshire Regiment, tutor, soldier and mentor.

QUORUM PIETATES NON

GEORGE·H·BARKER

in the closing months of the war. The three groups – officers, NCOs and privates – were even in size, with 20 officers (15 second lieutenants, two lieutenants and three captains), 20 NCOs (eight were sergeants and two sergeant majors), 16 privates, two gunners and an able seaman.

T. E. Adlam started off in the ranks, but was commissioned as an officer during the War. He earned the Victoria Cross for action on 27 September 1916. His decoration rewarded heroism on the Western Front in the thick mud and shellholes near Thiepval where, despite his wounds, he showed exceptional bravery in fighting while leading his men. His devotion to duty is noteworthy in that his mother died in the late summer of 1916, but Adlam, rather than return home, stayed with his platoon and made a heroic contribution to the capture of an enemy position in late September. He was wounded and was back in England when his VC was gazetted on 25 November. Unaware of the recommendation and the outcome, he learnt the news from his father over the phone (see p58).

George Barker MC of the Hampshire Regiment is commemorated by a fine window at the north-west corner of the Winton Memorial Room, now reinstated as the Chapel, on the King Alfred campus (see p54). His connection with the Hampshire Regiment is signalled by the presence, in the lower left-hand corner, of the regimental badge. Barker, as the window proclaims, was a student at the College 1900–2, and thereafter did some teaching there and maintained his links with the College Company of Volunteers, becoming colour sergeant in

1912. A territorial at the outbreak of the war and Headmaster of Holy Trinity School, Winchester (situated among the poorest people of the city), he continued learning, becoming one of only three people to pass the General Diploma Hygiene (with Special Honours) during the war in the 1917 awards, achieving a mark of over 90 per cent. He was rewarded with a Fellowship of the Institute, which noted his special work in 'Hygiene and Physical Training'. His training at the College and his lecturing there meant he was well prepared for these exams and had probably taught the prize winners, W. E. Jackson and M. W. Simmonds, as listed in the College in the Midsummer 1914 awards. His fitness no doubt contributed to his war service.

At Passchendaele in early September 1917 Barker was one of two subalterns of the Hampshire Regiment to be decorated for their bravery in an action in which the 15th Battalion was 'practically wiped out', facing terrible odds while attacking machine guns and blockhouses. Monty Moore – not a Winchester alumnus – who had left Sandhurst only the previous year, was awarded the VC for 'dashing gallantry and cool determination' amidst the carnage around him in capturing an enemy position, equipment and ammunition. George Barker, the more experienced officer, in the same action 'reached his objective with a few men' and held out there for 18 hours against bombing and frontal attacks, in the course of which he was wounded. He displayed 'good leading and initiative' and 'great courage and resource', for which he was awarded the MC. He returned to convalesce at Hursley, but the wounds to his hip and thigh dogged him for the rest of his life. He returned to work for the College after the war, and took on the role of 'General Secretary' of the various geographically scattered branches of the Winton Club in the 1920s. He lived on until 1932, when he died 'very suddenly' at Winchester. It is likely that the window

'Temporary Second Lieutenant' Tom Edwin Adlam, VC.

Tom Edwin Adlam, VC ....

Adlam was born in 1894 in Salisbury, one of a large family, and was recorded at home in the 1911 census. He was at the Training College from 1912 to 1914 and no doubt joined the Volunteers, as his first regiment was the Hampshire Regiment, in which he became a sergeant. From 1914, he served with distinction in the Bedfordshire Regiment, serving as a temporary second lieutenant with the 7th Battalion at the time of his VC. (It was recorded that his great expertise in throwing grenades 40 yards arose from many years of playing cricket.)

Towards the end of the war he transferred to the Royal Flying Corps. He was among the 400 officers who formed the Army Education Corps founded in 1920, before returning to civilian life as a teacher, and in time became Headmaster at Blackmoor in Hampshire. He returned to military service in the Second World War and rose to the rank of lieutenant colonel. He died in 1975 aged 81.

The citation for his VC won at Thiepval reads:

Temporary Second Lieutenant Tom Edwin Adlam, Bedfordshire Regiment.

For the most conspicuous bravery during operations.

A portion of a village which had defied capture on the previous day had to be captured at all costs to permit subsequent operations to develop.

This minor operation came under very heavy machine gun and rifle fire.

Second Lieutenant Adlam realising that time was all important, rushed from shell hole to shell hole collecting men for the sudden rush, and for this purpose also collected many enemy grenades. At this stage he was wounded in the leg, but nevertheless he was able to out throw the enemy and then seizing his opportunity, and in spite of his wound, he led a rush, captured the position and killed the occupants. Throughout the day he continued to lead his men in bombing attacks.

On the following day he again displayed courage of the highest order, and although wounded and unable to throw bombs he continued to lead his men.

His magnificent example and valour, coupled with the skilful handling of the situation, produced far reaching results.

Cross presented by the King on 2nd December 1916

in the Chapel was subscribed soon afterwards, one of the embellishments of the 1927 extension of the Chapel.

A second MC was won by Second Lieutenant Merton A. Rose, who gave his life in September 1918 in the closing battles of the war in France. Attwood, the College servant, joined the Hampshire Regiment on the outbreak of war in August 1914, and went to the North-West Frontier in India and also Mesopotamia. His brother William joined the Sussex Regiment at the same time, and was killed in France in 1915. When Albert returned after the war in 1919 his career did not flourish, for although the Vice-Principal (Lockton) and Matron 'tried to keep me', Principal Wainwright 'said I must go' – surely an example of Attwood's claim that Wainwright overrode advice?

As for those students not immediately involved in the war, they were scattered far and wide, to Durham, Exeter and elsewhere, and once it became apparent that the war would not be over by Christmas, or even within a year, the decision was taken to close the College. This led G. R. Crawford, the Honorary Treasurer of the College, to the view that lengthy closure could well lead to extinction. Closure was apparently not immediate in 1914, as V. S. Manley, in his detailed account of his own and others' service in the war, recorded that the Volunteers' adjutant had addressed him among others in the Common Room at the College on 23 November, perhaps still in the hope that the war would be over by Christmas.

V. S. Manley, with the Hampshire Regiment, in Egypt in 1919. He left a remarkable multi-volume account of his experiences and those of his Training College contemporaries. His letter from Bernard Goddard of 1929 *(see p49)* shows how, ten years on, the experiences of the Great War were still taking their toll on Manley.

A BURIAL PARTY ....

Wed. 14th Nov. 1917

I have hesitated to pen this chapter of horrors – a brief account of the work of a burial party at Gaza – because it has never ceased to be a continual nightmare to me, but I have hoped, and most likely in vain, that by recording it here, I might be more able to rid myself of the thought of the gruesome experience…

A fortnight ago I had made the last patrol of the ground in the small hours, with a firm grip of my rifle. This day I sauntered along in daylight. The Turkish listening posts, near which our patrols normally halted, were then visible.

The sun lit up a valley of death in which nearly eight hundred rotting corpses of British chivalry putrefied the air. At first there seemed to be lines of mounds, almost like mole heaps, but on coming nearer each was seen to be a corpse. The men had been mown down by machine-gun fire like grass before a scythe. Everywhere the ground was littered with shell cases showing what a hell of fire they had passed through.

Our party collected the corpses as best they could on stretchers and laid them in lines alongside the graves. Those who had fallen on the higher ground were mummified, their hair, and even a moustache, having remained intact, and their clothes still remained. But men who had fallen in low and damp parts had been reduced to bleached bones, with barely a shred of clothing remaining. My job was, perhaps, ghoulish. As it was necessary to secure the identity disc, and the buttons refused to undo, I armed myself with a large wire-cutter and cut the buttons off the tunic and shirt. Then began the hunt for the disc which was always worn around the neck. In many cases the string had rotted and the disc disappeared in consequence. I did not, however, hurry over such an unpalatable occupation, as I kept in mind those at home who were anxiously waiting news of these men. Only after an exhaustive search did I put back any corpse as "Unknown".

As an example of devotion we found a Colonel, his Adjutant and their batman lying side by side…. Most of the corpses had a peaceful expression, but the look of horror on one man's face haunts me still. He had been shot clean through the neck, and had gripped the place in a frenzied attempt…

Lieut C. J. Law (son of Bonar Law, Prime Minister) 5th K.O.S.B. was found and buried in the cemetery near the Burnt Tank.

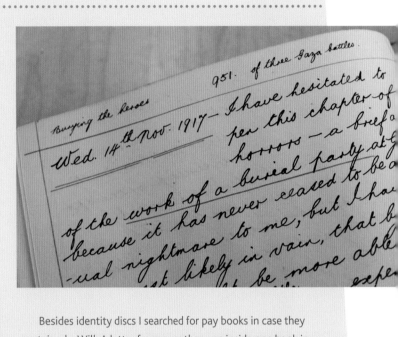

Besides identity discs I searched for pay books in case they contained a Will. A letter from a mother was inside one book in which she commended her boy to God. The unposted reply was there, too, in which he stated his expectation of 'going over the top' shortly. A strange case occurred when an officer passed by at the moment his son was identified. One must draw a veil over such a pathetic scene. Only one Turk did we find, a giant who had been killed very recently, and he disappeared over-night.

V. S. Manley

The burial party and a tank in Gaza.

Below: A group of students in Mesopotamia. Oakley, Rose, Warne and Tarrant (seated) died; Walter (right) survived.

Bottom: Advance of the 75th Division in Palestine, 6–10 November 1917.

Right: Manley's Roll of Honour, 1915, emblazoned with the College crest.

Wintonians who volunteered for service in Mesopotamia - Oct. 1915.

3381 Purkis. H. S, Pte. Jersey - (Died of disease whilst Prisoner of War at Kut-el-Amara.)
1865 Smith. Ralph, L. Cpl. - Swindon - (Shot in elbow 21.1.1916)
3084 Singleton. C. F, Pte. Codford, Wilts - Died.
2167 Bolwell. F. W. J, Pte. Radstock - Killed.
1869 Windust. A. H, Pte. Eastleigh, Hants - (Survived).
2185 Oakley. E. R, Pte. Broseley, Shrop - (Shot thro' shoulder. 21.1.1916)
1862 Rose. H. W, Pte. Ongar, Essex - (Killed in action
3078 Hurst. G. F, L. Cpl. - London S. E. - (Wounded 21.1.1916.
3611 Richardson J. J, Pte. I. of W. -
3616 Soper W. F, Pte. - Cowes, I. of W. -
2195 Tarrant. A, Pte. Wroughton, Swindon (Killed in action
1867 Clifford. W. C, Pte. Charlton S.E. -
1867 Warne. A. Pte. Brighstone I. of W. (Killed in action
2199 Woodfield. A, Pte.   (Died of disease 8th/1916).
        Rodd. E. W.   Shanklin I. of W.
        Butcher. J. Pte. Canterbury.
(Westminster Training College. — 3081 Pittuck. B, Pte. - London).

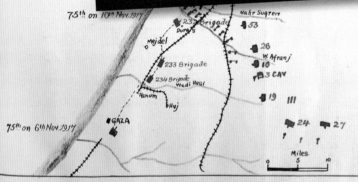

75th on 10th Nov. 1917.
233 Brigade
Nahr Sugreir
53
Mejdel
Durg's
26
W. Afranj
10
233 Brigade
234 Brigade
Wadi Hesi
3 CAV
Hanum
Hyj
19   III
75th on 6th Nov. 1917.
GAZA
24   27
Miles
5   10

Advance of the 75th Division – 6th –10th Nov. 1917.

Manley, among much else, recorded Wintonians serving with him in India, and included transcribed letters by staff such as Goddard, with whom he corresponded in 1929, and from Captain Kirby, head of the Wintonians in the war, as well as compiling a Roll of Honour of war service by his Wintonian contemporaries. Troops, mainly members of the Army Pay Department, occupied the College buildings, relinquishing them only in 1919. Their departure was followed by significant refurbishment, including electric lighting and central heating, and the College was able to open for 72 students in the autumn of that year.

DEVELOPMENTS AFTER THE WAR

Change followed the Great War. Changes in legislation, for example the raising of the school leaving age and the Teachers' Superannuation Act of 1918, were among many reasons for a surge in applications for training. Among the men who joined in the post-war period was Reginald George Wing, who made a lasting contribution to the College in a variety of ways, first as a student from 1922 to 1924 and subsequently as Secretary of the Winton Club from 1934 to 1960; he also acted as a representative and provided a 'communal memory' on the Governing Body. In 1949 he completed a short history of the College through its first 109 years. The Chapel was enhanced by a fine wooden statue of King Alfred, which is now centrally located between the four west windows *(see p81)*. These windows depict the evangelists, in memory of Wing, whose connection with the College spanned the change from Diocesan Training College to King Alfred's College in 1928.

Proposals to increase numbers from 80 to 100 were made, and it was further proposed to enlarge to 200, 'a proper economic size', by 1925 – the perennial issue of 'critical mass' –

William Leach's memorial in the Chapel. Born near Salisbury, he left the College in 1909. During the War he served as an RSM in the Hampshire Regiment, leaving from 2, Alswitha Terrace, Hyde. Captured by Turks af the seige of Kut, he performed 'outstanding work for his fellow captives' and was allowed to travel to different camps in support of his men. He caught typhus and died in Turkey aged 30. He is also commemmorated in Baghdad and at St Bartholemew's church, Hyde.

via an interim 150. Principal Wainwright successfully pioneered the admission of nonconformists; Catholics were also admitted. These Roman Catholics, initially with the nonconformists, were marginalised to live at 'Edgehill', renamed St Swithun's Lodge and acquired in early 1920 to house an additional 20 students. It lay a short distance west of the Anglican stronghold of the Main Building, and the presence of Catholics there no doubt explains the appellation 'the Vatican'. When a lecturer and chaplain, the Rev. Paul Kingdon, lived there in the 1950s he was known therefore as 'the Pope'. The St Swithun's Lodge property included two acres of land and its staff cottage (The Cottage), a significant addition to the site of the Main Building, itself originally only a five-acre parcel of land. The 1920 purchase cost £4,000 and was the precursor of many such purchases of properties nearby and further afield in Winchester, providing a template for expansion towards a platform of long-term mass and viability.

Among changes to the College teaching accommodation in the decade after the First World War was the addition of an Art Room, completed and in use by 1926, when the visiting Board of Education inspector recommended that new workshops be erected on site, and improvements were duly and promptly carried out. The inspector also noted that a proposed increase in numbers would ahve an impact on existing spaces, picking out the Dining Hall and the Chapel – maybe he was prompted to refer to these areas,

Henry Thatcher (R) with his contemporaries standing outside their dormitory cubicles, 1932.

as resources to address these precise matters were speedily forthcoming.

Plans were drawn up for extension to the Dining Hall on 1 July 1927, were submitted to the City Council on 5 July, and passed on 28 July. The Dining Hall, situated in 1862 in the Main Building opposite the main entrance from the south from the Terrace, was enlarged by encroaching further on the original 'Exercising Court' at its south-east corner to allow covered space for more dining tables there. In addition, the whole of the kitchen (north) side of the Main Building was 'overhauled'. This area and associated spaces are now known as MB Room 11.

A fine coloured plan of the proposed extension to the Chapel was submitted at the same time, with a ground plan showing how the extension would require cutting back the bank to the west and removing the hedgerow there. The extension was to add 68 new seats to the 86 already there, for a total of 154 – a recognition that the College was not growing as fast as had been hoped. Much of the old west end of the original chapel was preserved and reused: the Rose Window was taken down and re-inserted in the new west wall, which includes a line of carved heads of ecclesiastical and lay figures on a string course where the former western entrance would have been. Who do they

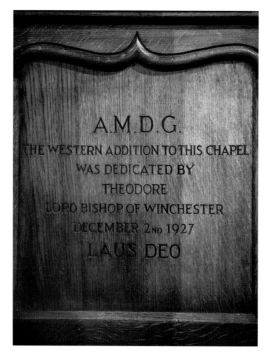

Above: Chapel extension dedication panel, 1927.

Right: Staff and students after the Great War in 1920: Wainwright, with Lockton on his right, Davies, and Goddard on his left.

represent? We don't know. The west doors were recycled on the north side, there being no longer a western entrance; on the south-east corner buttress the original carved heads are to be seen. Today there are uncarved blocks in the western extension bay of the Chapel, ready for, but having never received, the carvings they deserve. Internally the panelling from the west wall was re-erected against the new west wall, with additional panelling being supplied on the north and south walls, and centrally where the west door had formerly stood. A carved panel inside the south door of the Chapel records 'AMDG The west addition to this Chapel was Dedicated by Theodore [Woods] Lord Bishop of Winchester December 2nd 1927.'

Wainwright's plan to increase to 200 by 1925 was frustrated, with only 103 enrolled at inspection in 1926. Growth was still the Principal's main preoccupation, as revealed in his proposal to increase to 150 in three years starting on 1 August 1927.

Carved heads from the western wall of the 1881 Chapel, rebuilt in 1927.

Holm Lodge, purchased in 1926.

With this proposed expansion in view further property was acquired, while borrowing was comparatively easy before the crash of 1929 – but only comparatively so. When the Diocesan Finance Committee purchased Holm Lodge, north of St James's Lane (1925–7), this was achieved only by balancing College finances 'in face of considerable financial difficulties'. Student fees were raised from £15 to £20 a head and considerable savings were demanded in office expenditure, on replacement of furniture and repairs, and on lighting, heating and other basics. Nonetheless, the purchase went ahead to accommodate the growing number of students, and Christchurch Vicarage, just south of the Lane and renamed St James's Hall *(see p72)*, was subsequently bought in 1928 to accommodate 28 students. In fact plans changed, and Holm Lodge was made a residence for the Principal, while the east end of the Main Building was converted to accommodate the students.

The inspector's report of February 1926 was written while the purchase of St Swithun's was demonstrating the value of increased space, and negotiation for the purchase of Holm Lodge was in progress. This report provides a snapshot of the College after nearly 65 years in the 1862 buildings. The inspector noted that the numbers, 80 at the end of the Great War, had by 1926 risen to 103. There was some criticism of music provision and resourcing. The chapel music was reported, somewhat opaquely, to be 'in a traditional stage' (did he mean 'transitional stage'?). More precisely he stated 'simpler and more dignified music is gradually ousting the unworthy', and advised 'a better hymn book'. This hints at some conflict in liturgical matters within the College chaplaincy and community, a recurrent theme in the history of the institution.

A student from the early 1930s opined that Principal Wainwright, who retired in 1933, 'left much to be desired': this may have been one such area of concern. The inspector noted an orchestra conducted by a student, and that more and better pianos were required, as well as a music library. It was pleasing that the College had obtained a 'gramophone', in common with national trends at that time. Music was also a social activity, with

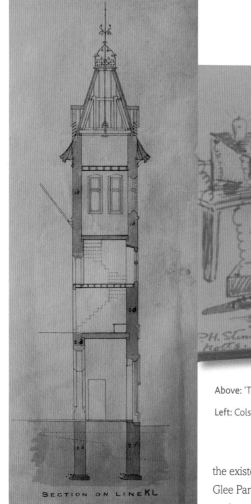

SECTION ON LINE KL

Above: 'The Princes in the Tower', Stimpson and Newnham transmitting in 1924.

Left: Colson's 1860 section for the College tower.

the existence of a Glee Party of College students and nurses (to enhance the range of voices, among other attractions), and dances arranged by the Winchester School of Art. Beyond these activities a French Society, a Dramatic Society and a Shakespearean Society were noted. On a very positive note the report concluded that 'The College has every right to be proud of the reputation it has earned'. The teachers were undoubtedly fulfilling the original purpose: 35 who had completed their course were working in the two dioceses, 20 in Winchester and 15 in Salisbury, with four placed in The Midlands and two and four respectively in 'The West' and 'The East'. At this period a number of students were working towards degrees as opposed to the teaching certificate. These men clearly enhanced the College in the inspector's eyes – 'setting the pace' and 'creating varied interests'. Their degrees were London University, some BA, mainly BSc, while one – no doubt a leading light in the French Society – had completed a successful third year at 'Paris University'.

A NEW NAME, AND UNEASY ALLIANCES

The reporting inspector noted the strong connections with, and influence of, Winchester College school, from which 'the active portion' of the Governing Body was drawn. Rules on conduct in the town were similar in both institutions, sporting fixtures took place between them, collegers attended classes in the school,

and the older boys at the school were reported to influence 'considerably yet indirectly' the behaviour of the students (!). This relationship was not at all surprising, as the links between the two went back to the opening of the Diocesan School in 1840. Added to this was the close proximity and shared educational purposes, not to mention the fact that the buildings of both institutions had strong architectural resonances with the fourteenth century *(see p27 and p40–1)*.

Winchester College remained the much larger, and infinitely better funded, of the two institutions. In 1925–6 there were 476 boys and 45 dons (masters), a ratio of some one to ten. The governing

H. A. L. Fisher.

C. A. Cripps.

Bishop Alwyn Williams.

body of ten (not including the Warden, the Director of the British Museum Sir Frederic Kenyon), included men with an interest in education and social change, such as H. A. L. Fisher, Warden of New College, who had been involved in framing the 1918 Education Act, and the Labour peer C. A. Cripps (Baron Parmoor), who had a special interest in the Church of England as a High Anglican and archiepiscopal official. The governors were national figures, however, and it was the practical assistance of successive heads that drew the institutions together. The Rev. Alwyn Williams was Headmaster of Winchester College 1924–34, where he had taught for many years previously. A canon of Winchester Cathedral – as were

KING ALFRED (d. 599) ....

It proved a truly inspired and prescient choice when the Diocesan Training College added King Alfred to its name in 1928. Alfred's life was dominated by the conflict in his mind between secular and clerical callings. In certain respects the struggles of the college to which this long-dead king gave his name reflect similar conflicts of interest from time to time, whether viewed from an ecclesiastical or secular standpoint. The choice of Alfred sent a series of messages, antiquity being one, and the royal status of Winchester another, although Alfred is only recorded once in the city in his lifetime, sentencing Danish marauders to death. He became much more secure in Winchester after his death, when he was buried first in Old Minster then New Minster, ultimately being moved to Hyde Abbey in 1110.

Thornycroft's 'Christian warrior peasant' statue of 1901 re-established a visible presence for the king in the city and continues to do so. Alfred is associated with laying the foundations of what became England. His learning is well attested, his military prowess acknowledged (the Danes conquered or mauled most of the other kingdoms in England) and his Christianity paramount. Even his lack of culinary expertise would have struck a chord with the hungry students at the time of the Great Depression and thereafter. While the cakes were burning (if we believe the story), Alfred was planning guerrilla tactics. Later he oversaw the construction of the great system of forts in Wessex, and he also organised the army into a viable force and, tradition has it, developed a navy.

The king was clearly adept at business administration, leaving a significant fortune in his will, and was also a renowned law-maker, whose innovations began to set the English law system 'apart from every other'. His 'court of scholars' was a step in reviving education in England: the 'Alfred Jewel' bears a legend stating 'Alfred had me made', and may depict Christ personifying wisdom. His deeply religious and scholarly output 'more certainly than any other work in Europe's middle ages … bear the impress of a single, royal, mind'. He remains the best documented Englishman of the Anglo-Saxon era, and before Becket (d. 1170) the most written-about man in the Middle Ages. The choice of Alfred as a patron of a college – now a university – teaching a wide selection of Alfred's known skills in a secular environment based on a Christian ethos, was a move full of *wisdom ond lar*. Alfred would feel at home here.

The Alfred Jewel and Thornycroft's statue of Alfred.

Right: Winchester 'Voluntary Corps' students on the SS *Aquitania*, 1926.

Far right: Summer teaching outside the Assembly Hall, 1933.

successive Principals of the Training College/King Alfred's, such as Wainwright – Williams was very familiar with King Alfred's College, and after a spell at Durham returned as Bishop of Winchester from 1952 to 1961. Alwyn Hall is named after him in recognition of his long association with and support of the College.

In the mid-1920s, the growth in numbers of students to over 100 and the use of the term 'College' for the Winchester Training College on West Hill were causing confusion with Winchester College, the College of St Mary *prope Winton*, down in the valley. Discussions involving Williams and Wainwright led to the renaming of the West Hill institution King Alfred's College in 1928, when a further 21 students joined the complement. Economics, social change, legislation and developments in higher education all contributed to a period of exceptional, and often unpredictable, change.

King Alfred's was one of a group of colleges of education scattered across the south of England. Some, like King Alfred's Anglican, the Training College of the Immaculate Conception, otherwise La Sainte Union (Roman Catholic), Southampton, and the Anglican women's colleges at Chichester and Salisbury, were also denominational. Others, such as the municipal college at Portsmouth, were secular foundations. Universities and university colleges had developed in the wake of the early training colleges. The legacy of Henry Robinson Hartley (d. 1850), who despite having his 'obscene and blasphemous' anti-Christian writings destroyed against his wishes after his death, provided for a secular polytechnic adult school in Southampton which opened in 1862, and became Hartley University College in 1902, but was not to become a university until 1952, when it received its Royal Charter.

Nonetheless, discussions were already in the wind in 1926 proposing 'attempts to create a real connection between the two colleges' – the Diocesan Training College at Winchester and Southampton. However, then as during the next eight decades on and off, the same basic issue emerged: 'difficulties in travelling have prevented a fruitful cooperation up to the present time and tentative measures have had to be abandoned'. The Winchester educational

fraternity of institutions, St Mary's College in the valley and King Alfred's College at the top of the hill, were self-supporting, with much in the way of shared Christian philosophy, chapels and so on. Southampton University College, on the other hand, had grown up from different root stock, and was not readily discernible as an obvious partner. Elsewhere in the region, a Reading-based arts and sciences college of the 1860s and 1870s became an extension college of Christ Church, Oxford, in 1892, and received a royal charter in 1926 – the only such institution to achieve this distinction in the inter-war years. Further afield London and Bristol universities were respectively active and potential validators of courses.

Despite the issue of distance, links were envisaged with universities for the purposes of framing and conducting examinations in academic subjects. In 1928 Winchester, prompted by the government, was still investigating links with Southampton, and a draft scheme of co-operation had been agreed. However, government plans changed, and a joint examining board was established in each of 11 regions, with the Board of Education assessing practical teaching. The Training College at Winchester was linked under this scheme with the University of Bristol, giving a south-west regional focus, Southampton not then being a fully fledged university. Later the Vice-Chancellor of Bristol and Professor Lawton of Southampton joined the Winchester Governing Body.

The more academic Bristol-based Joint Board was welcomed by Principal White (1933–46), who described it as 'representatives of Bristol University, University College, Southampton and a number of training colleges

Hartley University College Southampton

Hartley University College Southampton, *c.*1900.

(including ours) and three domestic colleges' with its 'finances made up of grants and students examination fees. The colleges have no financial responsibility'. However, the Joint Board provided a welcome link with 'highly developed' university education, at Bristol. Disputes between the institutions arose periodically, including on one occasion while King Alfred's was subject to Southampton (from which White was delighted to escape into the welcoming arms of the Bristol Joint Board). In White's words:

> *On the History Board of Studies there was myself, a nun and a Chairman and the latter was afraid of the nun, who raised a fuss because the World Outline of History paper had a question on the Reformation epoch, and he ordered it to be struck out but the same paper could contain a question (framed by the nun) on Thomas More… They couldn't apparently see at the Convent that we had to regard History as something of an objective study and anyhow (to take that one example) whatever you think of the Reformation, it did happen and a history student might be expected to know of it.*

What 'infuriated' Principal White was that the external examiner (presumably the Chairman) argued that he was '"trying to compose denominational differences" as he put it'. However, White feared that 'the Romans' would take the battle to Bristol 'and marshal their forces to scare the Joint Board'. The archive contains a sheaf of copies, no doubt prepared by White for the governors and others, of the proposal to join the Bristol Joint Board which culminated in the statement, 'The conditions for passing the examination of the Board are those of Bristol – slightly harder than at Southampton.'

THE INTER-WAR YEARS: POLITICAL AND SOCIAL INFLUENCES

External events affecting staff and students during the inter-war period included the General Strike (1926) and the Crash of 1929, followed by the Great Depression. Social change after the Great War resulted in a less compliant student body. Many had witnessed the horrors of war at first hand, so these attitudes were predictable but not easily managed. Personal and institutional problems for students and staff in the early 1920s were soon sidelined by national and international events. The General Strike of 1926 provided an opportunity for the trainee schoolmasters to put their shoulders to the wheel of authority. Travelling in a canvas-covered lorry, students went to Southampton docks in May 1926, breaking the strike and receiving abuse from strikers. The 'Voluntary Service Corps T C Battalion' from Winchester unloaded ships ranging from the 'spud [potato] boat' to the liner SS *Aquitania*. Some used their payments to purchase fashionable 'Oxford bags' to replace clothes damaged in the rough dock work.

From 1919 to 1930 the College had doubled in size, to over 160 students, and despite the crash in the world economy,

St Grimbald and education ....

St Grimbald (d. ?901)

Grimbald of St Bertin (St Omer, Pas de Calais) was a Benedictine monk who helped King Alfred with his literary work. Grimbald's mission it has been suggested was to help Alfred counter 'cultural as well as political barbarism.' He was described by Alfred as 'my mass-priest' and is credited with bringing the precious relics of St Judoc from Picardy to Winchester. He may also have brought manuscripts from the Continent and if so may have been a key figure in Alfred's revitalisation of English culture in the tenth century. Through a programme of translations key elements of Christian Latin texts were rendered into English vernacular. In addition a continental scholar such as Grimbald may have passed the literary and artistic culture of the Carolingian Renaissance into the England of Alfred and his successors. Grimbald is traditionally considered a co-founder of New Minster at Winchester, dedicated in 903, but that was two years after Grimbald's death. A cult grew up in his honour at New Minster. Grimbald's remains, and those of Alfred, were removed to Hyde when that abbey was established by Henry I in 1110 and New Minster destroyed. Perhaps the best account of Grimbald's life dates from c.1300 in a Breviary of Hyde Abbey. St Grimbald's day is 8 July.

(after R. W. Pfaff, ODNB*)*

funding from the Church of England held up. Further phased building development was planned to include an expansion of the Dining Hall (£600), a new wing added to St Swithun's Lodge (£3,300), and a new Assembly Hall west of the Chapel (£2,400). The Assembly Hall was achieved in 1930 by creating a flexible space that could act as three classrooms with partitions, capable of conversion into a single space. This hall, with its arcaded frontage, is also described as the 'Lecture Loggia' *(see p67)*. These new works cost in the range of £6,000 to £7,000.

St Grimbald's Court was begun in 1930 with funds drawn from a loan of £20,000 from the Central Board of Finance and opened in 1932. It was described some years later as 'a modern brick building of pleasing appearance containing no less than 40 study-bedrooms and a modern library, the fine oak shelving the gift of the Winton Club, being designed by Messrs James Laverty ... the Winchester cathedral craftsmen. Also ... rooms for a resident tutor and a Common Room for students.' This presaged emergent change as numbers increased, namely the devolution of common rooms to

St Grimbald's Court from the north, 1934.

Richard Clement White, Principal 1933–46.

residences. Encouraged by Principal White, this innovation reduced the central role of the Main Building.

Various matters, including the Depression, conspired to result in a reduction in numbers: the 160 noted in 1931 was down to 130 in 1933 and 129 in 1936, with a notable fall in the number of degree candidates. It also led to curriculum changes. In History, for example, the curriculum changed from a general global outline (including the Renaissance and Reformation) to a focus on the period since the Congress of Vienna in 1815 which followed the end of the Napoleonic wars. The upside of these reduced numbers was that the students could live in more comfort, both at St Grimbald's and in the Main Building, where the former cubicles were converted into study bedrooms.

PRINCIPAL WHITE: A NEW VISION

Principal Ernest Wainwright's 21-year Principalship ended in 1933. It was time for a younger man, and the governors settled on the Rev. Richard Clement White, a 32-year-old graduate of Exeter College, Oxford, who brought experience of work at St Luke's College, Exeter, and latterly as a warden and lecturer at Sheffield University. There was also a change at this time at Winchester College, with the Rev. Spencer Leeson arriving in 1934, and White and Leeson established a friendly working relationship.

White was a High Churchman who did not favour recent changes in the service book of the Church of England – presumably the hotly debated 1928 Prayer Book – which had had to be promoted through Parliament when it failed to achieve acceptance within the Church community. White found its language 'banal', perhaps compounding divisions noted in the guarded criticisms of the chapel activities recorded in the inspection of 1926. White's mission was that the College should be an educational institution, and not merely a place that 'peddled tips for teachers'. Some of his ideas (for example that the College should aspire to be a mixed community) were well ahead of their time, and were fiercely opposed by 'First World War-influenced' members of the Winton Club.

The increased size of the Chapel in 1927 had provided sufficient seating for 154 people. Perhaps it was White's experience in the secular university at Sheffield (which had grown exponentially since 1919) that persuaded him that

if Winchester was to expand – part of its mission – it would soon outstrip the available seating in the Chapel. It was White therefore who took the decision to do away with compulsory chapel, probably in 1934.

The 1936 inspection by the Board of Education, called for by the new Principal, highlighted the inadequacy of the Library and the need for an Assembly Hall and a larger Gymnasium, with asphalt provision for outside activities. The comparatively new Assembly Hall/Lecture Loggia of 1930 suffered from the

TWENTY YEARS AFTER ....

The July College Reunion at Winchester in 1934 was the most remarkable ever held at The Training College, for there we saw a gathering of Survivors of the Great War. A bugle sounded on The Terrace, and Capt. B. R. Goddard took command of his last Parade. Subdued emotional flashes passed through our minds – of the happy Pre-War days here, and to some there was a sense of North-West India, of Mesopotamia or of France. And unconsciously there were none apparently missing as we stood in company with those who, in reality, lay in heroes graves. The Roll was called....

After Roll Call the Parade adjourned to the Hall for a Camp Supper, the only illumination being candles, stuck on ration tins...

V. S. Manley

Right: Bar End Playing Fields, purchased 1935.

Below: Physical Training on the Dytche, 1933. Generations of students loved sporting activity at the College. At least one is known to have had his ashes scattered on the sports field in recent years.

inevitable drawbacks of such 'flexible spaces', the inspector noting that change of use from classrooms to Assembly Hall involved the heavy labour of clearing furniture and so on.

Similar problems were noted in the Library/Common Room at St Grimbald's. In a clear warning for the future he noted that the laboratories and other buildings were not constructed of permanent materials, 'and will have to be replaced'. The College had purchased playing fields at Bar End, about a mile from the main site in 1935, at a cost of £2,000, to which was added a heavy legal charge of £420. These fields, while not ideally situated, were a great boon, and were to become exceptionally valuable in the great era of expansion after 1958. Consequent upon the inspection, the first-floor Common Room in St Grimbald's Court

KING ALFRED'S COLLEGE, WINCHESTER.

was converted into the Library, and provision was made for the building of a new Gymnasium on the Dytche, with two tennis courts to the west, and a large new Assembly Hall.

Such major projects required additional funding, which was addressed by raising fees, which were more than doubled from the £20 of 1926 to £50 ten years later, although the blow was to an extent alleviated by the intervention of the Church Training College Common Fund, which contributed £9 to fees in each case. The new Gymnasium was opened in May 1938; its gas heating was a particular novel feature of the day. The Assembly Hall, built end-on to the Gymnasium, to the east, down slope from the east end of the Main Building, was delayed because of the shortage of steel, but was successfully completed during the war in 1940.

In the uncertain times of the 1930s the College men may have become more introverted. A contemporary recorded that student intakes included boys whose families had lost their money in the financial crash, and so, presumably, were sending their sons into a more stable and affordable profession. The 'Bishop's Court', in which seniors 'tried' and tested uppity (or indeed any) juniors they could lay hands on, and the St Luke's

night celebrations of 18 October, provided an opportunity early in the academic year for the seniors to exercise their authority over the recently arrived juniors.

These occasions were understandably feared by juniors, with corporal punishment being meted out by the seniors in some cases. 'Slow-serving' was a particularly heinous offence in the eyes of senior men. In 1935 a student paying the penalty in the slow-servers' race, in which he was required to participate with a chamber pot on his head, fell and gashed his knee so badly on the broken china that he was hospitalised. W. D. Wickson, in the newly designated post of Senior Student (formerly Senior Prefect, a term in use at, and drawn from, Winchester College), took the lead and banned future activities of this kind. He recorded his extreme disgust that he had been obliged 'to watch the appalling obscenities which my fellow first-year students had to suffer' in 1933. Subsequent attempts to resurrect these practices in the years immediately prior to the Second World War were mocked by other students, and the revival failed.

Principal White was sympathetic to these student-led reforms. Surviving evidence suggests that most got on well together, and in many activities – singing and sport, for example – staff and students had good relationships. Plays were put on, which were initially selected by senior students but later, from the mid-1930s, fell under the auspices of the Irving Club. In 1936 103 of 129 students in the College were members of the club, and it was around this time that younger students were called upon to reflect on the Great War, in R. C. Sherriff's 'Journey's End'.

Right: St Luke's night group from 1919–20. These fearsome 'celebrations' involving the 'Bishop's Court' continued into the 1930s, striking terror into the hearts of some 'juniors'.

Left: The College on a summer's evening in the 1940s.

A MID-1930s FRESHMAN

I first came to Winchester on a wet September evening in 1935. My trunk had been despatched days before. Now, only a suitcase stood in the hall, waiting to be taken to the station. After tea my father drove me through the rain into my life's work…

St James's Lane climbed over the railway bridge and up the hill. At the top, in a ragged, shady garden stood a decrepit Victorian house. Once it had been the elegant home of affluent families [formerly Christchurch Rectory. Ed.]. Now it had declined into a hostel for first-year students at their training college, chaperoned by a pair of second-year men behaving like prefects, and a tutor who darted in and out like an apologetic bird and did nobody any harm. St James's Hall was bleak. The ground-floor study-bedroom was shared with three other freshmen who either grew into close friendship, or gradually reached screaming-point at the sight of one another. It was a far cry from home. Just iron bedsteads with a strip of frayed carpet beside each one, metal lockers for clothes, a kitchen table with rickety chairs in the centre of the room, and drab curtains hanging at high windows which went down to the bare floor and should have opened from a gracious drawing-room on to a verandah. Now they served as an escape-route to the local pub…

Early in that first term we were thrown in at the deep end. With a partner we were turned loose in the city schools for a month of practice. This was an effort to discover if we could ever become teachers. It was four weeks of a peculiar kind of hell. The children knew who and what we were, and why we had come; they, from past experience, knew what they might do and get away with from the command-posts of their desks. They recognised as trusted conspirators our tutors, who crept into our lessons without warning, and had closely guarded signs for when havoc should break loose. We were the innocents led each day to the slaughter.

Worse torture lay ahead. Classes were brought to the college. In our turn we gave demonstration lessons before a jury of tutors and students who scribbled copious criticisms, and sniggered loudly at our discomfort when we dried up through lack of material. After the pupils had left, judgements and abuse were hurled from every direction in the lecture-room. But from such sessions came the generations of schoolmasters who followed all that was worthy in their profession – properly prepared lessons, conscientious attitudes, discipline.

John Melville Smith, 1935–7

St James's, 'the decrepit Victorian house', with its floor-to-ceiling windows opening on to the verandah.

WHITE'S ASSESSMENT: THE MEMORANDUM OF 1937

In August 1937 Principal White wrote a general confidential memorandum for the governors in which he reflected on the College since c.1930. He also took this opportunity to respond to the inspections by the Board of Education and the Board of Supervision of Church Colleges in 1936. This memorandum provides a handy snapshot of the position 20 years after the First World War, including the issues that predominated as another world war loomed.

Among the future developments suggested, White opened by addressing the issue of 'concentration' of Church Colleges: Cheltenham, Culham and King Alfred's had then recently been considered for closure, and the 'matter was still *sub judice*'. White himself favoured the closure of Culham, though in fact all survived, despite the fact that they were deemed expendable, as they were 'isolated training colleges'. White perceptively characterised Winchester as being 'semi-rural' and located 'near a city containing few people who are likely to be very much interested in the kind of social and educational work a training college seeks to do'.

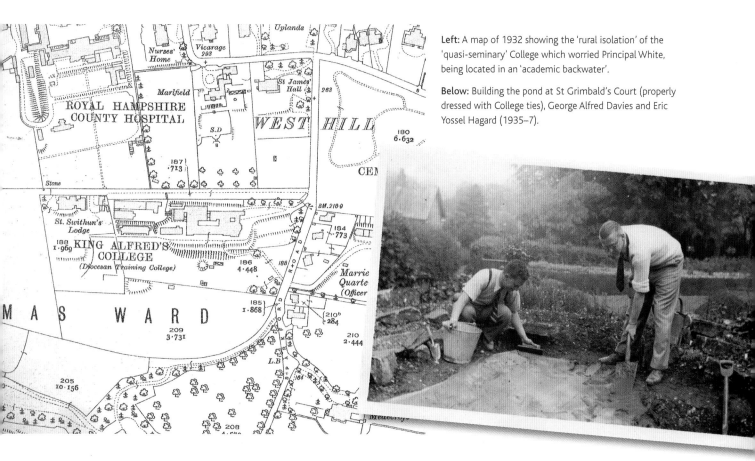

Left: A map of 1932 showing the 'rural isolation' of the 'quasi-seminary' College which worried Principal White, being located in an 'academic backwater'.

Below: Building the pond at St Grimbald's Court (properly dressed with College ties), George Alfred Davies and Eric Yossel Hagard (1935–7).

The inspectors in 1936, without reference to the Principal, had been highly critical of certain members of staff, who had 'mostly been at the College too long' and were 'hopelessly antiquated' – verbal accusations which White found 'unkind'. Nonetheless, within a year Lockton, who had served since 1910, and Burfitt, who had been in place since 1920, were both gone. White moved on to consider the 'quasi-seminary' nature of the College in a neighbourhood 'with which the College has no great affinity', which had led to isolation in contrast to colleges in Exeter, Birmingham, London and elsewhere, where there were university and other cultural attractions unavailable in Winchester, which was considered to be an 'academic backwater'. This location therefore inhibited opportunities for staff for research, and the requirement that five of the seven full-time tutors (distinguished from part-time 'lecturers') were obliged to live in prevented them getting married, although an experiment was under way with a married couple at St James's. The stipulation that staff should sympathise with the Christian work of the College was a 'limitation on those applying', while the salary arrangements were 'stupid', being those of a secondary school teacher. No other experience counted, and the peculiar nature of the College work rendered staff unsuited to migrate to state, public school or university posts – though they might, if clergymen, find parish work later in life.

As for the students, they had formerly led a very regimented and restricted life. The management of their time was comparable to 'a barracks, a monastery or a public school' – two or three compulsory chapel attendances each day including Sunday – except in the case of applicants who requested to be excused, presumably because they came from other denominations, rather than none. There were also compulsory lectures for the Archbishops' Certificate, and these took place in the morning and part of the evening, or otherwise as supervised study in two large groups. There was no privacy, as the cubicle walls of the dormitories were very thin. Nor was there to be any

> *When I was at College, the Vice Principal [Lockton] rarely left his study cum cell. If one was reading in Chapel, one had to go to his austere room and read the passage. I rushed in, just in time, and read. He didn't look up from what he was doing. 'Very well read,' he said. 'Wrong passage. Fined a shilling.' He lectured twice a week – few students understood him, and occasionally he went for a walk, holding his flat hat on with his walking stick. I understand that he was a great scholar, and Albert Dodd, a great name for many years in the Winton Club, named his house after him, 'Lockton's'.*
>
> John Shannon, 1935–7

Tutor Abbott (left), supervising Rural Science work, 1933.

'social intercourse etc with Principal or tutors; [but rather] a rigid system of control by student officials' – the 'Bishop's Court' and boisterous St Luketide activities resonate here. White hoped that younger tutors might be found who could relate more readily to the men they were teaching.

Echoes of all these experiences, synthesised from colleges beyond Winchester and under previous regimes, were to be found in the late 1930s at Winchester, despite White's best efforts. By contrast to this former regime, King Alfred's had made some (if not extensive) progress since White was appointed in 1933. Although there were still no facilities for welcoming guests (even the 'new' residence at St Grimbald's lacked pantry facilities to make a cup of tea), there were common rooms in the residences and a general games room with table tennis and billiards, and around half of students had single cubicles. The College, with its long corridors, 'remain[ed] very noisy', and abundant clubs and societies existed, as did sporting competitions, held with Southampton, Portsmouth and Culham colleges among other institutions.

One major problem troubling Principal White was the 'really isolated' location of the College. He suggested that the location of the College, especially in winter, should enable it to develop not in its role at that time as an Arts and Science College, but as an Arts and 'rural side' college. As such it should train teachers to go into the countryside, rather than drift there 'because he cannot get a town post'. The Winchester and Salisbury dioceses were historically for the most part rural. At that date changes in the academic regime had led to the phasing out of degree students, who had, he opined, occupied a disproportionate amount of tutors' time. In any case, the isolation of the College required almost constant supervision of students. The change to the Bristol Board had removed 'general elementary science' from the curriculum, thus limiting the science instruction. Work was therefore diverted towards biology, contributing to White's vision of the isolated, semi-rural college engaging in arts and rural affairs. So far as arts and crafts were concerned, his hope was that these subjects would, following discussions that had taken place with governors, be removed 'to the new County School of Art (when in being)… The gain will be incalculable from all points of view.'

WAR RETURNS

These plans, however, were frustrated by the outbreak of the long-predicted European war in September 1939, exacerbating uncertainties at King Alfred's. One strong possibility – although not ultimately realised – was that women from areas vulnerable to bombing might require admission. These were to have been from St Gabriel's College, Camberwell, and would have realised Principal White's controversial goal of engineering a mixed college. But although their college was bombed, they did not come, but rather went to Doncaster. King Alfred's was requisitioned, at 48 hours' notice, from June 1940 to 1946. Thus within nine months of the outbreak of war the College was closed once more, and its site commandeered for military personnel. Staff who were given notice included some who were still active in and around Winchester as late as the 1970s. Mr Beecroft, who arrived as the second bursar in the College's history in 1935, retired later to a property bordering Sarum Road and Chilbolton

Culham College, seen here in 1890, founded by Bishop Wilberforce, 1853.

Below: Students exiled to Culham celebrate the centenary in 1940 with King Alfred at Wantage.

Below right: Asa Briggs in khaki.

Avenue, and was still to be seen walking his dogs near the College in the 1970s. The Rev. K. W. H. Felstead (Mathematics before the war) moved to a living in Southampton before returning as Master of St Cross Hospital in Winchester in the 1970s.

Those who moved into the College included first the Intelligence Corps and subsequently the Auxiliary Territorial Service (ATS). Among the many Intelligence Corps men who passed through Winchester was the young Asa (now Lord) Briggs, the distinguished historian *(see box)*. Another bright young man based at Winchester was Allan Merson, subsequently lecturer in History at Southampton University. By political inclination a communist (students

ASA BRIGGS AT WINCHESTER ....

Lord Briggs, Baron Briggs of Lewes (b. 1921), was based at Winchester in the early years of his service with the Intelligence Corps, before moving on to Hut 6 at Bletchley Park. He recalls:

I had never been to Winchester before and I made the most of it wearing uniform. I was impressed by the Cathedral … I confess, however, that what I remember best while there for the first time is a visit that I made to the biggest cinema to watch Vivien Leigh and Clark Gable in Gone with the Wind. *When I went back to Winchester after the War and got an Honorary Doctorate of Southampton University in the Cathedral I knew about Winchester College and what Wykehamists were. I did not know who they were in 1942.*

Besides being Vice-Chancellor of Sussex University, whose interdisciplinary arts degree structures King Alfred's was to reference as it diversified in the 1970s, Lord Briggs held many senior posts as a distinguished historian, both in England, for example as Provost of Worcester College, Oxford and in the US, focusing first on the nineteenth century, and later on the BBC and other media. He returned to Winchester as an examiner of both undergraduate and postgraduate work, and was called upon to open the new library in 1978 *(see p111 and p116).*

Auxiliary Territorial Service women were at Winchester 1942–6. Back: Sheila White (Pacey), Martha 'Mac' Kennedy. Front: Joan Smith, Joan Batterby, Ethel Belshaw.

"

We're the Old Boys of Winton, the boys of K.A.C.
and though what we're here for we're damned if we can see
We leave here to teach the kids to write
But most of us only learnt last night
The students of King Alfred's
The boys of K.A.C.

When this term has ended happy we shall be,
No more oats for breakfast, no more buns for tea
We'll tell them to keep their beetroot
And stuff them down the Matron's throat
The students of King Alfred's
The boys of K.A.C.

Finals come next summer, time for us to part
We are getting older both in mind and heart.
And when we leave this lovely place
We know we'll surely bring disgrace.
The students of King Alfred's
The boys of K.A.C.

Dudley Pickles's mocking paean on
'the Carmarthen Experience' (to the tune of 'Lili Marlene')

recall Merson engaging in public debates on religion with clergy at Southampton University), Merson's ideology was reinforced by attendance as a guard at the Nuremberg trial of the Nazi leaders in 1946. An exhibition in *c.*1970 entitled 'Homes of the Intelligence Corps' featured a picture of King Alfred's, and it was noted there that it was 'the Other Ranks element' of the Corps that was located at King Alfred's early in the war.

When the Intelligence Corps was replaced by the ATS, the women's branch of the army, the first cohort of women who were neither servants nor family members of senior staff came to reside at the College. ATS work at Winchester involved keeping War Office Records and assisting soldiers and their families to keep in touch. They used the Main Building, with additional offices in Nissen huts at West Hayes on Sarum Road (soon to be purchased by King Alfred's), and were also accommodated at St Grimbald's, recalling the basic comfort of stone floors and a lack of carpets in the buildings. They carried out 'route marches' including some to St Thomas's Church in Southgate Street. They also strayed further from the site, discovering, like their student counterparts, the town cafés, such as Dumpers (in Market Street) and The Cadena (in The Pentice), where they could obtain better tea and cakes than that served in 'The Old Dining Hall' from the College kitchen and its tea urns. Entertainment included talks, for example from the journalist and writer (also in the ATS) Pamela Frankau, and a talk on fashion by Mrs Heathcote of Hursley, whose family there had contributed to the College building in 1862. Like their male predecessors on the site they developed a strong sense of belonging, and many kept in touch and returned for reunions (especially in 1995, when they

celebrated 50 years since the end of the war) all the way into the present century: some, diminished in numbers if not in enthusiasm, were present at the Winton Lunch in July 2011. Martial Rose noted that at first the male students from before the Second World War found the ATS women's presence at reunions unsettling, although the two groups had shared the common experience of life on West Hill in series, if not in tandem.

WINTONIANS IN THE SECOND WORLD WAR

'At least 27' men from the College gave their lives in the Second World War, according to Principal William Dickinson in 1948, when the number was still uncertain and the Winton Club was moving towards a decision on providing a matching memorial to that for those who had given their lives in 1914–18. It was later reckoned some 60 had given their lives. Either way the Winton Club took a leading role in establishing a suitable commemoration of their contemporaries, with the Winton Club War Memorial Committee researching memorials at other colleges, including those at Chester and Saltley.

Students and staff at saw war service in a variety of theatres. Not least among these was John Stripe, who was to become Principal in 1958. Stripe joined the RAF and was sent to North Africa, where he was Mentioned in Despatches, before going on to become a member of the intelligence staff of Earl Mountbatten, the Supreme Allied Commander in South-East Asia. Thomas Graty, who was recruited to teach horticulture in 1948, brought with him experience in RAF liaison during the Second World War, following his degree in botany and zoology from Downing College, Cambridge. L. E. Newnham (c.1922) progressed to be a Squadron Leader and made an impact in the field of radio work, 'G6 NZ'.

F. Saunders (1928–30) joined RAF intelligence and, in the course of duty, was sent clandestinely to Ireland to blow up a crashed plane containing secret documents. He also spent a period in the United States, in Maryland, engaged in work on anti-submarine detection. After the war he became Principal of the St Austell, Cornwall, Technical College, from which he retired in 1970. Philip Le Bas, a lecturer in the 1980s, was likewise a wartime pilot. These RAF examples give a flavour of the shared Second World War fighting experience both of those who had studied and those who taught.

Other survivors, such as T. G. Hull, found themselves in prisoner of war camps. But even in captivity their enthusiasm and affection for their *alma mater* was undimmed. Hull's student career at Winchester had spanned 1938–40. On King Alfred's Day, 26 October 1944, while in the third year of captivity at Camp VI, Pakan Baroe in Sumatra, he composed an '"Ode" for King Alfred's Day' *(see p81)*. No doubt he recalled the traditional chapel service and celebrations that, since 1928, had accompanied that patronal festival.

On the home front, whether as students or staff, life was disrupted and bleak during the war. Some were sent to Culham, Oxfordshire, whence they were able to make an expedition to the King Alfred Statue at Wantage in October 1940. One alumnus, recalling those far-off days in Oxfordshire, remembered that they continued to celebrate Rag Week while in exile. Students would dress up as a 'type' from about half a dozen stock characters – bishop, executioner, man about town (he recalled dressing in his dinner jacket in October 1940 to be 'the man about town') – and thus disguised would collect for the Red Cross. In this way seniors and juniors alike echoed what went on in Winchester. There was a difference in distance to a statue of King Alfred: our informant had to bicycle from Culham to Wantage (over ten miles away) where he found a convenient place to change into costume, activities being nostalgically centred on the statue of King Alfred. One wonders about the return journey after festivities! In this way the centenary of the foundation of the College was marked by the exiles *(see p75)*.

Some went to Saltley College, Birmingham, others to Trinity College, Carmarthen. A number of registered students never set foot in Winchester. At Culham, Principal White was prevented even from seeing his own students. At Trinity College, Carmarthen, the students were borne down by the primitive conditions, homesickness for Winchester and notoriously poor food. Nonetheless, the Winchester governors were grateful to these institutions, especially Trinity College, for helping out.

> *Rationing was still in vogue, of course, and the amount of food served to the students was just abysmal and hopelessly inadequate … parcels from home and visits to cafes in Carmarthen were part of our survival strategy… After 'the Carmarthen Experience', Winchester seemed almost heavenly. A different atmosphere altogether, a feeling of civilisation.*
>
> *It was bliss.*
>
> Winchester alumnus at Carmarthen

Trinity College, Carmarthen, another neo-Gothic Training College.

3

The College was run down during the War.

From Triumph to Tragedy ......

POST-WAR DESOLATION AND A
CHANGE OF PRINCIPAL

Relief and celebration greeted the end of hostilities. But as
the war ended, returning to and reopening King Alfred's
did not prove simple and straightforward. On the contrary,
negotiations to persuade the Ministry of Defence to hand
back the College were protracted. When the Army eventually
moved out and the new Principal and his staff moved in,
they were met by a scene of desolation. The College was
left without equipment and almost without furniture – a
shell of its former self. For example, the first floor of the

Main Building, which had formerly contained the students'
study bedrooms, had been converted into one long room.
During this period the Nissen hut, on what was formerly the
Principal's tennis court, and where the University Centre
and Main Reception now stands, served as the emergency
cookhouse. The playing fields at Bar End were also in a
desperate state, having been rented out during the war as
pastureland, but in 1946 they were prepared once more for
student games.

   During the delays occasioned by the negotiations to rid
the site of military functions, the governors decided a new
start was required, and Principal White's contract was not

1946–1958

renewed, nor were other staff contracts. White was taken aback by this, for he had already begun negotiating for the successful purchase of West Hayes, a mansion in Sarum Road and a former preparatory school, partly funded by compensation under Section 2(1)b of the Compensation (Defence) Act of 1939 and the 1944 Education Act. White's contract was nonetheless terminated by the governors. A former chaplain from before the war commented in the 1980s that White's 'attitude towards staff and students alike was that they were rather inferior mortals', which no doubt contributed to his downfall. Despite the termination of White's tenure, West Hayes was successfully purchased by the College in 1946, for conversion

Clifford Nolloth (1956–8) at HMS Collingwood on his first day in the Royal Navy.

into accommodation for 40 students. The first students took up residence in the summer term of 1948 (despite the lack of a boiler, which had failed to materialise), and the building was dedicated by the Bishop of Winchester, Mervyn Haigh, on 7 March 1949. The total cost of the purchase, alteration and furnishings was £15,000. A right of way for West Hayes students was negotiated through the hospital grounds to the main site.

The new Principal, W. P. Dickinson, formerly headmaster of Ormskirk Grammar School, was appointed to 'pick up the pieces'. William Dickinson was not, as his predecessors, an Anglican clergyman, breaking a tradition of over a century. He was a former scholar of Corpus Christi College, Oxford, founded by Bishop Fox of Winchester, and a lay preacher, who did much to restore and sustain the fundamental Christian ethos of the College, and to encourage collegiate life among the men. He distanced himself from Principal White's 'decentralisation' of common rooms to the residences, and worked towards a college in which students dined, studied and worshipped centrally. He appointed some staff from Oxbridge, such as Harry Blamires, a former student of C. S. Lewis at Oxford (English), and Thomas Graty from Cambridge. Others, such as Blackburn (Loughborough) and Lamb (London) had different backgrounds and skills.

Dickinson met the challenge of military personnel returning to civilian and academic life, and managed successive generations of national servicemen who came into the College. Many of these men probably had a wider experience of the world than Principal Dickinson

William Parker Dickinson, the first lay Principal (1946–58).

himself. Cliff Nolloth (1956–8), for example, who was to marry WPD's secretary Joy, was sent to the Korean War in the Navy before training as a teacher. Anxieties Dickinson may have had about potential friction between 'ex-servicemen and younger students' were soon allayed, though, and he was able to report in June 1948 that he was 'happy about the general tone of the College at present', and that 'students of all ages have lived and worked together very happily'.

This was a relief: despite Wickson and White's largely successful efforts in the 1930s to banish the wilder excesses of inter-student friction, anxiety remained that these would be reinstated post-war. Many of the customs were lost – even the sceptre of the residence competition, which had been hidden in the roof before the war, but was not found afterwards – and it was 'doubtful if the mood was there for frivolity after the war'.

POST-WAR EDUCATION POLICY AND ITS IMPACT

During the war the future of education had not been forgotten, and change was set in train. In 1944, the McNair Report complained that the teacher training institutions were 'not related to one another in such a way as to produce a coherent training service', and recommended that 'each university should establish a School of Education – responsible for training and assessment of all students in its area who were seeking recognition as Qualified Teachers'. The recommendation was implemented nationally between 1947 and 1951, although the plan for Schools of Education was dropped in favour of 'Area Training Organizations' (ATOs) 'serviced by an Institute of Education staffed and housed by the University'. King Alfred's College was thus linked once more with Southampton, which became a university in 1952.

'Ode' for King Alfred's Day.

And we, far scattered on this Earth's wide face,
No matter 'mid what strange and unfamiliar scene,
Nor how far sundered from our fellow men,
Do now remember, on this patron day
Our past estate.
Gone now the carefree hours when, as we pleased,
We idled, worked, or played, free of that shade
Of stern responsibility that now o'er-hangs,
And dominates our lives.
Now, older, clearer-sighted, sober, calm,
We view those days that, maybe,
Once we held in scorn.
Or frittered lightly, without thought that soon
We should regret the opportunity,
The life we let slip thoughtlessly away;
The Beauty that around us lay
In stone, or wood, or simple country-side:
The worth of books, of music, or of art,
All things now long foregone.
Now, do we know
That there was happiness, and peace of mind,
A spaciousness made for content,
Our youth - to some, the best they knew -
That, passing, leaves regret for chances past,
Yet mixed with happiness in reminiscence,
Fond talk that ends with sighs for good days done,
And binds us close wherever we are met.

Far left: A statue of King Alfred made as a memorial for the Chapel after the Second World War.

Left: '"Ode" for King Alfred's Day', composed by T. G. Hull (1938–40) in 1944 in a prisoner of war camp in Sumatra.

Below: Spencer Leeson (left) and Walter Oakeshott, heads of Winchester College who helped King Alfred's to recover after the War.

The fundamentals of the College's mission and purpose remained the same after the war. Although the 1944 'Butler' Education Act had encouraged widening participation in secondary education, the main role of the training colleges remained as the preparation of candidates for primary teaching. As White had noted in 1937, 'A majority of our primary teachers are trained in Church colleges,' while 'The very efficiency of the state educational machine constitutes a possible danger to the Christian tradition of English civilization by lessening parental and Church influence over the rising generation.' Church colleges, both before and after the war, were knocking on the door of secondary training through their work in Handicrafts (later Design and Technology), Physical Education (P.E.), Maths and Science. Work with older pupils may have been more attractive to these returning military men and their contemporaries than a life in primary school teaching, however idealistic they were. The existence of these subjects in the colleges provided a basis on which secondary training, and even diversification beyond mono-technic work, might be constructed.

Despite change and the privations of post-war Britain, the decade or so that followed 1945 was a positive time at Winchester, student testimony bearing powerful witness to the strong spiritual and educational values of the institution under William Dickinson's leadership. However, there were problems behind this facade. A recurring issue was the size of the College, which had still not attained the 200 set as a target in the mid-1920s, languishing at some 130 before the war. After the war the new Principal had been unable to start work because his predecessor was in place.

Fortunately the Rev. Spencer Leeson, Headmaster of Winchester College, was able to help. He advised on property availability, and further properties were bought to add to the accommodation for 130 on the main site. Leeson was replaced by Walter Oakeshott at Winchester College in 1946 and went

on to be Bishop of Peterborough in 1949. Oakeshott, a former master at Winchester College, was, like Dickinson, a layman.

By mid-1948 numbers at King Alfred's were on the rise, with a complement of 166 and a target of 170 for the autumn of that year. Successful recruitment of 180 – more than the Chapel, Dining Hall and teaching space could adequately accommodate – was welcome but problematic. Nor were all the students of high quality. In 1949 one student, thrashing about to explain failure, implied his poor performance was due to having been brought up 'in a monastery' – a statement that led his tutor to comment that he was 'disinclined to believe anything' the miscreant said. Comments noted from the same long-serving member of staff on another particularly exasperating student that year indicate that this tutor thought him 'the worst ever' and 'extremely lazy or stupid'. Tom Atkinson, another senior tutor who had served since 1927, by contrast suspected there was 'no will power'.

One reason for the presence of such weak performers may well have been the new secular colleges, with more modern facilities, which brought unexpected and unwelcome competition for King Alfred's. In all there were an additional 55 new colleges founded by the government after the war to address teacher shortages, including those at Worcester and at Bognor (West Sussex), largely Local Education Authority-based. In this reorganisation a special place for the religious-based voluntary colleges was acknowledged, but the secular outlook of the new foundations constituted a threat. In December 1949 it was noted that seven of the new colleges were taking both men and women, with three of them, at Bath, Bognor and Bristol, competing in the south.

Above: Herbert Jarman, who served the College from 1911 to 1951.

CHANGES UNDER PRINCIPAL DICKINSON

The Principal debated with himself the strengths and weaknesses of his staff. 'What staff do we want?' he wrote. As is common for new managers he wondered about the quality of the very long-serving members of staff, questioning no doubt whether they were appropriately qualified in the post-war world. Herbert Jarman, aged 62 in 1949, had worked in the College since 1911, nearly 40 years, and yet had 'no diploma'. Should he be required to make way for a younger, better-qualified man? This concern echoed White's memorandum of 1937. A detailed account of his factotum role pre-war as Vice-Principal Senior Tutor, Director of Studies, Lecturer in Geography and manager of the playing fields, as well as leader of the 'rural' side of the curriculum, along with the roles of all the other pre-war staff, was recorded in a letter from Jarman at his Margate

" I'm afraid we don't find Feathe

home in 1946. In the end William Dickinson allowed compassion to take precedence, conceding that 'Jarman loved the College, and has only two years to run': he retired in 1951. It was a sign of the times that Principal Dickinson had to find out what Jarman's, and others', duties were not from former Principal White but through an intermediary, Leeson of Winchester College.

Some younger staff were appointed, such as Thomas Graty, tutor in Biology and 'rural science', in the cause espoused by Principal White a decade earlier. Graty served at the College until 1978, in which time he trained many students in the art of horticulture – one, from the 1950s, recalls that another student, anxious to impress Graty during inspection of the gardens on the slope north of St Grimbald's, resorted to using hairspray on his lettuces to create the best effect! Another student hijacked a wheelbarrow from the horticulture store to wheel his belongings to the railway station. Yet another recalled that Graty was enraged to see, despite his best efforts to instruct otherwise, a student

watering the trunk of a tree, rather than the roots spread out at its base.

Graty loved the trees, and his greatest legacy was the planting of trees such as productive walnut trees, tulip trees and many varied shrubs and other enhancements of the King Alfred site. Martial Rose recalls tasting 'the first walnut plucked directly from a Graty walnut tree above the Dytche. Milky, and so unlike any Christmas commercial walnut!' His planting books bear the record of these works, which included many rare and exotic trees. (Many of these trees have necessarily been lost as building density has increased on the site.)

Graty also taught Douglas Randlesome (1946–8), the father of a future Vice-Chancellor of the University, perhaps contributing to the 'green' environmental ethos that Randlesome's daughter reintroduced to the new university at Winchester, together with

Above: A sports team in 1947, from Douglas Randlesome's (second from left, back row) collection. Legible signatures include Page, Wright, Smith, Hughes, Vass, Busby, Branson, Crelow and Boydell.

Left: Inspecting Teaching Practice: a *Wintonian* cartoon of 1949.

at his best on Friday afternoons."

"

There was much friendship and companionship, which has been maintained by many. In the General Election in my second year we invented the candidate Alfred King the Communist, and some dozen of us covered the city with red paint posters on newspaper and a banner outside Winchester Prison, 'Vote for King and get your freedom'. After lunching one day the Principal stated that a Detective Sergeant and Detective Constable wished to interview those responsible. I am pleased – and was relieved – to say 143 out of 178 students attended and were waved out by the D.S. – 'I expected as much.' We also carved a question mark on St Catherine's Hill which made all the national as well as local press.

Intellectually, Physically, Socially, Emotionally, Morally, Aesthetically and Religiously we could gain much: and some time after leaving, I received my certificate – in a cardboard tube through the post – which, until I retired in 1992, some 37 years later, I was never asked to produce.

Howard Horstead, 1953–5

Below: Howard Horstead (referee, right) with the unbeaten 1954–5 football team.

Right: John Allen's picture of preparations for the levelling of the east end of the Dytche, c. 1951.

Left: Howard Horstead, indefatigable champion of the Winton Club, speaking at the 'senior' graduation as part of the 175th anniversary celebrations in 2015.

ethical care for the environment. He certainly would have approved. Tutors such as Graty contributed much to College life beyond the classroom, leading the violin section of the College orchestra for many years as well as performing in the area with his eponymous Graty string quartet, in which his wife played the cello.

The buildings to which the College community returned, besides being in a battered and forlorn state after its use during the Second World War, were mostly over 80 years old. Principal and staff, sometimes directing German prisoners of war, returned furniture to the Main Building that had been locked in the Chapel, where it had been in storage for the duration of the war. They were also at times to be found on their knees scrubbing, in preparation for the return of students.

A hunt ensued for an inventory of what had existed in 1940. Beds, blankets, sheets and other items had been disposed of in a 'forced sale' in 1940, and had to be replaced. As late as 1948 there were still no coverings on the study-bedroom floors in the Main Building; the Ministry of Education was 'unable to issue a permit for linoleum', so the best that could be hoped for was that the floors in the many rooms which had to be scrubbed could, in time, be polished. The financial austerity of the time is further

exemplified by the Principal's feeling that the College 'ought ... to obtain a refrigerator as soon as we can afford it'.

Measures were taken to capitalise on assets and to make extra charges. Principal William Dickinson noted in February 1948 that vacation lettings had produced a satisfying extra £300 during the year. Electricity in student accommodation brought both opportunities and anxieties. Students were allowed one 60-watt bulb, but if they had trailing wires they had to sign a disclaimer for the College, and if they had more than one bulb they incurred an extra charge. Such restrictions were short-lived, however, as new technologies became more familiar to the authorities. The dilapidated post-war state of the 1862 building was a reflection of the austerity of those days, and beyond the buildings the College still relied on its own vegetable garden.

Not everything was found after the war. Among the losses Principal Dickinson noted were the chapel vestments; as an interim measure when they did not turn up, appropriate vestments were borrowed from a former chaplain. The lectern Bible was in poor condition and required rebinding. Despite this, and appropriately on King Alfred's Day, 26 October 1946, staff and students gathered at 9.45am, William Dickinson recording,

'I want this College to be a Christian family where each works for the good of all.' One such aspect central to Dickinson's vision was that the staff and students should eat together, to which end he commissioned plans for the Dining Hall in 1951, which were amended at the end of the academic year in June 1952.

In 1951 the Dytche, the playing field south of the Terrace containing the Main Building and Chapel, was purchased from the Dean and Chapter of Winchester Cathedral. Work started straight away at the end of the summer term of 1951 on levelling and removing 'the enormous chalk mound which so long disfigured the field and made a large part of it quite useless'. It was hoped to plant flowering trees on the north side of the field near the tennis courts and kitchen garden and perhaps some sort of screen on the west side, where the field adjoined the hospital's poultry runs. There were tennis courts opposite the Chapel, where the Library now stands.

The new Elizabethan age began at King Alfred's, with some minor changes emphasising continuity. Drainage work and grass seeding on the recently purchased Dytche were carried out in 1952, when the cost of purchasing the field, professional fees and shifting the chalk had risen to £2,650. The following year 4,000 cubic yards of chalk were needed to bring the level of the lower part of the field up to something like the level of the adjacent Sparkford Road, where in 1952 the old wild rural hedges had been replaced with privet. Elsewhere on the site, in 1952 the old menservants' quarters

were adapted to a flat for the Vice-Principal, and new steel windows were installed in the Main Building between 1952 and 1955.

The major developments in the early 1950s, however, came in 1953, when the Dining Hall, still in the Main Building, was improved and upwards of £14,500 was spent on the kitchens; William Dickinson placed great value on 'having the whole College together for meals'. In the same year improvements to the Chapel were completed, including new furnishings. It is probable that these 'improvements' involved plastering/painting over two ceramic reredos panels dating from 1905: one each side of the altar.

The chaplain at this time was the Rev. H. Paul Kingdon, who, on the face of it, was a good choice to revitalise the spiritual life of the College along the lines advocated by Principal Dickinson. Kingdon had graduated from Exeter College, Oxford (Principal White's *alma mater*), where he had been chaplain before the war and fellow from 1933 to 1945. He also knew Winchester well, as his father had been a boy at Winchester College as early as 1874, and he himself had studied at Winchester College as a boy from 1920 to 1926.

Paul Kingdon was a crack shot at school and continued to take part in shooting for Winchester College Old Boys during his time at King Alfred's. As an expert on German theology, it was no doubt hoped that he would contribute both to the revitalised Christian ethos of the College (where the role of Principal was no longer filled by a man of the cloth) and as a teacher in Divinity, as he had lectured at Corpus Christi College, Oxford – Dickinson's own college.

The Coronation Procession makes its way up Sparkford Road in 1953.

H. Paul Kingdon, with the Cup and the Winchester College Shooting Team, 1926.

But the relationship failed, and they fell out. The chaplain used his position in the pulpit to attack the Principal, who kept copious notes of what happened, noting on more than one occasion, 'Am I a leper?', and elsewhere 'a lot of stuff in chapel about spiritual wickedness in high places'. Principal Dickinson felt trapped in his stall during these attacks. Among much else the chaplain criticised the Principal's Old Testament lectures on the grounds that they were the same for second-year students as for the first years, with no progression. This unfortunate situation endured for ten years, involving the Bishop of Winchester, the bishops of Fulham and Bristol, and other governors and intermediaries, who sought to find a way forward. Kingdon finally left in 1956. When he died aged 82 in 1989 – a letter in the file recording that he was a millionaire – in one bizarre press obituary it was stated that Kingdon had failed in everything he attempted: his teaching had been 'in terms so obscure' as to be incomprehensible; he had failed in relations with students, with members of the hostel he had been in charge of, in dealings with colleagues and with the Principal and later on with his parishioners.

Despite all this, students from the 1950s recall that the Principal clearly usually relished chapel, singing with a loud and robust voice while fixing a penetrating stare on the students to ensure that they too were singing. His method of keeping an eye on student chapel attendance was to allocate resident students a seat alphabetically (students also had a set place in the Dining Hall). This made it easy for him to spot when a student was absent, and on next encountering said absent student he would demand an explanation. Sometimes students would themselves draw attention to absenteeism, as in the case of the poster drawn up in 1953, complete with a picture of the miscreant Ken Butcher on the occasion of his 'First Appearance in Chapel This Year'.

Opprobrium for Ken Butcher's failure of religious observance, 1953 – with a picture to identify him to Principal Dickinson.

The Hockey First 'XI', 1956–7. Back: Jeff Turton, Roy Wilcox, Hugh Vickers, Arthur Wall, Tony Kellaway, Geoff Macey, Robin Harcourt. Front: Grant Wilmot, Tom Dry, Alan Wise (capt), Colin Aslett, Harry Burden (white Merchant Navy socks from his previous career).

Over a period of three years, from 1954 to 1957, a large part of the Main Building roof was repaired. At St Grimbald's Court floors were levelled with asphalt and covered with thick linoleum, which made for a 'quieter building'. With the maintenance and painting of several other College buildings, it was noted in 1957 that 'considerable progress has recently been made'. This included work carried out at St Swithun's Lodge, Holm Lodge, the Great Hall (Assembly Hall), the Gymnasium, St James's Hall, the chaplain's quarters at St Swithun's Lodge and The Cottage near St Swithun's (which was occupied for some years by the fearsome Bill Gibson, Head Porter either side of the Second World War, who held sway over students by his fierce military demeanour), as well as the laboratories and workshops.

In 1955 the remaining balance of the compensation received from the War Department in return for the wartime requisitioning of the College (£350) was used to update the 'very dilapidated' main entrance with a new gateway, which included wrought iron gates. These were both designed and made by College personnel. The gates were later removed, probably because of access issues as vehicles grew in size. As the 1950s progressed, there developed a pattern of sound recruitment, a collegiate atmosphere and improvements. Not everything was smooth, however, for in 1955 Principal William

"

On KA Day in October there was usually some rag organised by students – such as Winchester waking up one morning to a town full of pink elephants, and on another occasion painted footsteps from the King Alfred statue across The Broadway to the public toilets by the (then) police station, and back to his plinth. Social happenings were all kinds of sport (Bar End grounds extensively used), meetings at the Black Swan in Southgate Street (where they made double decker sandwiches at special rates for hungry students), and of two organisations in particular. One was a political club, and the other, the Scripture Union, a radical evangelical body, whose members were to be found knocking on cubicle doors in the evening and trying to get students on their knees asking Jesus into their hearts. Both had very small followings. The Saturday night dances with the nurses were very popular, and it was always a subject of discussion as to who was going out with whom. Also on a Saturday night there was always a large attendance of nurses and students at the Lido (the local open air swimming pool and buildings) – that was when 'Rock Around the Clock' was at its zenith. There was a college Skiffle group which was very popular and performed on Saturdays at a pub in St George's Street. Students were allowed to have their own transport. Old motorbikes like mine were discreetly stored at the west end of the Chapel where they could not be seen.

Richard James, 1956–8

Richard James conducting the Male Voice Choir on the Terrace, July 1958.

It was mid-morning on Monday 18 February 1952. I was in my last year at Sir James Smith's Grammar School at Camelford in north Cornwall and had applied to go to King Alfred's College, after serving two years' National Service, to train to be a schoolmaster. I had sneaked to the school 'coal hole' for a sly puff of a Woodbine when the door burst open and there was Headmaster Kenneth Sprayson. 'You can put that away Pearce. A visitor has arrived and would like to see you in my office.'

1952 was of course long before the days of mobile phones, when roadside red telephone boxes were a major means of communication. College Principal W. P. Dickinson had spent the weekend in Truro visiting former KAC Chaplain Rev. Guy Bowden, who in 1951 had taken the role of residentiary canon at the Cathedral. Aware of my application, he drove the A39 to Camelford on his way back to Winchester and arrived unheralded at my school. It would appear the interview went well because he offered me a place when I returned from National Service in 1954, the first student from Cornwall to go to King Alfred's. My acceptance was considered to be such an achievement the local press carried reports at the time. In May of that year for health reasons I was to fail the examination for National Service and consequently arrived at KAC in September 1952, two years earlier than expected.

Headmaster Sprayson was a very pleased man on the day, because Prinny had been duly impressed with what he saw on a tour of the school – so pleased he never mentioned the forbidden Woodbine.

Bill Pearce, 1952–4

The Coronation Procession, 1953. Top, the banner on the float (occupied by children at desks) reads 'Today's children – Tomorrow's citizens'. Below, 'Dickie's Dragon' honouring Principal Dickinson.

Dickinson commented that the 'rising cost of food prevented work on buildings and equipment'. Minor projects, however, could be implemented, such as more levelling work carried out on the Dytche in 1957, allowing the installation of two concrete cricket wickets, jumping pits for athletics, etc. Such additions enabled the Principal to describe it as 'an increasingly valuable asset'.

THE CHALLENGE OF INCREASING NUMBERS

In the decade following the reopening of the College, the tide had flowed strongly for teacher training in general and for King Alfred's in particular: the raising of the school leaving age (ROSLA) to fifteen (1947), a rising birth rate, and the realisation in government of the implications of this latter development

fuelled a decision to increase teacher provision. In 1956, taking steps that had been long recommended by the McNair Report of 1944, the government announced that it planned both to double teacher training capacity by the end of the decade to reduce class sizes, and to increase the teacher training course from two to three years (the latter of which was confirmed in June 1957 to be implemented from 1960). These early signs of a revitalised expansionist policy in education were catalysts for change.

This decision was to have major implications for the College, which was already struggling for space in the late 1940s, though with only 180 students. The expansion continued, to almost 200 students in 1950, after which there was a momentary decline, with the decision not to admit day students, in an attempt to return to a fully residential college. In 1952 there were 178 students, numbers having fallen since the previous year. In 1956–7 there were 196, but the big leap was between then and 1957–8, when the number rose to 239, only to rise by a further 41 students to 280 (46 day students) in total in 1958–9.

This great growth in student numbers put the buildings under severe pressure. A report on the state of buildings on 20 February 1957 by W. W. Chapman of the architects Woodroffe, Buchanan and Coulter concluded, 'The present situation presents one of the shabbiest sets of teaching rooms that I have seen in a Teachers Training College.' In a prescient comment Chapman observed that the scattered residential accommodation would not be suitable for women – presumably on the grounds of safety after dark – and that the 'depressing buildings cannot have anything but an adverse affect [sic] on the work of the College'. The worst was St James's, for which the report recommended demolition and replacement by a new hostel behind St Grimbald's, as well as a new teaching block. As it turned out, these architects designed a memorable and remarkable building on the site: a new Dining Room with a 'hyperbolic paraboloid roof'.

Further pressures emerged with the approach of the new academic year in the autumn of 1958, as it became known to the Principal that Hampshire County Council was contemplating making a bid for an additional teacher training college to contribute to the predicted national shortfall of 12,000 teachers by 1962, and that such a college should be located in Winchester. This confronted Principal Dickinson with a seemingly insurmountable dilemma. On the one hand he could preserve the community on the scale and of the type for which he had prayed on that King Alfred's Day in 1946, but this option might be blighted by a local education training college on his doorstep in Winchester that held values different from his own. Alternatively he could go for massive expansion at King Alfred's and, it seemed to him, by so doing bring about the end of much for which he had worked since 1946. In reply to the governors' enquiry about maximum size, he presented his proposal, which was that in moving from a two- to a three-year training programme, the size of the College could expand to 250, the maximum he could envisage on the site.

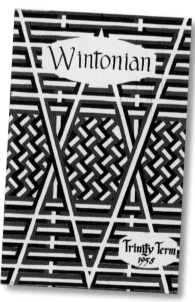

Above: The *Wintonian*, Trinity Term 1958, the calm before the storm.

Left: Interior of the new Dining Room, showing the remarkable 'collapsed tent' roof, High Table and the doors (right) to the crush hall where the diners waited (impatiently) to eat.

A TRAGIC DÉNOUEMENT

On 9 October 1958 the executive committee of the governors had conducted a site tour of the College to explore for themselves possibilities for expansion in view of ongoing debates about the future. On the eve of King Alfred's Day, 25 October, the full governing body met to receive their report and took the decision to forward a proposal much bolder than the small increase in numbers favoured by the Principal: to increase to 400–500 male students. On the very same day the plan for the second college in Winchester and the wider proposals for expansion of teacher education were printed in the *Hampshire Chronicle*. But Principal Dickinson was no longer alive to hear the outcome of the deliberations, for on 14 October, to great shock in the College and wider community of Winchester, these stresses had overwhelmed him and he had taken his own life by drowning in the River Itchen.

In the view of his widow, worries about the future, such as the capacity of the building stock, the size of the site, the threat of a competitor built anew with modern accommodation elsewhere in Winchester – quite apart from predictable difficulties in placing students for teaching practice in Hampshire schools – were just too much for him, and he had become increasingly depressed. His deputy added in retrospect that these threats, especially that of managing a rapidly and

significantly enlarged college, may have brought out a latent insecurity in him. His secretary suspected he was challenged in particular by the looming threat of a Local Education Authority college in Winchester and the necessity of expansion at King Alfred's. Although she did not know whether he was aware of the pressing question of the admission of 'young women', she suspected this may have contributed to the mix of anxieties as he made his fateful final journey to the Water Meadows. In retrospect a comment remains on file that his end had been brought forward by the debilitating and long-term struggle with the chaplain, which had taken a significant mental toll on him.

This tragedy was a heavy blow to the students as well. Some questioned how a Christian could do such a thing. They found it hard to believe. The Senior Student at the time recalls William Dickinson's great kindness not only towards the community of students but also to him personally. His death

The
Wintonian

Michaelmas
1958

was 'unbelievable, shattering news' which 'I, along with many others, found … very difficult to accept… It was as though everything was unstable.' However, the College had to move forward, and all pulled together. He concluded, 'Of course the College on the surface proceeded as before, everyone trying to ensure that "life went on!"'

Looking at photographs of students relaxing at the College in 1958 – particularly the iconic picture of Dick Martin with his straw boater (with College crest), blazer (with pocket-crest), baggy grey trousers, suede shoes and furled umbrella – nothing in the College's identity seemed unsettled or unstable. In the background of the photo of Martin, the Main Building shows that much of its flamboyant 1860s 'true Christian' Gothic, including the tower and the roof furniture, remained intact. The 1950s was a period of austerity, a decade in which the College worked hard under Principal William Dickinson with make-do-and-mend to get back on its feet after the war. The core structure, the Main Building, was to an extent refurbished, but the benign neglect of the age of rationing had contributed to the preservation of many of its original features. And after a century in existence it was not only the College's physical structures that were primed for development; in curriculum (with its possibilities for secondary teachers in Maths, Science, P.E., etc.), student experience, dress and outlook, change was imminent.

Three snaps of the College in May 1959 (note the film stars above the bed). The picture of St Swithun's dates from 1956–7.

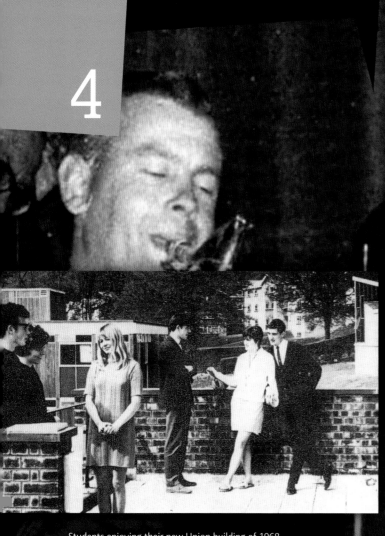

Students enjoying their new Union building of 1968.

Gender and Growth......................

A MIXED COLLEGE

Change was already inevitable for the College in the late 1950s, even before the momentous events of October 1958. One aspect of the change, suspected by at least one of those around him, and which preyed on William Dickinson's mind, was the matter of admitting women students. After his death, events moved quickly. On 22 December, following the decision to expand to 400 students, a statement from the governors was issued to staff by their secretary, Kenneth Kettle. It began by stating the known: that the College would expand over the next four years, taking into

account the lengthening of the course to three years from 1960. The second paragraph, however, will have caused significant discussion during the Christmas holiday that year: 'King Alfred's College will become a mixed College for approximately 250 men and 150 women students', it announced – a change conforming 'with national policy' – before stating that 'life will become more similar to that of a university student'.

It should be noted that this bold decision taken by the governors was not what William Dickinson would have hoped for, and indeed at the time it was agreed there was no Principal. Vice-Principal H. H. Humphrey was then acting

1958–c.1970

KING ALFRED'S COLLEGE,
WINCHESTER.

Dear Sir,

I have set out below a statement by the Governors of the College for your information.

Yours sincerely,

K. B. KETTLE.

Hon. Secretary to the Governing Body.

KING ALFRED'S COLLEGE

With the approval of the Ministry of Education, the Governors of the College have agreed upon a programme of expansion, beginning almost at once and being concluded before September, 1962. The College's decision has been taken in the context of the Government's intention to increase the supply of teachers and also to extend the teachers' training course from two to three years. The three year course begins in 1960.

King Alfred's College will become a mixed College for approximately 250 men and 150 women students. This change in the make-up of the student body conforms with national policy. Recruitment will be more flexible and the life will become more similar to that of a university student. There are also evident advantages, from this point of view, of being situated in a city such as Winchester. The College is a Church of England foundation and already benefits greatly from being in a Cathedral city.

With four hundred students and the appropriate staff the College will be able to offer a wide range of subjects at a high level and in particular the necessary workshops and laboratories will be provided for this to be done in Handicraft and Science.

Not all Training Colleges will have this equipment, so that King Alfred's will be one of a number to which a student must come if he wishes to specialise in these subjects. At the same time most students will find whatever courses they need in the College.

The cost of rebuilding will be borne partly by the Ministry of Education and partly by the Council of Church Training Colleges. The scheme will involve alterations upon the present site; more hostel and teaching accommodation will be built; and new kitchen and dining halls and an administrative block will be necessary. Building is likely to begin during 1959.

The Governors intend to appoint a Principal as successor to the late Mr. W. P. Dickinson in the very near future.

22nd December, 1958.

Above: Vice-Principal Robina Macintyre with a student band before 1965. Life was not always easy for her in this new role: students once threw her Mini into the bushes 'because she was a woman'.

Principal, as the incoming John Stripe was not formally appointed until a week later on 29 December – although it is presumed he was invited to accept the position in the knowledge of these new departures.

The proposal for the addition of an LEA training college in Winchester had already been abandoned by 8 December, and the Governors' Executive Committee led by Sir Desmond Lee (Headmaster of Winchester College) seized the moment to grasp the opportunity of admitting women. This followed 'the Ministry's view' on the

The letter announcing plans to expand and to admit women, Christmas 1958, this copy issued to Thomas Graty, who preserved it.

matter, which (as will be seen) was key to the expansion of the
institution and in time led to University Title. King Alfred's was
among the last institutions of Higher Education to admit women,
but by 1960 the Ministry was pressing for equal numbers of 200
men and 200 women.

The admission of women was not acclaimed with joy
by all male students. In January 1960 a boisterous (and
Freudian?) protest took place in the form of a three-legged
race from Westgate in Winchester to Bargate in Southampton.
Contemporary photographs show the men, festooned in College
scarves and colours, bearing placards calling for 'Clean Living'
and 'No Women'. But their protest fell on deaf ears: the changing
tide overwhelmed them. Female governors were appointed in
1960, as were the first women academic staff: Jennifer Nias,
an Oxford MA, to teach History, and Patricia Pemberton BA
(London) in Geography. Patricia was designated warden of the
new residence for women at St Elizabeth's, along with Robina
Macintyre, a Southampton graduate, who was also appointed as
a second Vice-Principal.

Desmond Lee, Headmaster of Winchester
College and on the Governors' Executive
Committee, led support for 'the Ministry's
view' to admit women.

Principal Stripe, Vice-Principals Hugh Humphrey
(at the Principal's right hand) and Robina
Macintyre.

In a charming memoir Robina Macintyre recalled her experience prior to King Alfred's, aspects of her appointment and also her life at the College. Her prior experience was at first sight rather surprising. According to her own account, after university she had started out as a journalist and also as a 'dancing partner' at a London nightclub run by Mrs Merrick, who was notorious for bribery and corruption and for breaching licensing laws. Merrick's fines and prison sentences were reported not only in the UK, but also widely in the US and Canada. Robina then took up the ukulele, appearing in variety billed as 'Bina Theodore and her Uke', after which she spent a year with a circus as a snake-charmer's assistant – 'I provided what we hoped was an exotic Eastern flavour.' Recent work has provided a gloss on this CV, revealing that these events were probably part of her journalistic efforts to obtain copy as a reporter on the *Sunday Express* in the late 1920s. Otherwise she was involved in education. At this point Miss Macintyre renewed

acquaintance with one of her lecturers at Southampton, the deeply religious Anglican Professor A. A. Cock. He urged her to 'settle down'. By 1930 she was Headmistress of Southbourne High School, Bournemouth, and went on to lecture at Truro Training College. Thereafter she spent nine years at Homerton College, Cambridge, and then, after a spell at the Ministry of Education ('not cut out to be a civil servant'), 11 years at the Catholic Maria Assumpta College in London where, despite not being a Roman Catholic, she rose to be deputy to the Principal, a nun. At this point she decided that time was moving on, and applied for the job in Winchester, for which she was interviewed by John Stripe, after which silence fell. When she telephoned she was was airily reassured, 'Of course you're appointed. All the others wore cardigans.' This was a striking contrast to her nun-Principal in London, and she quickly established a rapport with the relaxed and humorous Stripe. On the back of his report to the governors in October 1960, when women had just set foot on the campus as students, Stripe noted as his mission the basis of his concluding remarks: 'the creation of a new community of almost 450 men & women with the Chapel at the centre, & the Library as another focus'.

ARCHITECTURAL AND SOCIAL CHANGES

Suitable accommodation was required for the new bachelor Principal, John Stripe (1958–67). In 1959, soon after his arrival, considerable work was carried out at Holm Lodge so that it contained an 'attractive flat' for the use of the Principal and rooms for 11 resident students. Expansion required such extra student accommodation and also enhanced teaching areas, a new kitchen, Dining Hall and an administration block. 'Unceasing activity by the Governors in discussing and agreeing plans with the Ministry of Education' led to work on the Main Building beginning on 30 November 1959.

The needs of the new co-educational institution resulted in a wide-ranging and disruptive campaign of rebuilding and refurbishment between 1959 and 1964. A new chapel already envisaged in 1958 was planned and a model existed both of it

Arriving at Southampton Bargate. One student
said, 'it was too snowy to do sport.'

Hockey 2nd team, 1960–1 – the last season of men-only sport.

and of the proposed new Dining Room in 1960. Work on the new hostel for women, St Elizabeth's Hall, began in January 1960, while construction of a hall for men, Alwyn Hall (named after Bishop Alwyn Williams, who had for decades been such a good friend of the College) began in July on land purchased from the hospital. This transaction was only possible because of sustained pressure on the hospital authorities to sell from the Ministry of Education and the Ministry of Health.

The expansion programme meant the loss of the Main Building, with the exception of the Dining Hall, the Sick Block (Sanatorium) and the offices, 'so that its adaptation in the new plan for the College could begin'. Work on a new Dining Room was planned to begin in September 1960, but because of delays with the architects' plans (Woodroffe, Buchanan and Coulter), work did not begin until January 1961. During the building works extra space needed to be found, particularly three large lecture rooms, space for the Studio and the Pottery Department and sleeping accommodation for 40 students. The Great Hall (Assembly Hall) had often been used for lectures, a large ground-floor room at West Hayes became the Studio and a disused hut in its grounds housed the Metalwork and Pottery Departments. The previous Pottery facility had been in the Nissen hut situated below the east end of the Main Building (once the Principal's tennis court/lawn). Extra rooms were made at West Hayes and St Swithun's Lodge, and two classrooms were lent by St Thomas's School by permission of the Hampshire County Council.

Provision was also required for extra sports facilities. In 1960 some games pitches were transferred to larger facilities at Bar End to enable, for example, a new hockey pitch for women. The Principal reported to the governors that 'the College will have to provide additional games facilities for the large number of women who will be in the College by 1962'. By the end of 1960 the College had 'regained' the part of the Main Building that had been under reconstruction the previous year. The adaptation provided a large students' Common Room, with coffee bar and stationery shop, which 'were provided for the first time in the College's history'. Originally in 1862, these had

The former teaching spaces of 1862 by The Terrace, converted to the Junior Common Room, c. 1960.

been teaching rooms, with rising, tiered seating. As redecoration began the ghost of the former raked seating reappeared as stepped shadows on the walls, and was soon covered by new wallpaper. The original design of the seating explains the high windows there. Following use as the students' Junior Common Room these spaces became a part of the library, then the Senior Common Room and now, at the heart of the campus approached from the Terrace, the Student Centre.

Among the other Main Building areas noted in 1960 were eight lecture rooms, nine tutorial rooms, three store rooms, a Music Room with 11 practice rooms, three Geography lecture rooms with darkroom and store, a large English lecture room and a tutor's room. A new flat-roofed extension at the east end of the Main Building, consisting of the Principal's study and administration centre, with offices on the first floor and the new Senior Common Room on the ground floor, came into use during the Easter vacation of 1961. Temporary libraries were set up in these offices so that the library in St Grimbald's Court could be converted into five study bedrooms. Work began at the end of July 1961 to convert St Grimbald's into an additional hostel for women.

St Elizabeth's Hall was to have been completed by September 1960 (perhaps for her saint's day on 5 September), but the deadline was missed. Temporary accommodation was therefore required for the 42 women and two tutors, Robina Macintyre and Patricia Pemberton. Robina provides a vivid account of what happened, as the scramble for readiness occurred amidst the mud of the building site – where construction was taking place of not only the women's hostel but also a chapel, a Dining Room and a hostel for men – all amidst 'rain, rain, rain' in St Swithun's city. A casual enquiry the night before the women arrived about whether lavatory provision had been made for women elicited a look of horror from her male opposite number, followed by a scene straight out of the film *The Happiest Days of Your Life*, when, in

Above: A bold extension to the Main Building for the Principal's and other offices, 1961.

Left: The Main Building, May 1959, scarcely altered from 1862.

A valedictory dinner, 1965.

such circumstances, similar measures were adopted: the 'Gents' sign was substituted with 'Ladies'.

These early women students were on occasion disparaged by some as 'vicars' daughters'. Though some may have been just that, their widely experienced Warden found them, in certain respects, to be somewhat surprising. True, they had unsuitable shoes, but what they found was not what they had packed for: they were strongly opposed to the Warden locking the doors at 10pm (knowing that the men's doors remained unlocked), and refused at first to elect any representatives or have a house committee. On the other hand they devoted themselves to washing, ironing and behaving like 'real slave types', for which Robina Macintyre, 'from a mildly feminist point of view', chided them by pointing out there were three men to each girl, a comment that elicited an unexpected response: 'We each want three men.'

One of these pioneering women recalls arriving for the first time in the Dining Hall expecting a welcome, only to find that the men had arranged the benches and tables to prevent ready access to the spare seats lower down. The new girl, on enquiring if she could pass, was advised to walk along the table. Things soon settled down, except after rugby matches, when teams of men would appear, encouraged by the notion 'of beds in the sitting rooms which put ideas into their heads'. Macintyre was a match for this type of siege: 'On one occasion I stationed myself at an upper window with an air rifle and potted at behinds trying to insert themselves through ground floor windows … the action got noised abroad and seemed to do something to discourage these escapades.' In time the women 'douched with cold water poured on them from above' visiting rugby players trying to break in.

At the opposite end of the site one wing of the men's hostel, Alywn Hall (what would Bishop Alwyn Williams have made of all this?), accommodating 48 students, was ready in September 1961. Another wing for 33 students was occupied at the end of November 1961, and the final wing was in use by January 1962, in total providing accommodation for 116 students. In addition,

I was unaware of any anti-women feeling when I went, as a pioneer woman, to King Alfred's College. I loved the place, had enormous fun and was always hungry.

The staff, in the main, were well qualified, industrious, multi-talented and inspiring. The imposing Principal, John Stripe, often said 'I love all my students', but one wouldn't have risked putting it to the test. We went, in groups, for a drop of sherry with him after Sunday chapel.

The formal structure was helpful, I thought, when fresh from home. We 'ladies' lived in St Elizabeth's Hall with the diminutive but formidable Miss Mcintyre in loco parentis. *We were, after all, under 21. Men wore jackets and ties to lectures and main meals; no jeans for us. Formal meals began with grace (usually in Latin). If late we had to 'bow in'*

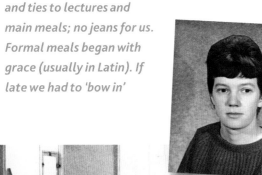

– and 'bow out' if we had to leave early. One could, if unlucky, have lectures until 6.30pm and on Saturday mornings. Being called 'Miss Thorpe' felt very odd. I seriously wondered whether I would have a report at the end of the first term!

Chapel was important. Everyone was supposed to take a turn at reading the lesson. Sunday services were well attended by staff and students and there was Morning and Evening Prayer in the week. I loved singing in the choir, though my musical ability was limited. They were rather short of women!

We had formal dinners – one at Christmas, when the staff did a turn, and the Valedictory in the summer. They were fun, as were the corresponding balls.

I hated leaving after three years and had learnt far more than just how to be a teacher.

Pat Brockway (née Thorpe), 1960–3

there were initially two staff flats there, one married and one single. Students resident at St James's Hall, St Grimbald's Court and the Main Building moved into Alwyn Hall. Further west, West Hayes also accommodated men, developing a reputation for a laddish sporting culture, encouraged by the P.E. students.

Also in January 1962 the new Dining Room was completed, if not quite soon enough for term to start on time (it began a week late). It was a great success, this building with 'a pure neo-Gothic structure complete with buttresses and large windows. The collapsed tent roof has occasioned much comment.' There was a small, private 'Principal's' dining room to the east, Stripe being a bachelor. Although this new Gothic building was a success, it was in the course of these large-scale, financially demanding works on tight deadlines that the destruction of more of the Gothic detail of the original 1860s Main Building occurred. As the new Dining Room came into use in January 1962, work began to convert the old Dining Hall and kitchens in the Main Building into library accommodation, with a completion date set for September 1962.

With the completion of Alwyn Hall work could begin on updating and adapting St James's, which had been

Mixed meals in the new Dining Room in the 1960s: waiting on the benches to be served.

When I arrived at King Alfred's College there was still a male ethos. I lodged in St Grimbald's Court and the old dining hall was in use. Every Friday the stale food was presented and there was literally a bun fight. There were three main social circles in Winchester in the 1960s: KAC, Winchester College (I lodged with a tutor's family in the Close) and Winchester Prison. The Prison Officers organised social events for us and were heavily into evangelical activities.

I was a Certificate of Education student at KAC. I took English as my main subject and was fortunate enough to have Harry Blamires as my supervisor. He already had an international reputation for his work on James Joyce and at that time he was working on The Christian Mind.

I chose as the subject of my long essay the work of a comparatively obscure eighteenth-century novelist, Samuel Richardson. The only reason I ended up with Richardson was that by the time I reached the library all the twentieth-century novelists had been taken out. It could have been a disaster.

I had a tutorial with Blamires for an hour every week. He had the knack of drawing out students so they took ownership of new ideas. Thus I wrote a chapter comparing the treatment of sexual exploitation by Richardson and D. H. Lawrence. I was so excited by this world of ideas that I would work through the night in preparation for tutorials. I was honoured to be asked my opinion of arguments in his book.

Since that time I have attended five universities as a student or tutor. I am grateful that in the 1960s the staffing levels gave me the opportunity for individual tuition.

Clare Debenham, 1961–4

As captain of the Rugby Club in 1963/4 I was instructed by Jack Stripe to appear at the Magistrates' Court in Winchester as a character witness for one of the junior members of the club who had been apprehended after a fracas in the Turk's Head on the Broadway.

Immediately after that I had to appear before the magistrates as the College Bar Manager to apply for the temporary transfer of the liquor licence from the pavilion at Bar End for the purposes of a dance being held in the College buildings. Both events filled me with some apprehension, the first being a novel experience, the second on account of what had preceded it.

The post of Bar Manager came about because I had persuaded the College authorities that the new pavilion at Bar End needed a bar to entertain visiting teams after matches.

Roger Hailwood, 1961–4

summed up as 'appalling' in 1957, but had survived to become in part a sanatorium, as well as accommodation for residential staff; conversion was also due to be completed by September 1962. In addition, immediately at end of term in July 1962 a scheme to convert St Swithun's Lodge into a women's hostel was put into operation. Meanwhile, the new pavilion at Bar End was completed and opened by the Mayor of Winchester on 16 June 1962. In 1963 permission was given for a licensed bar to be opened here – the first on a College site – and beer (or coffee) and chat were no longer the only recreations off the sports field open to students, as television became more prominent.

With arrangements to house and feed the ever-growing student numbers and accommodate the newly arrived women on site, attention could then turn to expanding accommodation for students' minds and souls. A new chapel was dedicated on 2 July 1964 by 'our Bishop', Falkner Allison, with a service described by Principal Stripe as 'moving'. The Science and Handicraft teaching accommodation west of the Chapel, later named the Herbert Jarman Building, came into use in September 1963. This was 'most invaluable', one reason being that it replaced the need for the hut at West Hayes and St Thomas's Annexe. Stripe reported: 'It is a happy experience to wander round these rooms and to see the students so completely immersed in their work.' This was built on the site of the corrugated hut to the west of the Chapel and of the former 'Lecture Loggia', which had contained three classrooms separated by sliding, folding partitions.

> *We are magnificently equipped for a College of 400, the original target, but we shall be 639 next September, and while the lecture rooms just cope, tutorial rooms and student common rooms are overcrowded.*
>
> John Stripe, 1964

The five-year plan completed in 1964 saw the end of that phase of expansion. As far as the curriculum was concerned, in that same year, when Philip Ray arrived to join John Jameson (later godfather to Pat Brockway's daughter), there were two Education tutors doing secondary work in the traditional subjects of Maths, Physics, Design and Technology, as well as P.E., for which a 'useful' physical education room was added to the south of the Great Hall (Assembly Hall) in the mid-1960s. Although the method of these subjects was taught by specialists, the tutors had experience in secondary schools.

Meanwhile, the hope that colleges would attract aspirant Maths and Science teachers in significant numbers was frustrated,

THE COLLEGE ON-SCREEN ....

King Alfred's made it to television on Sunday 2 February 1964, when producers, with spaces in the schedule for religious broadcasting, hit on the idea of a programme on church colleges. The programme, part of the BBC *Meeting Point* series, featured King Alfred's, and included an interview with Robina Macintyre. This was the year in which (Dame) Joan Bakewell began her television career with the show. Macintyre was enthusiastic about the possibilities of radio and television for teaching students, and ordered up pamphlets that supported programmes for the Library.

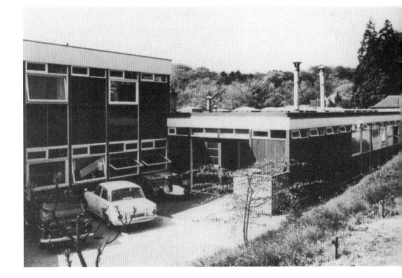

Top: The rear of the Herbert Jarman Building, with varied staff transport, late 1960s.

Above: The New Chapel, with its purpose-built organ, opened in 1964.

"

Teaching practice was always one of the challenges for a student at King Alfred's College, and yet it could also produce some memorable highlights. I shared my penultimate teaching practice at Whitchurch Secondary School with other colleagues. Bill Hayward and I studied the same course of Advanced Maths and Physics and shared the same teaching practice. Knowing that he was due for a visit from a tutor I agreed to act as lab technician while he taught. When Mr Meredith [a Music Tutor] arrived he came to talk to me at the back of the lab, assuming I was a member of staff – our paths had not crossed previously – and of course I gave Bill a fulsome, glowing report. Transport to teaching practice was by coach, and Whitchurch was the last destination. After my first journey, as an enthusiastic cyclist I opted to ride, saving half an hour. Bill took my briefcase each day and placed it on the back seat beside him. On one of the return journeys the coach was very late in returning, as there had been a crash on the way; a somewhat shaken Bill handed back my briefcase with apologies for the gash down its side, where a shard of the roof light had embedded itself in the seat where I should have been sitting. On the afternoon we left, Mr Potter the Headmaster thanked us and gave the following advice, 'Whatever you do in life be an enthusiast.' A maxim which has influenced the rest of my life.

Roger Hailwood, 1961–4

Below: Women's sports flourished: a tennis team in the 1960s. Back: Pat Thorpe, Celia Packer, Terry Parsons. Front: Fay Watts, Kate Sowerby, Carolyn Lloyd, Linda Saunders.

so numbers had to be found elsewhere. Traditional arts subjects such as English, French, Geography and History meanwhile recruited solidly, and so these departments each appointed a specialist to undertake method training for secondary work. With the growth in construction of secondary schools in Hampshire at that time, and also of middle schools in some Local Education Authorities, it was not difficult for these students to find work in secondary schools – especially in junior secondary work, although in the government's eyes they were not officially trained as secondary teachers. It was a complex situation, but one that provided opportunities for students to come to Winchester, and by taking two of the three teaching practices in secondary schools they could find careers in that sector.

Likewise in Drama, an interest of the new Vice-Principal Martial Rose (who had studied Education among other subjects at Cambridge, and so was called upon immediately to teach Philosophy of Education), students could find work in secondary schools. Patterns of recruitment in the Arts and Drama signalled the way forward for the College in the coming decades, as science declined.

WOMEN ON THE RISE

The table opposite shows how the gender balance developed from 1957 – it is clear that expansion occurred at a faster pace than initially planned. This was a period of great optimism: during the

election campaign of 1959 the Conservative Prime Minister, Harold Macmillan, chaffed the nation that they 'had never had it so good'.

As the table opposite shows, already at Winchester in 1959 numbers exceeded the proposed 250 by over 10 per cent, and the planned 400 for 1962 was exceeded by 22 in 1961, although the number of women grew slowly at first and fell short of the proposed 60 in 1960 and of the 250:150 split envisaged in 1958 for 1962. However, by 1967 women already represented some 40 per cent, and in 1968 at 418 men to 412 women equilibrium was reached. In

Below: Numbers of men and women 1957–2014.
Figures for some dates and periods were not found.
(Bracketed figures are known targets.)

YEAR	MEN	WOMEN	TOTAL
1957	230	0	230
1958	239	0	239
1959	279	0	279
1960	330	60 (42)	390
1961	302	120	422 (400)
1962	304	203	507
1963	335	231	566
1964	367	263	630
1965	398	290	688
1966	434	321	755
1967	425	354	779
1968	418	412	830
1969	402	569	971
1970	362	634	996
1971	370	629	999
1972	404	603	1,007
1973	393	631	1,024
1974	395	690	1,085
1975	390	650	1,040
1976	344	620	964
1977	333	631	964
1978	336	635	971
1979	301	592	893
1980	286 (663)	592 (1,055)	878 (1,718)
1981	281	626	907
1982	262	661	923 (1,000)
1995	990	3,452	4,442
1996	1,071	3,693	4,764
1997	1,111	3,995	5,106
1998	990	3,452	4,442
1999	1,120	3,750	4,870
2000	1,170	3,980	5,150
2001	1,160	4,120	5,280
2002	1,415	4,912	6,327
2013	2,093	4,302	6,395
2014	2,255	4,621	6,876

Medecroft, a Victorian villa, purchased in 1965.

1969, women sprang ahead numerically following a fourth year of marginal decline among the male student numbers to 402, with 569 women. This trend continued as numbers grew, with men falling back towards 250 and the numbers of women growing swiftly in the early 1980s, when there is a break in the available data.

By 1990 women were outnumbering men by 3:1, and they have remained predominant ever since in a similar ratio. One of the key changes in the early years was that it was clearly impossible to accommodate all the students as boarders on site, and equally impossible to sustain the high percentage of resident students as opposed to day students. While there had been a long tradition of daily attendance, this now contributed significantly to numbers so that, for example in 1965, when there were 688 students, 296 were resident, 195 in approved lodgings and 197 were day students. The lodgings tutor Dorothy Smithson was especially valuable in recruiting long-term landladies.

FURTHER EXPANSION

Stripe had reported to the governors in August 1965 at the end of academic year 1964–5 that King Alfred's College, with 630 students, continued to be the largest Church of England college for men and women in the country. However, although 1964–5, in which there was no building work, was a 'quiet' and 'peaceful' year, this only served to highlight the necessity for increased accommodation for students and study areas.

In 1965 Medecroft, a private house built on a two-and-a-half-acre site in Sparkford Road in 1868 and subsequently used as a preparatory section of St Swithun's School for girls, was bought by the College at public auction, the purchase being eased with the assistance of the Headmaster of Winchester College, Sir Desmond Lee. Medecroft, a few hundred metres south-west of the King Alfred's site, was developed in 1966 into the Art and Craft Department, together with the addition of two purpose-built art studios there, their

Carfax Hotel, by the station, provided accommodation in the late 1960s.

Principal Stripe and Vice-Principal Macintyre welcoming a toga-clad group of Romans.

PRINCIPAL STRIPE'S LEADERSHIP

During these rapid and seismic changes Principals and staff continued to promote the fundamentals of the Christian foundation. Principal Stripe (1958–67) provided, in Martial Rose's words, both 'spiritual and academic leadership'. In addition Stripe made it his business to try to be familiar with staff and students, and to know their names so that he might welcome them to Holm Lodge, especially for sherry parties after Sunday chapel. This was no mean feat in a period of rapid expansion – a threefold expansion of the College in the eight years he was Principal. He did his best, but confessed that when defeated in recalling names of the female students he would refer to them as 'Flossie'!

In essence, however, Stripe was a traditionalist. For example, he maintained High Table in the new Dining Room and would lunch strictly at 1pm. Staff who wished to eat with him would assemble in the crush hall, on the north-west corner of the Dining Room, and he would lead them in, taking his reserved seat. This arrangement enabled staff who wished to catch his eye to raise a topic without a formal appointment, and he in turn

characteristic saw-toothed roofline lighting the exhibition area from the north. This enabled a whole floor of the Herbert Jarman Building to be freed for additional science laboratories, with the ground floor being extended in the late 1960s/early 1970s.

In August 1966 negotiations for the renting of the Carfax Hotel and Wellington House had been satisfactorily completed, and according to the report of 1966/7 they were both used extensively. Carfax (reputedly haunted) provided accommodation for 45 students and two resident tutors/wardens between 1966 and 1970 (Lois Haynes, Warden), and Wellington House was to be used for the Education Department for two years, until the main College building was completed. The Carfax, now demolished, was near the railway station where the Hampshire Archives and Local Studies Centre now stands, at the corner of Sussex Street. Wellington House is a large building on the corner of Kingsgate Street and Canon Street, opposite the Wykeham Arms. Three other properties were leased for residence: 1 Christchurch Road – Spicer Lodge; 6 St James's Lane, which came to be known as The Crescent; and St Faith's (formerly the St Cross Hotel), situated at the corner of Barnes Close and St Cross Road.

Tony Garnett, artist, potter and musician (he sang at the Coronation at Westminster Abbey), with a group of mature students in the pottery room at Medecroft, c. 1975.

could then think about it. After he had taken his seat no student left the hall without a slight bow to the Principal, leaving through the crush hall. Staff, on the other hand, left by the exit to the Principal's right.

Conversation might centre on a London Ballet or theatre production he had seen. If conversation lapsed, Stripe, a fast eater, would be on to his second course ahead of other staff and on occasion would leave, causing an unceremonious scramble of staff after him, some puddingless!

Philip Ray, Education Tutor from 1964

On Wednesday afternoons his support for sports teams, especially rugby, became legendary. Indeed, he took an interest in all aspects of College life. Joyce Tuffill, a young part-time recruit to the Library staff in October 1966, recalls being visited by Principal Stripe while at work so that he could welcome her personally. Stripe was especially keen that the Library should

be an academic, but also welcoming place, adorned with student art and ceramics atop the shelves (a case of ceramic art is located immediately inside the entrance to the Library to this day, with further items on the shelves behind the counter, continuing this tradition). In addition there was a limit neither on the number of books that could be borrowed, nor on the length of time students could keep them. In the last year that he reported to the governors, in August 1966, Stripe noted when discussing the Library that, whereas in 1959 there were 239 students and a budget of £350, in 1966 there were 688 students, a budget of £5,500 and an increase in stock of 6,000 books and pamphlets (including academic journals, it would appear). Such extraordinary growth and development across the College undoubtedly took their toll on him: he succumbed to chronic illness and died in May 1967.

The Education Department and its predecessors had established overseas links for many years previous to, as well as in Stripe's day. The College visitors' book since the Second World War reveals a stream of visitors from overseas, including some former students and/or their families, such as two daughters of Ibrahim Takla Bey (a student 1907–9 in Principal Martin's time, who went on to be Minister of Education in Egypt), who visited in 1951. During William Dickinson's and John Stripe's time educationists, including inspectors and teachers, came from all

I have had a good time during my one year course at King Alfred's College, Winchester. It reminds me of the old Chinese proverb which goes 'There are brothers in the Four Seas.' ... I will remember you, my dear Principal, and King Alfred's all the time.'

Letter from a visiting student from Hong Kong, 1966

Ceramics have remained attractive decorations in successive libraries ever since, as this 2015 photograph shows.

Beech Glade, a modernist house, built for the Vice-Principal c. 1967.

over the world. Signatures of visitors include the Principal of Ghazi College in Kabul, Afghanistan (1961), preceded by visitors from Antigua, Burma, Canada, Egypt, Germany, Iran, Malaya, Northern Nigeria, Sudan, Switzerland, Tasmania, Uganda and the USA. In 1958 there was a delegation of Russians from Moscow, including a reporter from *Pravda*, who all signed in. In addition to those who signed in, students came to study from far and wide, for example Alex Yorke from Ghana in 1957. Such visitors and students give a flavour of those welcomed to the College by Principals and their staff between *c.*1950 and 1960. John Stripe, an English graduate, had an interest in promoting English Studies for teachers in France, for which he had been appointed *Chevalier de l'Ordre des Palmes Académiques*.

MARTIAL ROSE BECOMES PRINCIPAL

Following John Stripe's untimely death, his deputy Martial Rose stepped up. Rose had been appointed as senior Vice-Principal and acted as Principal during Stripe's illness. He was a natural choice in the circumstances, and although initially reticent to apply, he was persuaded, providing continuity and making the change as seamless as possible. A graduate of King's College, Cambridge, Rose had experience both in schools and far from Winchester at Bretton Hall College in Yorkshire, where he had put on a production of the Medieval Wakefield Mystery Cycle of plays on which he was expert and which he was to repeat in the grounds of Wolvesey Palace in 1974. He became only the ninth Principal since 1840.

A new, 'modernist' house, Beech Glade, was built on the lawn west of Medecroft for the incoming Vice-Principal, Guy Barnes – a provision called for nearly 30 years previously, by Principal White in 1937. These new managers found themselves in a rapidly changing world, captured in the photographic record of the 1960s: changing social mores and long-haired men and short-skirted women, strongly contrasting with the church parades,

A View From the Bridge by Arthur Miller, performed by the student Irving Club, December 1967. Roy Faithful as Eddie Carbone, Ron Berry (with chair) as Marko. It was the last production in the Great Hall (above).

Left: The Stripe today.

Below: *The Proposal* by Anton Chekov, performed at the opening of the John Stripe Theatre in October 1969. Roy Faithful (centre) with Drama students Pam Bagguley and John Sykes.

suits and jackets and ties of their servicemen predecessors. In 1968 students' end-of-term celebrations included the successful innovation of an Open Day, 'the students' brainchild', which was a great success despite torrential rain. It was also an Open Day in the sense that outside people could come and see the College to take a tour, rather than Open Days now, which are designed specifically for prospective students.

Martial Rose, Principal 1967–1984, as many recall him in his gown.

Rose, meanwhile, provided a strong spiritual example, attending morning chapel on a daily basis and always wearing his gown. His experience at King's College, Cambridge, would have informed his view of the Chapel as a central part of the College, just as his predecessors had emphasised. By the time he became Principal compulsory attendance at chapel had long since ceased, not least because the numbers at the College were far more than could be accommodated in a single act of worship. W. P. Dickinson's vision of a College dining and praying together had gone for ever within a few years of his death; R. C. White's vision of a mixed College with a devolved social structure had triumphed.

Rose did much to draw the various constituencies of the College together. An early achievement was to engineer the creation of the John Stripe Theatre, which he had helped to plan with his predecessor, whose name it took. The theatre, it was said, was achieved by the clever expedient of surrounding a courtyard with offices and then – when the authorities had refused to fund a theatre – roofing the central space to provide the new major auditorium, which opened in 1969. Rose recalls with pleasure celebrating its opening by Sir Alec Clegg, another Cambridge man and founder of Rose's former work place – Bretton Hall near Wakefield, Yorkshire – as an Arts teacher training college in 1949. Clegg was among the outstanding educationists of his day.

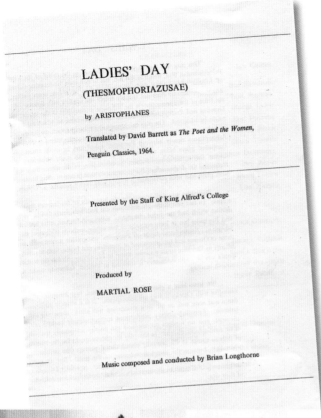

LADIES' DAY
(THESMOPHORIAZUSAE)

by ARISTOPHANES

Translated by David Barrett as *The Poet and the Women*,
Penguin Classics, 1964.

Presented by the Staff of King Alfred's College

Produced by
MARTIAL ROSE

Music composed and conducted by Brian Longthorne

The earliest productions in the new John Stripe Theatre included a Greek play, *Thesmophoriazusae* (*Ladies' Day*), produced by Rose in 1970, with a cast of both female and male staff. This was well received by most, but was sufficiently risqué that the script, spoken by a young member of the English Department, was altered when Bishop Allison, a classicist who chaired the governors, attended. Archdeacon Beynon, also a governor, felt that such a pagan enterprise was an unwise choice for a Church College. In recent years Rose recalled the pleasure

Programme and scene from Aristophanes's *Thesmophoriazusae*, directed by Martial Rose: a 'pagan' and 'unwise' enterprise for a Church College according to the Archdeacon, but staff and students loved it.

of that production, which brought together a wide range of some 32 staff: Sonia Carver, who delighted colleagues and students with her mastery of movement and dance, the Design and Technology Department, who prepared the stage and the effects, and the teaching staff, including the academic ladies in the chorus. The play helped establish the College as a local venue for drama, acknowledged the culmination of the building works and set a joyous seal on the opening of a new era. 'It was a riot,' Rose recalled recently with a laugh.

EDUCATIONAL POLICY CHANGES AND THEIR IMPACT

Beyond these changes there were challenges from the outside world to be addressed. Government-sponsored reports included that of Robbins (1963) and its successor by Weaver (1966), which allowed colleges more autonomy, as close relationships with universities and external controls of curricula were restrictive. Robbins drew the student teacher training experience more closely to the university experience, by enabling validation of 'a three-year concurrent certificate course … and a four-year BEd course'. The colleges were to be 'dignified' with the name 'college of education'.

However, the report at the same time noted that liaisons with universities had not been advantageous to colleges, and proposed the setting up of independent governing bodies. The Weaver report gave further autonomy to the College by handing 'ultimate responsibility for the academic direction of the institution' to its own academic staff and allowing the appointment of a clerk to the governors, who was to be the senior administrative officer of the College, and would not, as previously, be an elected governor.

Weaver had a further modernising impact on the College. A flustered new member of staff in the mid-1960s was asked by the Vice-Principal to order materials for the College. At a loss as to how to get the order funded, he found himself outside the Principal's office, and asked John Stripe for a cheque, only to be met with the surprising response: 'Do you think I sign College cheques?' Even at that date all cheques had to be signed by the College Treasurer, as had been the case since foundation. At that date Arthur Edmonds, a town draper, former mayor and a governor, was Treasurer. This antiquated system was superseded in 1967 when, following the Weaver Report, the chief administrative officer (finance) of the College became Clerk

Women trained at Winchester proved to be much in demand as primary teachers as the population grew.

to the Governors assuming these responsibilities. At the same time the Principal, technically still at that time invited to attend the Governors meetings, was enabled to attend in his own right, formalising a practice already in place.

These reports no doubt encouraged the College management to reflect on what was best for their curriculum, and whether validation by Southampton University might be ideal. However, the road towards any such independence was blocked in 1965 by the minister, Tony Crosland, when he effectively prevented the development of a 'unitary' Higher Education system, creating instead the 'binary' system. This left colleges and polytechnics on the other side of the tracks from the universities, tracks that were to prove difficult for many to cross in the next generation. There was a danger, unrealised as it happened, that the colleges would become a 'third sector' behind universities and polytechnics.

There were already seven new universities established in the early 1960s, in East Anglia, Kent, Lancaster, Essex, Sussex, Warwick and York, to cater for the baby-boomers of the post-war generation. Locations of some of these new universities (Canterbury, Norwich and York) were cathedral cities like Winchester. Their curricula, for example at Sussex, might involve a 'Main Subject' and 'Associated Subjects' – the first course model adopted by King Alfred's a decade later. Although for the moment the possibility of University Title was

closed by the changes in 1965, these institutions provided a model that could be adapted across the binary line in a 'College of Higher Education', or in one of the polytechnics that had also begun to flourish in the 1960s, with validation of their degrees by the CNAA (Council for National Academic Awards), which had been founded in 1965 to enable institutions without a royal charter to award degrees. Rose realised that there was danger in sole reliance on a teacher-training income stream, and planned to widen the institution towards being a College of Higher Education, but it was to be in 1975, ten years after the foundation of the CNAA, that Winchester was to join the ranks of institutions whose courses it validated.

Arts A

The Asa Briggs Theatre at Sussex University: King Alfred's drew on the traditions and strengths of the new universities both for curriculum and campus developments.

Sonia Carver (pale dress), whose 'Movement' sessions were treasured by John Rogers, flanked by Donald Venning and by Peter Holden.

NEW DEVELOPMENTS

As the decade progressed more new buildings were completed at King Alfred's. In 1968 the Tom Atkinson Building was built on the hillside facing the Herbert Jarman Building. This new teaching block was used at first mainly for Education and French. The Herbert Jarman and Tom Atkinson buildings, incorporating respectively science and television facilities, did much to ease teaching-space pressure on the site, as did the establishment of an 'outpost' for 25–35 students in Basingstoke, as the College sought wider horizons for its courses. In September 1968 the 'Basingstoke Outpost' opened its doors to 26 students, with an average age of 35. This was a base for teacher training purposes, with one day a week in Winchester and half a day in school, and addressed a teacher shortage current at that time. These Basingstoke students were mainly married women, thus contributing to the changing gender balance outlined above. The 'outpost' occupied a former Civil Defence building and closed in 1977.

A short course in training, implemented to address the shortage of teachers, was also offered at Winchester in the late 1960s for people such as those at Basingstoke who found themselves, rather to their surprise, termed 'mature' students, in order to distinguish them from their younger counterparts. This brought some noteworthy as well as inspiring encounters, typified by John Rogers, a mature student.

Rogers also tried to start a student political newspaper with the younger students, but found them remarkably 'unpolitical',

I found many of the staff very stimulating. My Pottery tutor, Tony Garnett, was truly inspiring and opened up in me a side I had long since forgotten. And Dr Foster, my 'Divinity' tutor, was differently inspiring – a brilliant teacher who spoke with authority yet stood, as it were, at the pupil's elbow. It was called Divinity in keeping, I expect, with old university tradition, but it was really academic theology and not in the slightest pietistic. Then, Sonia Carver was a very beautiful teacher of P.E. (I think, or it may have been called Movement for the mature folk) and I think I looked forward to her sessions even more than everything else – even more than well-cooked chips at lunchtime.

John Rogers, mature student 1968–70

Students from the Basinkstoke Outpost on an Environmental Studies expedition to RAF Odiham, supervised by John Hird and Ruby Chambers.

"

Perhaps the most memorable tutor was Lois Haynes in 'Education'. I was tremendously interested in all her statistics and, for me, revolutionary ideas – as well as the practical matters of teaching. There was one session, however, which nearly resulted in a riot. She had been telling us about a new alphabet called ITA [Initial Teaching Alphabet, a reading support fashionable in the 1960s] designed to make the learning of reading easier. At the end, one of our number, a retired Naval Commander (whose wife was also a student in that room, and their daughter a 'normal' student elsewhere in the College) asked about children arriving at such schools already able to read. Miss Haynes drew herself up to her full height and proclaimed, 'Any child who can read at the age of five is the unfortunate victim of a nasty, thrusting, middle-class attitude.' Great laughter and the room was cleared rather quickly.

John Rogers, mature student 1968–70

COLLEGE GASTRONOMY ....

Complaints about food have a very long history at Winchester, as in most other institutions. C. E. Creese (1892–4) recalled that breakfast and tea were identical: a pat of butter the size of a penny, hunks of bread and tea from an urn. Breakfast could be augmented with porridge and/or an egg (with the owner's name written on it), which could be provided to the kitchen for cooking. The midday meal started with rice pudding, 'a solid hard mass – very little milk was used'. There was a joint on each table (no doubt where Attwood learnt his carving skills in the years before the First World War), potatoes and a very small dish of cabbage. The 15 men on each table watched eagle-eyed to ensure equal division of this fare. The smell of cabbage, which percolated from the kitchens to the upper floors of the Main Building, remained ingrained on early students' olfactory senses.

Examples of many food-related grouses included Wickson, writing of the 1930s, who recalled how the 'first time [he] had food which could be eaten with pleasure' was when he was sent to stay in the Cathedral Close, where he took part in a pageant. ATS girls in the war, served by College servants kept on by the War Office who slept above the kitchens, also found the diet inadequate. While Asa Briggs was Provost of Worcester College, Oxford in the 1980s, one of his special achievements was to secure funding for significant improvement to the College's food, perhaps echoing his experience of the poor College food at King Alfred's for 'other ranks' in the 1940s. King Alfred's students complained bitterly of the scanty amount and poor quality of the diet at Trinity College, Carmarthen during the war. In the late 1950s there was a food boycott, and as in the late 1960s, food remained a contentious issue for the ever-hungry student body as numbers grew, pressuring the kitchen.

College-wide communal meals were by this time limited to Christmas and the Valedictory in the summer, where students booked tables and invited staff to join them. They were marked by high spirits: it was at such an occasion in 1956 that Chaplain Paul Kingdon was reminded of his insistence on blackboard-watching by a student breaking a (paper) blackboard over his head. Loud cheers regularly occurred when the kitchen staff appeared with flaming Christmas puddings lit with brandy, as one honoured top-table guest put it, 'warmed on Hazel Crooke's thigh', Hazel at that time being head of catering. (She attended Martial Rose's farewell lunch in 1984 and a staff reunion in 2014). By the 1990s even these dinners had ceased, one explanation being that the Principal's wife had been struck by a flying bread roll. It was more likely that there was little demand for such formality by then, and senior staff became more removed from the student body.

Geographers en route to the Valedictory Dinner, 1972. Includes staff Dennis Fancett (left), Edmund Dobson (centre) and Jean Sawyerr (right). Smith, the student of Dobson's right, became an acclaimed BBC American Football reporter.

94 Christchurch Road, named Allison Lodge after Bishop Falkner Allison and purchased in 1968, provided additional accommodation for students.

and concluded that 'there were only three things that stirred the student body to action: the breakdown of the heating or of the TV or the chips being soggy at lunch'.

One reason for the comparative contentment of the student body of this period, food apart, may have been that their building, the Student Union Block, now St Edburga's, was completed in 1968. Such provision was a wise move in a tumultuous era of international and national student unrest. Nonetheless, Principal Rose was able to report to the governors (no doubt with some relief) that 'in a year [1968/9] marked throughout the country by student unrest, this College managed to remain relatively quiet. Students were invited to Academic Board and to meet Governors to discuss student representation.' Significant change was afoot among the staff at this time: 23 appointments of new staff were made in 1968 alone, and over the next decade ten of the senior members of staff, many appointed after the war, made way for younger people. The Crombie arrangements from 1975 for redundancy payments for those whose jobs had disappeared were generous, and many needed little persuasion to retire.

From 1969 a system of 'hot-desking' was introduced on the main site, where cohorts of students were recruited to attend while their seniors were out in school teaching practice, emphasising the pressure on space at that time, as student numbers soared from 779 in 1967 to 999 in 1971. As numbers grew new courses and areas of study emerged in a consensual way under Rose, arising, for example, from a day conference

'involving the whole of the College's academic staff'. One such course was the four-year BEd (1968), initially for children with learning difficulties, for the majority still took the certificate. Such measures and responses to changing government policy showed how senior staff needed to be aware of changes, and how the lengthening of courses enabled the institution to capitalise on the numbers of students coming forward.

As mentioned above, the John Stripe Theatre had opened in October 1969, not long after the Student Union building was completed. 'It has since been used intensively for plays and concerts and has proved a most useful amenity for both students and citizens of Winchester' (Martial Rose). Offsite, the most significant building development was the purchase of Winchester property with Department of Education and Science approval and support, beginning with No. 4 Christchurch Road (Macintyre Lodge), which was converted to a hostel in 1968. In fairly rapid succession the following properties were purchased and converted: 94 Christchurch Road (Allison Lodge), Gifford House (across the town on St Giles's Hill), 14 Christchurch Road (Cotswold), and 78 Christchurch Road (Denstone). 86 Christchurch Road (Edmonds Lodge) was an exception; it was left to the College by Mr Edmonds, mayor 1935–6, College treasurer and governor (who owned an eponymous drapery business in the city), in a valuable and unusual act of philanthropy by a citizen of Winchester towards King Alfred's. They were all large freehold properties set in spacious grounds, providing shared accommodation for between 20 and 35 students.

A tug-of-war from Dick Allwood's remarkable archive (1970–3). Apart from the 1970s clothes, this snap epitomises the struggles of the College at the time.

TROUBLED TIMES – THE MERGER YEARS

Despite the best efforts to consolidate and promote unity among staff and students, dark clouds on the horizon were to bring threats and a struggle for survival over the next few years. Meanwhile in 1971, a memorandum sent down the road to Southampton University proposed that Winchester would expand to 2,000 students (i.e. double in size), 'half of whom would enter the teaching profession'. This suggested departure from the mono-technic model was prescient. The James Report of 1972 proposed a complex system of training based on a series of 'cycles' – two-year diplomas, three-year degrees, return years in training institutions, and so on. Its proposals were 'met with little enthusiasm'.

More seriously, in 1972 it became apparent that oversupply of teachers and a falling birth rate challenged the very existence of colleges of education. Rumours that colleges would close abounded, and a significant number did close in the following years. *The Times Higher Education Supplement* carried a front-page headline in the 1970s stating that King Alfred's was to close. This proved to be untrue, but fateful letters were arriving elsewhere, for example at the Froebelian College at Saffron Walden in Essex, where the Ministry's instruction that Initial Teacher Training should cease, received on 15 May 1974, rang the death knell.

Meanwhile at Winchester, in July 1974 the alumni Winton Club determinedly celebrated its centenary with a dance, chapel services and a *son et lumière* show – bed and breakfast in the College £1.20. Two years on, at Hockerill College, Bishop's Stortford, Hertfordshire, a similar doom-laden letter arrived from the Secretary of State citing 'national economic problems and a fall in the birth rate' as reasons for the College having no further intake of students from that autumn. This was an experience all too common in dozens of training colleges at that time.

The mid-1970s witnessed one of the periodic outbreaks of 'merger-fever' at Winchester and elsewhere, with mixed results. Principal Rose's report of 1975 details merger discussions between King Alfred's and the College of Sarum St Michael, Salisbury, founded to train male and female teachers respectively for their adjacent dioceses, and so potentially a natural partner. There was a precedent in the merger of the Colleges of Ripon (women) and York, St John (men), concluded in 1974. These were similar diocesan foundations to Salisbury and Winchester, the proposed merger of which was to start from 1 September 1976. Position papers to a staff working group and a student representative from each institution (Mr Dickenson and Miss Howie) included a 77-page report on King Alfred's and a 19-page report on St Michael's. Files show that discussions were vigorous, notably around the total of teacher training places, Principal Rose insisting that there would have to be 900 to make the institution viable. Another area of discussion was the ratio of representatives of each college on the proposed Academic Board, which was eventually settled in King Alfred's favour, at a ratio of ten (Winchester) to five (Salisbury).

There were differences also over the relationship with the University of Southampton as validating body. St Michael's remained in a relationship with Southampton, with which they enjoyed 'good relations', and would be 'sad to leave'. Mr Rose, however, stated that King

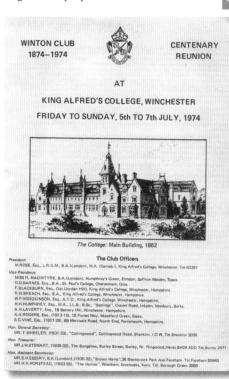

WINTON CLUB 1874–1974   CENTENARY REUNION

AT

KING ALFRED'S COLLEGE, WINCHESTER

FRIDAY TO SUNDAY, 5th TO 7th JULY, 1974

The College: Main Building, 1862

The letter apparently agreeing to a merger of King Alfred's with Sarum St Michael in Salisbury – but Salisbury chose closure instead.

> 21st July, 1975
>
> Secretary of State for Education and Science,
> Department of Education and Science,
> Elizabeth House,
> York Road,
> London, SE1 7PH.
>
> Dear Sir,
>
> We the undersigned, on behalf of our respective Governing Bodies, agree to the merger of King Alfred's College, Winchester and the College of Sarum St, Michael, Salisbury with effect from the 1st August, 1976. From the 1st August, 1976, there will be one Governing Body, one Academic Board, one Principal and one Administration of the new College.
>
> This agreement is made on the understanding that there should be within the merged College by 1981 no less than 900 places allotted to teacher education.
>
> Yours faithfully,
>
> Chairman of Governors,
> King Alfred's College.
>
> Chairman of Governors,
> College of Sarum St. Michael.

Alfred's had left validation by Southampton (for the Council for National Academic Awards) 'with trepidation', but 'would not go back'. In outlining the position at Winchester, Rose declared that King Alfred's 'hoped to be free-standing', but added that this was 'quite possibly not going to be so', indicating that discussions with the Winchester School of Art 'were at a rather turgid stage and the outcome uncertain'. Rose had concluded by this time that the future lay beyond the aegis of Southampton University – that he needed to press on the accelerator of change – and that through a diversified curriculum he could initiate a move towards creating a 'real' university.

A contrasting case was Bishop Grosseteste College in Lincoln, where the teacher-training staff retained more power over the curriculum than at Winchester for longer, with the result that there were initially fewer redundancies in the education area, but a less robust and diversified 'university' curriculum developed compared with Winchester. (Many education staff at Lincoln were to lose their jobs in the 1990s, however.) Nonetheless, in 2012 that college emerged as Bishop Grosseteste University in its own right, retaining a central focus on Education Studies, a different model from Winchester.

Negotiations between Salisbury and Winchester proceeded to the stage where a letter to the Secretary of State for Education and Science was drafted and signed jointly by the Chairmen of the Governors of Winchester and Salisbury, Bishop John Taylor and Dean Fenton Morley, closing with the statement that there should be within the merged college 'no less than 900 places allotted to teacher education'. But Salisbury drew back, and the women's college of Sarum St Michael closed with a service of commemoration on 25 June 1978, after negotiations with Winchester failed. What passed through Martial Rose's mind as the voices of staff, students and alumnae rang out in Salisbury Cathedral on that June Sunday can only be guessed at. Meanwhile the Ripon and York St John merger lasted for some 25 years, until between 1999 and 2001 functions were consolidated in York, and Ripon closed.

St Michael's Salisbury was one of many colleges to disappear in those years. At St Matthias Bristol, a women's Church of England College, men were admitted from 1966, and it had entered an apparent golden age, with a record 800 students and,

St Matthias Bristol at Fishponds. Originally founded in 1853 as the Gloucester and Bristol Diocesan Training School for school mistresses closed in 1978. The site and Gothic building were sold for development in 2014 by the University of the West of England.

The Crewe staff as seen by the Alsager staff.

Alsager staff as seen by the Crewe staff.

Stark contrast: Crewe and Alsager staff view one another with intense suspicion at the time of the merger.

and antiquated. Cartoons of the staff circulated emphasising the differences. The college of higher education that emerged was taken over by Manchester Metropolitan University in 1992, its numbers apparently contributing to making MMU the third-largest university in the country, with the cheapness of land in Cheshire, 35 miles from Manchester, a further incentive. Ten years later the Alsager campus was closed, the buildings boarded up or demolished, and now all its functions have been removed to Crewe.

At Cheltenham and Gloucester merger was followed by 'defederation' in rapid succession. In these years, 1970–80, when 'most polytechnics and all the former colleges of education were engaged in a virtually continuous process of institutional change', they secured impressive educational achievements despite successive cuts and 'increasing pessimism', one commentator observing gloomily from Cheshire that 'the major management agencies – the Government, the DES and the LEAs – have shown themselves either unwilling to make, or incapable of making proper rational policies'. Negotiations for merger at this time for King Alfred's also included the Winchester School of Art (WSA). In the event neither Sarum St Michael nor the WSA wished to merge with King Alfred's College, whose Principal now saw its future 'as a free-standing College of Higher Education offering teacher training and diversified courses to a student population of just over 1,000'.

as it felt its way towards involving students in decision making, limited 'investigation' into 'which areas of [college] government it is appropriate for students to take part [in]'. The government's humourlessly entitled White Paper, issued by Margaret Thatcher as Secretary of State for Education on 6 December 1972 in response to the James Report on Teacher Training – 'Education: A Framework for Expansion' – proposed, among much else, mergers for colleges, which in Bristol meant a reduction from 2,700 to 1,600 training places. After collapsed merger negotiations with Redland College and some 'unsavoury negotiations' with the county council, the college governors chose closure. The dream of 1966 was over and the college vanished, its service of Commemoration and Valediction occurring just a day before that in Salisbury, 24 June 1978.

Elsewhere others attempted wary and fractious mergers, for example at Crewe and Alsager, where the Crewe College (women) considered itself as senior in status and academic quality, while Alsager, a post-war College that had opened with 320 ex-servicemen, regarded Crewe as a nunnery – genteel

Asa Briggs's former doctoral student Grace Jones was head of History at King Alfred's (see p116).

Chilbolton Court, the first King Alfred's student village (since demolished), built on the former West Hayes playing fields c. 1978.

LOOKING TO THE FUTURE

With the future now clearer, attention turned once more to the estate. A new library was opened in 1978 by Lord Briggs, who had supervised the PhD of Dr Grace Jones, Head of History, accompanied at the opening by Bishop John Taylor. This freed up space in the Main Building for a new Senior Common Room in the central area of the ground floor by the Terrace, as well as providing space to accommodate an influx of books from the redundant library at Sarum St Michael. In 1978–9 College facilities were further extended with the opening of Chilbolton Court, near West Hayes. This field and yew-walk, west of West Hayes beside the Romsey Road, had formerly been the garden of that large house but had been cut off by the creation of Chilbolton Avenue in 1912. Purchased in 1963 – and thus reunited with the eastern area of the garden and the West Hayes house – Rannie's Field, as it was known, was a three-and-a-half-acre site on the corner of Chilbolton Avenue and Romsey Road. It was bought and developed in the 1970s as Chilbolton Court, providing further residential houses for students, including flats for married couples. Meanwhile Christchurch Lodge, in St James's Lane (formerly a Christchurch Vicarage), was purchased by the College in 1977 and opened in 1978 as a hostel for 20 students.

In 1979/80 the second phase of building at Chilbolton Court, consisting of a second block of ten study bedrooms and a further 'married flat', was completed, as was conversion to accommodation of the Coach House at Christchurch Lodge. In

Lord Briggs with Bishop Taylor, opening the Martial Rose Library in 1978.

1979 plans were made for the improvement of the Design and Technology Department (the Herbert Jarman Building), with Department of Education and Science support, and government finance was secured for the building project.

Ten years after the heady 1971 proposal of a College of 2,000 students numbers were stubbornly stuck at just under 900, only creeping over that number in the early 1980s. Threats and closures elsewhere had encouraged diversification of courses, and this had become a key concern when closure letters arrived on principals' desks after 1974. When the Anglican Colleges issued a joint prospectus for 1980–81, despite casualties such as St Michael's there was still a vigorous if diminished band of some ten free-standing colleges, including King Alfred's,

providing a 'network of Christian communities' in a core of areas and subjects – Education, English, Geography, Mathematics and Religious Studies. Some were drifting into associations, such as Bishop Otter College in Chichester, which had joined, following complex negotiations, with the post-war college at Bognor to form the West Sussex Institute of Higher Education. Beyond the standard teacher-training courses, the King Alfred's curriculum consisted of BA English; BA History; BA Drama, Theatre and Television; Dip.HE in Social and Environmental Studies; one-year PGCE; part-time and full-time courses for qualified teachers; BA History (part-time, evening); and retraining in Craft, Design and Technology. An 'Opportunity to Study in the United States on some courses' was highlighted.

Dr Foster, a 'brilliant teacher' of (non-pietistic) 'academic theology', leaving the Chapel with the congregation in the late 1960s.

The University television studio in 2015.

5

College of Higher Education ...

COLLEGE LIFE AND DEVELOPMENTS IN THE 1970s

While in the background the birth rate, economic problems and government were making the future hard to predict, life had to proceed at King Alfred's as best it could. It is for that reason worthwhile to reflect on what had been happening in the microcosm of the College and in its regional context. The buildings of the 1950s to the 1980s echo the uncertainties of those times. That Winchester survived was due to much blood, sweat and tears – a phrase used elsewhere in the college sector at the time. The late 1960s and early 1970s were an especially difficult period for

the College. In order to secure new buildings beyond a new Sports Hall, partners were sought.

One such venture was the Wessex Closed Circuit Television Consortium. The College had long taken an interest in audio-visual equipment necessary to the delivery of teaching on site and in schools. Edmund Dobson, in addition to his role as Head of Geography, presided over the 16mm cine facility. Already the value of closed circuit television was being emphasised, and in 1966 a letter of support from the Department of Education was received, giving a green light to using the facility for observation of teaching. By Trinity Term 1968, led

c.1970–1990

Tony Lee and staff receiving ex-military TV equipment for the Wessex TV studio in 1972.

by Derek Hill, finance had been obtained and a TV Studio constructed. The following year a partnership with four colleges of education in Salisbury, Southampton, Weymouth and Winchester was established, with its headquarters in a specially designed single-storey building housing the College's own television studio. The indefatigable Mr Hill pressed forward, obtaining further support from R. M. Marsh, the benign and far-sighted County Education Officer at the time, and was soon giving demonstrations of this cherished facility to the Army at Aldershot and the Navy at Portsmouth, resulting in enthusiastic letters seeking further training from the officers involved.

Peter Sykes, whose Hammer Films include *To the Devil a Daughter*, teaching camera work to BA English students Hodgkinson, Cameron and Mangell (with camera), *c.* 1950.

Right: At work in the Library in the 1980s.

Four relics from Liz Jones's scrapbook of life at King Alfred's, 1978–81: pub crawl record with Bar staff signatures (**bottom**); Liz Jones with a pint of cider (**below right**).

Thus the College began to enhance its position in the wider world of training provision locally, as well as making its presence known beyond trainee teachers in local schools. The basis for later diversified degrees in television and film with drama was laid, demonstrating that innovation could bring dividends. Technicians were employed, resulting in a sharp correspondence between Hill, as their manager, and Colin Fowkes the Secretary of the Senior Common Room on the subject of access to the Common Room for the technicians. Hill's proposal that they be included was firmly rebuffed, although they could be invited to social functions such as sherry parties (the staple of College celebration in Stripe's time and for a while thereafter). The technicians were not academics, and their admission would have required the SCR to admit 'at least fifteen administrative staff', who were almost all women as was common at that time.

The new Sports Hall was developed on the west side of the Dytche between 1971 and 1974, freeing the Gymnasium of 1938 for use as an Exam Hall. The Bursar, Ken Heyes, a very keen tennis and squash player (and always immaculately turned out), was a leading figure in the Winchester Tennis and Squash Club in Bereweeke Road, and his contacts there enabled the College to enter an agreement providing state-of-the-art squash courts on the south side of the Sports Hall in 1976 in return for access for external players. This model of sharing with external partners and providing public access proved useful, while also raising the profile of the institution in the local community. The community's erstwhile consciousness of the student population was of the noise 'the Alfs' made in the city while going about their pleasures during Freshers' Week, after exams, sports fixtures or other undergraduate events – particularly pub crawls, where signatures were obtained by bar staff to evidence consumption of a pint in each place.

In the late 1970s the calm of the College 'Ent[ertainment]s' Committee was broken by the booking of the punk band Johnny Thunders and the Heartbreakers,

3 LEGGED PUB CRAWL	
Heart in Hand	*ADDAMS*
Black Boy	*Murphy*
Cricketers	
Riverside Inn	
India Arms	
Bakers Arms	*K White*
The Old Vine	*S Conboy*
City Tavern	*Collins*
The Exchange	*Y Hooper*
Green Man	
College	*D Snell*

Please get the bar staff in each pub to sign the sheet.
Good Luck!

> *"Amazed we managed to fit so much in. As well as doing a bit of work – squash, swimming, walks in the water meadows and up to St Catherine's Hill. Half price Pernod evenings, toga parties, beer festival at Guildhall, folk club wassail, lots of different music, films and plays, hostel parties, Isle of Wight Hockey Club tour – they left a couple of people there by mistake! – Hockey Club dinners at Southgate Hotel with boat races and bar diving (dangerous game invented by Colin [Larby] I think), field trips to Old Sarum – seemed to be shut! – and Wales. Plus English outings to see plays in London. All in all a wonderful three years in a beautiful setting – so glad I found the right course in the right place.*

Liz Larby (née Jones), 1978–81

Left: Folk Club programme cover.

Below left: Anti-racism leaflet from a demonstration against the National Front, 1979.

in Winchester in support of Robert Relf, a notorious white supremacist imprisoned for publishing racial hatred materials, enlightened King Alfred's students turned out with their own leaflets: 'Why We Are Marching', which denounced racism.

An early partner in development at this time was the Hampshire County Council, which was able to fund the building of a centre for children with special educational needs on land made available by the College east of Medecroft. The College had developed an expertise in special needs education, with graduates in the area beginning to appear in 1971. A time-specific reversionary agreement was made that lasted 30 years, after which the building returned to College ownership. Meanwhile the Special Needs School was run independently, flagged by an HCC blue school sign identifying successive head teachers and caretakers at the end of the Medecroft drive. This was the 'Medecroft Opportunity Centre', which opened in 1976, housed in a building known as the Medecroft Annexe, initially a single-storey structure. However, 1976 was not all good news on the estates front, for in that year a fire damaged the original Medecroft building, resulting, it was said, from an overheating iron in the textile room.

Links with the local university at Southampton were, up to the mid-1970s, generally satisfactory. However, Southampton Vice-Chancellor Laurence Gower's suggestion in a personal memorandum that Winchester and other affiliated colleges (La Sainte Union, Southampton; West Sussex Institute, Chichester) should become the Education Faculty of the University, was met with alarm from educationists on the Southampton campus and opposition from the chairman of the University Grants Committee.

whose gig had to be hastily relocated from the 'plush-seated' John Stripe Theatre to the Great Hall, where there was less danger of damage by the assembled punks and students, gingered up by College rugby types stirring up fights. The lengthy debate within the committee on how to accommodate the band's demand for cash rather than the customary cheque, both to satisfy the vampire-like Thunders on the one hand and to prevent a riot by the assembled punks by last-minute cancellation on the other, became the stuff of legends.

Those wild days inspired a rise in political activity among the students. On 10 March 1979, when the National Front marched

Martin Doughty.

Geoff Ridden.

Below: Town and Gown – a historic procession forms in The Close in June 1979 prior to passing through the city to celebrate the 900th anniversary of the dedication of the cathedral. Æthelwold (John Marshall) in the hood, with Canute (Martin Doughty), Emma (Annette Williams) and others.

Staff and students at Winchester felt beleaguered and pessimistic, which no doubt contributed to the failure to expand beyond 1,000 students. Winchester's desire to validate new, non-education courses was welcome neither in Southampton University, which despite being largely scientific in focus had an Arts faculty as well as a theatre, nor to the Regional Advisory Council (RAC), which at that time had overview of what could be taught in higher education, and where it could be taught.

These hurdles were addressed in various ways by the autumn of 1976: first the College approached the Council for National Academic Awards (CNAA), which became its validating body. This organisation's 'insistence on qualitative parity with best practice Higher Education' was a highly formative influence on all subsequent developments, not only at Winchester but in institutions experiencing the undoubtedly 'arduous, bruising and stressful' process necessary to achieve CNAA validation. Principal Rose found the resources to employ young staff from

non-school-teaching backgrounds. These included Oxford graduates such as David Jarrett (Jesus College, English) and Martin Doughty (Worcester College, PhD in History from the London School of Economics).

Other young staff, such as Geoff Ridden (English), brought experience of university teaching both overseas (Africa) and in the UK, while John Marshall, like Ridden a Leeds graduate, brought expertise close to Martial Rose's heart, specialising in medieval drama. John subsequently moved to Bristol University, where he taught for many years.

The College responded to objections from the RAC (which, for example, opposed the teaching of single honours courses in subjects already offered in the region at Reading and Southampton) by offering joint degrees in History, first with Drama and English, later with Archaeology, and in English with Drama, History and then American Studies, alongside the BEd awards. Among the BEd History students at this time was one

STEPHEN HEWITT AND THE CNAA...

Stephen Hewitt, who had joined the King Alfred's staff in 1971, led the team that drew up the first successful submission to the CNAA. In October 1974 the College's proposals for validation of its education and arts courses to start in 1975 had been rejected. At the time it was clear that the College needed validation of both education and arts courses to stand any chance of survival. Visitors from the CNAA had initially indicated that such radical reforms to college structure and staffing were required that no course could expect validation before 1976, but they subsequently allowed a submission to be made

for a BEd degree to start in 1975. Hewitt and his colleagues worked under extreme pressure to prepare a preliminary submission, which was taken to London on 17 December 1974 and, subject to a few amendments, was granted validation for a start in September 1975. That great breakthrough led the way for the subsequent validation of the first diversified degrees in 1976. And it was from that critical undertaking that King Alfred's College not only survived the imminent threat of closure but started to grow in stature, as a college of Higher Education that would eventually gain university status.

Bishop Taylor awards the first CNAA
degree to Jane Yelland, November 1978.

Don Nutbeam, who became Vice-Chancellor of Southampton University in 2009. A DipHE began in 1977 in Social and Economic Studies, and the first CNAA graduation was held in the John Stripe Theatre in November 1978.

'Thoughts of bare survival are giving way to thoughts about academic standards, self-development, our College community and our place in the family of remaining Church Colleges,' Principal Rose reflected in a report to the Governors. Conferment of degrees (for the first time in the cathedral) was held on 3 November 1979. 'The occasion was deeply impressive.' Thus, as the decade closed, after such an unpromising start, this report by Principal Rose must have been once again a very considerable relief. He of all people must have known how close to extinction the College had moved in the early 1970s, to be saved by external sponsors, partnerships and the introduction of degree courses no longer harnessed to the ebb and flow of teacher training provision, where the drivers were demography – birth rate – and party political ideology.

Changes to the validating body enabled the institution to stand apart from others by answering to a national body. This key development was at least as fundamental as the admission of women. For the first time there were many students in the College who were not being trained for the teaching profession. These students had a different weekly timetable, and so to an extent used complementary resources, and were not being trained as professionals. In arguing the case for diversification the College had wisely made it known that the diversified courses provided an opportunity for student teachers unsuited to the profession to move sideways. This addressed a long-standing criticism of training colleges going back at least to the 1860s, and recalled the oath students had to take at that early date to teach, having been trained.

If life changed visibly for many students when they donned graduation robes in the style and colours of the CNAA (Oxford gown, Aberdeen-shaped hood in gold and turquoise) rather than Southampton University (London gown, Oxford hood, many colours), it also changed for staff, whose stresses suffered are apparent from their memories of those days. If the experience of the students was contrasting on the different courses, the Senior Common Room (SCR) was no less affected. The former timetable of stopping for coffee, for lunch and to take tea (with specially baked cakes) was a ritual. This and other traditions for academic staff, such as not sitting with your subject colleagues but rather

The robes of the Chancellor and Vice-Chancellor are a deep Winchester purple. The current university colours and student graduation robes are a black gown and mortar board, with a rich St Aidan purple hood edged with ivory silk, to reflect the antiquity of Higher Education at Winchester.

Japanese students of the Shoei residence playing the koto.

migrating round the SCR with the intention of learning from the differing skills of others present, are fondly remembered by staff of that era, such as Jenny Nias. However, an initial unsuccessful attempt to disrupt this cosy atmosphere had already been made for the admission of TV technicians *(see p 120)*.

Following diversification from 1976 some new subject area staff wished to sit together, and a lecturer in Philosophy of Education recalled a young member of the History Department in the late 1970s carrying an armchair from one end of the SCR to the other to sit with his colleagues. A new member of staff in 1976 recalls being approached by an established colleague with the request 'May I sit at the clever table?' No doubt new hierarchies were perceived, viewed from the perspective of those involved in primary education training. Some members of staff simply refused to have anything to do with this new departure, and turned their backs irrevocably, both physically and metaphorically. Others, initially sceptical, came in time to embrace the new ways, and in one case carved a meteoric career to a Vice-Chancellorship elsewhere. But, however painful these experiences were, the College survived because it diversified and – under Rose's leadership and with input from staff who could see ways to change the institution's curriculum – held on where many others failed or volunteered for closure.

INTO THE 1980s: NEW INITIATIVES

One of the ways the College attracted new funding and opened its doors was by the establishment of overseas links. Rose had visited Shoei College, a Christian foundation in Tokyo in 1982, and soon thereafter had established a link that sent groups of Japanese women from Shoei to Winchester each year to be accommodated and taught in their own, Shoei-funded, buildings. This forward-looking Asian link was a major event of the early 1980s and brought work for the staff who taught the Shoei girls, although their buildings were for their exclusive use.

This included the introduction of a two-year course for female Japanese students, and the Principal's report of 1980/1 states that this agreement would bring more funding, 'as well as additional buildings at no College expense'. September 1982 saw the first 20 Japanese students arrive from Shoei. One aspect of the agreement stipulated that the Japanese would fund the building of the necessary residential and teaching accommodation, and that the College would provide sites for the buildings. The buildings themselves would revert to the College after a 40-year period, or at an earlier stage if the joint enterprise ceased; it flourishes still today.

The site chosen for the residence was Chilbolton Court, the former West Hayes field, where development had already begun

The singular change in Claudia Armstrong's role at KAC came in 1982, with her appointment as head of the teaching group responsible for the Shoei students, female Japanese students who studied for a two-year course in cohorts of 20. These students at first comprised a college within a college, having their own separate teaching and residential accommodation. This totally new undertaking called for extraordinary qualities of patience, understanding and adaptability – and, indeed, imagination. Claudia, facing a challenge unmatched by any previous experience, rose magnificently to the occasion. Both the Japanese school directors and the students themselves responded with the strongest show of faith in her leadership and, for the students in particular, affection for their leader. The cultural chasms that had to be spanned were wide indeed. No member of staff at KAC could possibly have achieved so high a degree of success in so difficult a job as Claudia. The fact that the enterprise still thrives at the University today, over 30 years later, is in no small part due to Claudia's masterful handling of both the academic problems and the diplomatic issues attendant on the enterprise.

Martial Rose on the late Claudia Armstrong, August 2014

Claudia Armstrong working with Kiyonao Okami (left) and Shoei students (Reiko Mizukoshi, Miho Yamashita, Yoshiko Endo and Harumi Shinkawa) in 1985.

in the previous decade. Other than a vigorous debate about the architecture of the bathrooms in the Shoei residence (Japanese bathing arrangements being more communal than their Western counterparts), the plans were smoothly realised. Teaching accommodation was built as a first floor above the Medecroft Opportunity Centre at the opposite end of the College's estate. Here, to distinguish the Shoei space from the Opportunity Centre below, the new first floor was approached by an entirely separate staircase. This pleasing architectural feature meant that the ground and first floors remained entirely self-contained. Exchange links with American universities were also established,

such as with Chapman College, California, the University of Southern Maine, the University of Wisconsin and elsewhere. Links with Canada and Poland were also initiated and sustained.

The Principal's report goes on to say that the Japanese agreement and the inception of the Nursing Diploma, agreed with Winchester and Basingstoke Health Authority and providing a broader base for academic activity in the College, 'are measures which help to ensure the continuing viability of our College'. Funding worries are raised again in the report of October 1982, where there was

considerable apprehension about the consequences of the Government's determination to reduce initial teacher training throughout the public sector. In the event this College was given additional numbers from 1984 for PGCE and BEd courses, increasing the student population over four years by 160. The challenge of the year ahead is to acquire additional resources to meet this expansion.

One way of providing trainee teachers with experience contrasting with that of leafy Winchester and rural Hampshire schools was through another partnership, with the Urban Studies Centre in Bethnal Green, East London, which was incorporated in 1984 and became the Urban Learning Foundation (ULF) in 1989. Here students encountered new experiences while serving London

The opening of the Shoei residence by Bishop John Taylor and Canon Imai, October 1982.

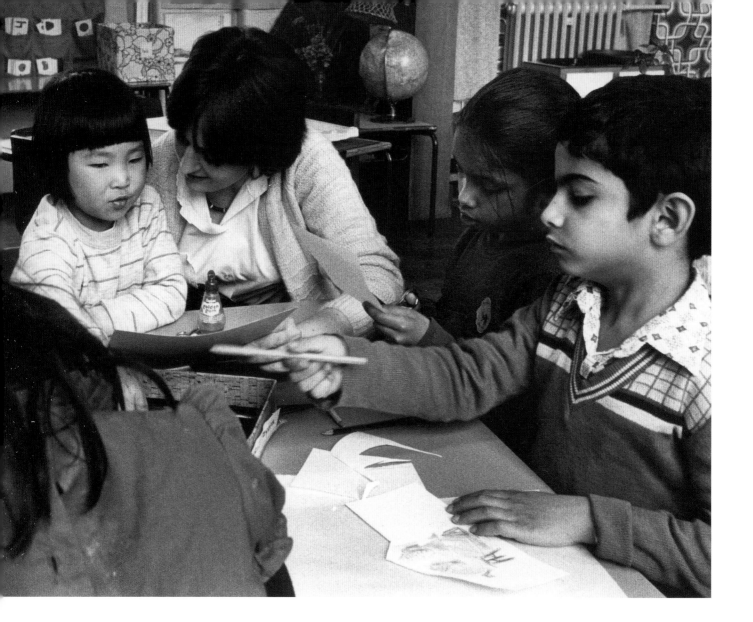

A student teacher at the Bethnal Green Urban Studies Centre in 1985. Up to 24 students at a time went to share the inner London teaching experience in the late 1980s.

schools, and thus were provided with a further career avenue, boosting employment outcomes. This became Newham Borough's major source of recruitment of teachers. The downside of this arrangement, as funding became tighter, was that the £4,000–£5,000 it cost to develop teaching practice through the ULF contrasted poorly with the £250 it cost for a similar experience in a Hampshire school. In due course Winchester relinquished its management and ownership shares of the ULF to a partner, the University of Gloucestershire, which incorporates former Church of England diocesan male and female training colleges.

The government's Department of Education and Science helped fund the building of a new Gymnasium and Movement Studio, together with new teaching accommodation, at a cost of £346,383. The Human Movement Centre, designed by Burford Marlow and Carden, was opened by Peter Brooke, the Under Secretary of State for Higher Education, on the morning of 27

Beryl Orchard, an expert in BBC computers and programming, took a lead in introducing Computer Studies training for students in the 1980s.

ACADEMIC EXPANSION ··

My years as Principal marked the change of a teacher training college to a College of Higher Education: from an institution that had first shown some reluctance to admit women staff and students to one that thrived particularly because of those admissions. The two-year course was replaced by three-year and four-year degree courses and a one-year postgraduate teacher's certificate, and provision was made for higher degrees. There were opportunities for staff to take sabbatical leave and for overseas experience. Many students also, as part of their course, studied in American universities. In addition there were courses for nurse education, extensive in-service provision, and a major venture into the training of teachers for children with special needs, which included the building on the College site of a school for such children.

These major institutional shifts coincided with a large expansion of student numbers, and a major building programme for provision of a student union, halls of residence, additional teaching and staff accommodation, a splendid new theatre and a library. In all this the DES and the Church of England were stalwart supporters and underwriters of the College's development. But beyond the growth in student numbers and the building developments were the deep concerns, under government pressure, to change the way our degrees were validated. The change from university validation to the CNAA was institutionally traumatic, resulting in staff redundancies and fundamental reorganisation of our academic structures.

During this period various new associations were proposed: that we should take responsibility for graduate teacher training at the University of Southampton; that both the Winchester School of Art and the Salisbury College of Sarum St Michael should amalgamate with King Alfred's. Negotiations failed. King Alfred's stood alone, and lived on.

In 1964 I was appointed Vice-Principal to John Stripe. He was then a sick man. When he died I continued to feel in a rather strange way that I was still acting on his behalf. And in 1984, when I retired, I felt that he had been at my elbow throughout.

Martial Rose, Principal 1967–84

Above: Martial Rose, on a visit to Shoei College in Japan in 1982, with members of the College including Kiyonao and Naoyuki Okami, who have been prime movers in the project for many years.

Below: Top floor of the Martial Rose Library today.

October 1984. In the afternoon he attended and spoke at the graduation in the cathedral. The Principal reported to the governors that the building received 'nothing but praise from the Specialist Staff and students who use it'.

A building linking the 'Learning Resources Area' to the 'Television Area' of the early 1970s was completed during 1983. This was followed in 1984 by a new building housing the Computer Centre, Geography and the Dip.HE in Social and Environmental Studies. Built on the two floors above the Television Area west of the Library, it consolidated in one central location the College's main learning resources – an acknowledgement of the growth of computer learning and audio-visual aids, in which the Library now became a part of the Learning Resources Area. The Department of Education and Science agreed to grant £312,620 for the building of the new Computer Centre. The Library was named after Martial Rose, who retired in 1984 after a tumultuous 17 years as Principal. In the following year Fred Wheeler, a governor and long-standing devotee of the College, died, and the Computer/AVA building was named in his memory.

John Cranmer with Tim Drey (left), Kenneth Kettle and Roger Richardson (right), seated with History and Archaeology staff, Dean Tippett (second left), Bursar Heyes (third right) and Estates Bursar Starkey (right) in 1989.

JOHN CRANMER BECOMES PRINCIPAL

Despite all these advances, when Martial Rose retired in 1984 the College was not free from problems. By contrast with the student unrest of the late 1960s this period was characterised by the staff unrest of the 1980s. This was over various matters, including pay and declining staff–student ratios, both of which arose because successive governments were unwilling to fund colleges of higher education with the same pay scales and staff–student ratios as in the 'traditional' universities. These issues continued through the decade, and the Education Reform Bill of 1988 once more raised the question of mergers and closures. Indeed Principal Cranmer, who replaced Rose in 1984 and was uniquely a Wintonian (i.e. alumnus) Principal, came to Winchester with the experience of closing down his previous college, and no doubt was cognisant that he might have to repeat the experience.

A new management team took office when Rose retired, and his deputy, former Head of History Bob Breach, did not become Principal, instead retiring the following year. John Cranmer was a traditionalist, and recalled his days as a student in the College in the late 1950s in William Dickinson's time with great pleasure. He knew the ways the institution had functioned in those days and was firmly on board for its Christian ethos. For example, having attended chapel on Sunday mornings, he then chaired a meeting of the Student Chapel Committee, a lengthy procedure that filled the morning until lunchtime.

One change Cranmer brought about with the governors was to appoint a new Vice-Principal, C. N. C. 'Tim' Drey, who arrived at the end of December 1985 and set about establishing a foundation on which the institution could build. In contrast to Cranmer, Drey, a chemist, was a technocrat. Like predecessors from Ireland, Yorkshire and elsewhere in the nineteenth and twentieth centuries, Drey came from far away, from the Robert Gordon Institute in Aberdeen, and was of Russian and French stock. He was not without common ground with the Principal, however, as he met the criterion for appointment of being a communicant member of the Church of England and also attended chapel.

The new management was soon drawn into the web of government policy changes. The Principal's report of 1985/6 reveals a year of financial restraint when unwelcome and unpopular measures were taken – cuts in the Library, the Student Union and the maintenance fund for buildings, as well as in staffing levels. However, steps were taken to protect the Library budgets of Arts areas such as English and History after complaints about the paucity of resources: a paper presented by the Vice-Principal was agreed by the Governing Body, and these areas benefited by a 10 per cent hike in library funding, and proof against inflation for some years.

The following year-end annual Principal's report was full of anxiety, however. Some money was available on this occasion, for a drive to recruit more teachers of Design and Technology, drawing on the developing skills of computer-aided drawing. Thus in 1987/8 the College's 'skyline' – as Principal Cranmer described it to the governors – was changing, as the new building development for the Department of Design and Technology took shape, in the form of a floor added at the rear of the Herbert

Staff (with some imports!) annual Over 40s vs Under 40s cricket match, 1985. Back: Jacobs, Foster (former Student Union President), Tramaseur, Nash, Firth, James, Quarendon, Breach Jr, Piper, Collins, Barton, Jardine, Martin, Clemson. Front: Eagling, Bowers, Breach Sr, Bentley, Dixon.

Jarman Building. Cranmer was especially aware of these changes in the appearance of the site since his days as a student at Winchester in the late 1950s, when the skyline was still the neo-Gothic extravagance of the Main Building and the old chapel.

At this point in 1989 Jose Chambers, a former English school teacher in Basingstoke, was seconded to the College to promote training technology in schools under the national curriculum, which she did with vigour. A signal of the gradual widening of the College's horizons was flagged by this appointment, and by the choice of the Annual Winton Lecturer 1988, the world historian, former Oxford academic and Vice-Chancellor at Southampton University, John Roberts. Roberts, in a detailed exposition, combined an analysis of development and decline in the breadth of the national history syllabus, which he argued had led to a lack of a minimum shared historical culture, with potential implications for social order.

Apart from changes to the skyline, in 1989 St James's Hall was converted from the Sick Bay and guest rooms to teaching accommodation for the History and Archaeology Department, which began at the same time to colonise Medecroft's old building with its storage facilities for excavation finds, in the former kiln buildings of the Art Department. Also at St James's in those days there were offices for the educational Comino Project and the Open University (OU), Southern Region. The latter co-operative venture led to a keenly contested annual cricket fixture between the staff of King Alfred's and an OU regional team, led by George Watts, who as well as working for the OU is a distinguished historian of medieval Hampshire.

By 1989 an urgent national need was identified to repair the Higher Education buildings, which had become dilapidated and unsafe as a consequence of systematic underfunding. As part of this wide-ranging survey, the College buildings at Winchester were inspected by the Polytechnics and Colleges Funding Council consultants in the summer of 1989. The skill with which the dwindling resources had been managed by Principals Rose and Cranmer, bursar Ken Heyes and their estate staff during these tough years was highlighted in this report, for King Alfred's buildings showed little need for any such urgent work on dilapidations and safety measures. So although the 1980s came to a close with more concern about lack of funds, Winchester was in pretty good shape. Clearly there was much focus on bare survival in these years, with a shortage of money and an ever-decreasing unit of resource.

From early in his tenure Tim Drey realised that danger lurked for the College if it failed to grow and to develop its curriculum. If Cranmer was the traditionalist, Drey was the moderniser. Starting quietly in an institution that was uncertain and fractious, and while suffering some poor health (he had a heart attack in 1988), he devised a method and a basis that enabled the College to expand and diversify. In this he was ably assisted by two long-standing staff members, Brian Bull and Brian Tippett. Both were old hands, Tippett having arrived among the large intake of staff in 1968. They spoke the same language as the new Vice-Principal, having seen the difficulties associated with funding for teacher education and demography as government pulled developments this way and that. Brian Tippett's guiding

5

principles were that 'the College should, if possible, grow in size, that it should further diversify its portfolio, and it should always maintain its reputation for quality'. This is exactly what was needed, and together these three set about shaping the future with the support of staff in the different subject areas.

In the late 1980s institutions were expected to take a view of their future, and to embody these proposals in two documents: a 'strategic plan' and a 'mission statement'. The strategic plan was begun by Tim Drey and his associates and completed in March 1992. This carefully constructed document created a five-year plan incorporating the six strands of the College's activities, academic courses, estates and so on, broken down into annual targets. It was praised as a model by the head of the Polytechnics and Colleges Funding Council (PCFC), Sir William Stubbs, and was in place when the new funding body, the Higher Education Funding Council (England) – HEFCE – came into existence the same year. This was, in Principal John Dickinson's words, a 'thankless task', but brought its rewards. It came at an important time, and while it seemed unnecessary to many, funding agencies such as HEFCE deemed such a document essential. Principal Cranmer had announced early in 1991 that he would be retiring at the end of the academic year in the summer of 1992. In these circumstances the new strategic plan was a blueprint for the course the College envisaged.

THE COLLEGE AT 150: ACHIEVEMENTS AND NEW DIRECTIONS

The College celebrated its 150th anniversary in 1990 and raised money for a lift for the disabled in the Students' Union building. There were commemorative mugs and a pictorial record of the first 150 years leading up to the sesquicentenary jamboree. Despite all the anxieties of the previous 25 years there was much to celebrate, through a breathless series of events.

Changing external constraints meant that, for example, by 1990 single honours Drama was permitted and had recruited very successfully. The College had been tested in the wider field of national higher education by its interaction with the CNAA, which required among much else a focus on research

Brian Bull in the 1960s.

Brian Tippett at a Shoei graduation in the 1990s.

and scholarship qualifications and interests of the specialist staff appointed to teach the diversified courses. It had consolidated its position on the world stage with overseas links in America, Japan, Poland and elsewhere. There was an ever-growing stream of publications from its academics, who attended international conferences and study tours literally all over the world, on all the continents from Drama in Africa to Computing in Russia to Medieval Studies conventions in America to visiting scholarships in Australia.

These developments, and in more recent times the work of Dr Charly Ryan, a chemist by training who taught science

Dr Charly Ryan.

"Access to scientific knowledge for peaceful purposes from a very early age is part of the right to education belonging to all men and women, [...] science education is essential for human development, for creating endogenous scientific capacity and for having active and informed citizens.

Science education, in the broad sense, without discrimination and encompassing all levels and modalities, is a fundamental prerequisite for democracy and for enduring development."

Declaration on Science – World Conference on Science
Budapest, 1999

UNESCO Science Education
Budapest Declaration, 1999.

in the College for over 30 years, and who was a fluent Spanish speaker, exemplify this cosmopolitan outlook. He has worked with partners from Spain and Ireland to establish the first European Union Erasmus Initial Teacher Education Primary link, which took students to work in as many as four different countries. This was followed by an intensive multinational study programme (1991) repeated in France, Denmark and Ireland, which was very well received and published, and is in progress in Austria 20 years on. With the same colleagues he has written the first ALFA (Spanish, translates as: Association for Latin American Academics' Development) Programme approved in Europe, which was to develop science teacher education in Argentina, Bolivia and Chile. The work in Argentina was most fruitful, with many participants on the programme now active university researchers with doctorates. It led to much more Latin American work and publications, including the UNESCO challenges for science education. UNESCO has subsequently established a Faculty for Science Education in Latin America and the Caribbean (Cátedra UNESCO). ALFA staff helped the development of national curricula, for example for the island of Trinidad in the Caribbean, where Dr Ryan contributed the science curriculum. He has recently written the new UNESCO Current Challenges in Basic Science Education document, and has been a visiting lecturer in ten countries.

Development of postgraduate courses began with the MEd (Master in Education) around 1980 and subsequently, from a start in the late 1980s, in MPhil and doctoral study, which contributed signally to the attainment of University Title in 2005. These changes derived initially from the teacher training curriculum, but a distinctive aspect of the church colleges has been the development of courses in the humanities and subsequently in the caring professions such as nursing. This contrasts with the polytechnics, which developed a broader curriculum with more scientific and vocational work starting from a larger student base.

Vice-Principal Drey repeated the mantra 'critical mass' – that is to say that in order to survive the College had to gain significant undergraduate numbers. Following his arrival in 1985, together with the efforts of the two Brians, the foundations of a modern, functioning institution of higher education were laid. These included creating quality control mechanisms and establishing quality assurance through course monitoring. Such changes were bitterly opposed in some quarters, notably among some administrative and education staff. This change was unavoidable, however, and fitted well with Brian Tippett's view that to survive the institution had to preserve quality. Tippett calls this consolidation programme of quality in the years following 1985 'the in-between years' – the years between diversification from mono-technic from c.1976 and the push for University status from 1995. The question of how to make the great leap forward in numbers to critical mass was answered in various ways. First it was clear that an institution with diversified strengths initially in History and English (with subsidiary American Studies, Archaeology, Drama, etc.) and with an Education Department would never be a university under the rules then current, as its base was too narrow.

The answer to this was to devise a programme that would encourage a spread of subjects and allow successful areas to grow. The way forward was to set in place a 'modular programme', led with great commitment and enthusiasm by Martin Doughty *(see p122)*, whose initiative this was. The modular programme allowed subject areas to recruit and to be tried. It was another stage on the road to establishing a well-founded institution that matched its aspirations with action. It liberated staff in subject areas it had previously found difficult to develop. Staff in areas that had previously provided 'special subject' expertise for teacher training students were enthusiastic for change, particularly as education reforms meant that there was less work. Among these education reforms had been local management of schools, which had freed schools to innovate and managers to manage, thereby opening new vistas for college staff.

Alongside the diverse modular programme, entirely new areas such as Psychology, with a new staff base, could be introduced. Business was also begun, with a mixture of external and internal staff, for example from the Maths Department, which after over 150 years finally passed away. Subjects such as

Archaeology became separate departments. Second, a way had to be found to obtain student numbers to populate these subject areas, in order to create the divisions or faculties which would in time form a university.

Drey and his colleagues, both on the academic side and in the Accounts Department, discovered that a route lay open through what was called 'marginal funding'. The College could bid for student numbers in a government 'auction' and in time these students, funded initially at a low level, could convert into full-cost places. The algorithm used at King Alfred's became sufficiently celebrated that a team from the College was invited to several other institutions to explain how Winchester had been so successful. Yet King Alfred's still had to grow and to demonstrate the quality of its courses to make its way towards University Title.

The need for a more broadly based curriculum and funding drew the College towards its neighbour, the Winchester and Basingstoke Health Authority, which ran the adjacent Winchester and other hospitals in the district and sought partnership in training its staff. The successful establishment of Nursing and Midwifery degrees emerged from these negotiations – invaluable to the College as an additional area in which to recruit students, and which drew on a different income stream from other courses at Winchester when the government, as had been the case with teaching around 1970, decided there should be all-graduate nursing and midwifery professions. At first all went well: negotiations with the Winchester and Basingstoke hospital trusts led to the establishment of these courses at King Alfred's, initially

under Magnus Shearer and subsequently under Cynthia Gilling. Internally the College was reforming its systems: in November 1990 new Articles of Government replaced Staff Conference, which had existed since the late 1970s, and College Council was replaced with a reconstituted Academic Board.

Managers at Winchester had to react to changing circumstances in the world outside. One such change was the demise of the CNAA as the validating body for Winchester courses in 1992, following the Further and Higher Education Act of that year. Again, forward planning had laid the foundation for what was known as 'partnership in validation'. In this scenario, rather than a visiting team of academics and others 'testing' the courses on offer, the validation process was chaired by senior staff from Winchester. Drey had pioneered this, and so by the time CNAA was defunct an 'accreditation' visit from CNAA had taken place. They had expressed satisfaction with Winchester's procedures, and so at last the College had control over validation of its courses. This was highly significant. When the College returned to Southampton in 1992 for validation it was under terms of accreditation, so that even if validations went wrong (and some certainly did), it was in the hands of the Winchester managers to sort the problems out, and with the breadth of the modular programme to introduce new areas of study. In fact 'public' sector institutions, such as colleges and ex-polytechnic universities, were further ahead on issues of quality control and quality assurance than most universities, which still relied very heavily on an 'old boy' network of external examiners.

The Vice-Chancellor of Southampton in the early 1990s, Sir Gordon Higginson, was supportive and sympathetic to what was being attempted at Winchester. He was conversant with the idea of the 'multiversity'

The chapel at what had previously been the
Westminster Methodist Training College, London.

that had been pioneered in California in which different, autonomous institutions in a region offered courses to students who came from all sorts of different academic backgrounds (in England this would be GCSE A level, BTEC and other vocational qualifications, access courses and so on) in a loose confederation of autonomous institutions within the regional 'multiversity'. However, when Higginson retired and was replaced by Howard Newby in 1994, the picture changed again, and Southampton University appeared more predatory, with talk once more of turning Winchester into a satellite Education Faculty for Southampton. This would have been the end of the College as it then existed, and would have meant major redundancies because of duplication. The Education faculty at Southampton University, once more, was unenthusiastic.

Winchester had explored regional links at this time with other colleges of education: with Westminster College, originally a Methodist College in London, and with Bulmershe College at Reading. Westminster had high hopes of becoming a college

of John Wesley's *alma mater* Oxford University: the Church of England College at Culham had become associated with the Education Faculty of the University in 1951. After lengthy negotiations with Oxford University and others Westminster relocated to North Hinksey, near Oxford, in 1959, a '15-minute' bicycle ride from the city. Hopes of becoming integrated into Oxford University were dashed, although some validation of courses was achieved, and the Sheldonian became a graduation location, all this agony dramatically catalogued by Jennifer Bone in her moving history of Westminster College 1951–2001, its 150th anniversary. A notable drawback for Westminster, in contrast with Winchester, was that, being a Methodist foundation, it was 'dry' – there was no bar. This severely inhibited out-of-term potential conference income. In the end the College merged in 2000 with Oxford Brookes University. The site was leased to Brookes, to form the Oxford Brookes Westminster Institute of Education and Human Development.

Bulmershe College at Reading had a different, but in some ways parallel, experience, having merged with Reading University in 1989. A latecomer on the scene, a College of Higher Education only since 1975, Bulmershe was a quality institution, especially under Harold Silver, a notable educationist, who developed specialist education for the deaf there. A successor, Brian Palmer, joined the governing body at Winchester – there was a tradition as late as 1998 of Reading and Southampton being represented on the Winchester Governing Body as the local universities. Palmer was vocal in urging Winchester to merge with Southampton, or indeed Reading. As at Ripon and York merger had worked for some 20 years after 1989. But at the end of academic year 2011–12 all courses at ex-Bulmershe ceased, and proposals were made to demolish all the buildings (including the Film Studies accommodation, which had been recently upgraded at a cost of £1 million), and the site developed, except for the student accommodation. This was converted to private apartments, as it was deemed too far from the other campuses of the university for student use. Only the sports fields were retained. Thus Westminster and Bulmershe joined that long roll call of colleges and institutes of education, and of Higher Education, like Alsager (mentioned above) and Matthias, Bristol, which survive now largely in archives and in the memory of former staff and alumni. Winchester decided to go it alone.

6

From Higher Education ....
to University

PRINCIPAL DICKINSON AND THE PUSH FOR UNIVERSITY TITLE

On its 150th anniversary in 1990 the College was more richly endowed to meet its academic and residential commitments than it had been ten years earlier, but it was still very far from the size and academic scope that could have allowed progress towards University Title. However, expansion in student numbers had been rapid since the mid-1980s, when there were 1,000 students, towards a goal of some 2,000 by 1992, when Principal Cranmer retired.

The new Principal, John Dickinson, like Vice-Principal Drey, came from a Scottish institution, this time Glasgow University where he was Professor and Dean of the Faculty of Business and Law having previously been Professor of Accountancy and Finance at Stirling. For the first time the College was headed by a Principal with a university pedigree. He took over in September 1992, opening his stewardship with a consultation paper in 1993 called 'A View of the Next Five Years', presented to the Academic Board and Governing Body. Proposals included expansion of student numbers to 4,500–5,000 full-time equivalent students – a larger number when translated into a head count of part- as well as full-time students. Expansion

1990—2015

WINCHESTER GAZETTE

EXTRA

THE NEWSPAPER FOR MID-HAMPSHIRE

THURSDAY NOVEMBER 25, 1993   TEL: (WIN) 867575   No. 649

Residents stand firm on retail park plan

Royal couple in city walkabout

College plan sparks hope of university

By PAUL STEVENS

of the physical estate was proposed. This task was top of the agenda for Tommy Geddes, a former Trades Union Congress scholar at the London School of Economics, who arrived as College Secretary (Assistant Principal) in 1993. This was a post that had developed from that of Clerk to the Governors, the head of administration and bursar, following the Weaver Report of 1966, when colleges began to create their own governing bodies.

The 1993 consultation paper also officially set down the notion of a mission for University Title in 2005. University status had been on the agenda for many years, as former Dean Professor Brian Tippett recalls, and moves such as increasing the breadth

Top: St Edburga entrance.

Above: *Winchester Gazette Extra* University project headline, November 1993.

of subjects offered and developing academic research had been quietly in progress. In September 1996 the Standing Committee of the Governors received a draft paper entitled 'University in Winchester', which set an agenda of aiming for Taught Degree Awarding Powers (TDAP: BA and MA, application to be made in 1997), and Research Degree Awarding Powers (RDAP: application to be made in 2001), with University Title to be achieved in 2005. The campaign, or Charter Board – reflecting the aim to gain a university royal charter for Winchester – was to be headed jointly by the newly appointed Bishop of Winchester, Michael Scott-Joynt, and the Lord Lieutenant of Hampshire, Mary Fagan, with a further 15 luminaries being invited to join, lured by a series of dinners for the 'Great and Good'.

Educational change is inevitably linked to politics, and never more so than in the last two decades. The CNAA, said to have been unpopular with former Prime Minister Margaret Thatcher, was abolished, and in 1992, the year in which Principal John Dickinson arrived, the College was obliged to return to accreditation of its degrees by Southampton University. This was uncomfortable and encouraged Winchester's leaders to seek a route to independence. When John Dickinson declared that the College would seek University Title, Southampton University declared itself 'surprised' and, as a validating body for Winchester degrees, took a paternalistic view of Winchester's aspirations, opposing not only 'University', but even 'Winchester' in the title of University College Winchester. While focus groups showed that the retention in some form of 'King Alfred's' in any new title was very popular, the use of 'Winchester' in any new title was deemed essential. An outcome of these negotiations was set for the end of 1996. In such choppy waters at that time, and with such opposition from Southampton, University Title seemed a distant and perhaps unrealistic goal. Opposition at Southampton to any course that duplicated their offerings was apparent.

In realising its aim of independent University Title, Winchester was helped by successive governments. Anxious over the titling of institutions, the Conservative government of the early 1990s became concerned that European Union and other overseas students might not be attracted to institutions not entitled 'University'. The result was that through legislation in 1992 the polytechnics were all designated universities, but dozens of other Higher Education institutions, including King

Alfred's, were omitted, and ways were sought in succeeding years to remedy this oversight.

Change also occurred in the area of teacher training, creating some ups and downs at that time. In September 1992 changes to in-school training looked potentially positive, but when the detail emerged in 1993 there was no money for the primary education training sector: a significant financial blow that reinforced the drive towards diversified income streams for King Alfred's. A further blow was the unwillingness of the Department of Education to allocate extra secondary education places to Winchester, resulting from a negative Inspector's report relating to staffing and other matters at that time. However, new possibilities of dual-stream funding also emerged in 1993, when the Teacher Training Agency (TTA) funding was separated from the Higher Education Funding Council (England) (HEFCE). With a strong surviving element of teacher education, the emergence of a TTA funding stream was of particular value to the institution. Such changes required the College to keep a sharp eye on government policy, and to tailor their internal policies and course designations to best local advantage, which in turn brought significant financial benefit.

The large and rapid expansion in student numbers from 1985 necessitated the development of the administration, registry and other aspects of support for students and management. Thus in

Left: The old and the new combine on campus.

Below: Students in The Stripe lecture theatre.

1993, when Tommy Geddes arrived, the east wing of the Main Building was adapted from 'The Principal's Suite' for an expanded senior management team, and planning for expansion of accommodation and infrastructure was necessary. Geddes moved quickly to design and implement a strategic plan for the College's estate, beginning with the sale of the old off-site hostels.

In 1994 a hasty government decision was taken that related to local government reorganisation. Its primary aim was to dispose of nomenclature deemed 'unpopular', such as Avon in the west and Cleveland in the north. The outcome was, however, quite different, and bombshells landed elsewhere: Berkshire ceased to exist, and Hampshire, previously among the most populous and wealthy local authorities, was broken up by the bestowing of 'unitary authority' status on Portsmouth and Southampton. This removed both its universities from Hampshire (Bournemouth having already been allocated to Dorset) and encouraged Hampshire County Council to focus on Winchester as the county's remaining institution of Higher Education.

EXPANSION AND EVOLUTION

What had started in the 1970s as a School of Arts and Sciences and a School of Education had been joined by a School of Nursing and Midwifery, but even with this addition there was an insufficiently broad curriculum base for a university application. In autumn 1994, therefore, in response to government guidelines insisting on a minimum of five Schools or Faculties, six Schools

Geddes recorded for posterity in a West Downs weathervane.

Principal John Dickinson and Kenneth Kettle sign the agreement for the purchase of West Downs in 1994.

were established, including Drama and Performing Arts, strong recruiting areas. Essential changes such as these were planks in the move towards University Title. Administrative areas were also consolidated to increase efficiency and effectiveness, and planning was enhanced by the introduction of a Learning and Resources Committee, instituted in 1994. The key to progress remained student recruitment, without which nothing could be achieved. This made ambitious building programmes essential. Building restructuring was significant, but had to be matched by the academic reorganisation.

By far the largest development was undertaken at West Downs, north-west of the College and hospital, along the Romsey Road. In 1994 King Alfred's was very short of good student accommodation, with many students in digs or out-dated off-site hostels scattered across the city, thus potentially endangering female students crossing the city late at night, as had been mentioned in the report of 1957. The redundant preparatory school with its extensive playing fields just a few minutes' walk from the College presented an ideal opportunity to expand the campus, and in particular to create a new student village for almost 1,000 residents, with its own community spirit. The West Downs purchase was concluded on 28 October 1994, when Principal John Dickinson and Kenneth Kettle, Secretary to the Governing Body, signed the papers. The price was £4.5 million, with a budget of £16 million required to complete the project. This was a key moment in the development of the institution.

The West Downs development was a challenging, high-risk venture, which had the capacity to make or break the College, and rigorously tested the recently appointed College Secretary Geddes and the new Director of Estates, Chris Higgins, the governors and other senior managers. However, the case was made successfully to the governors, then chaired by Bishop Colin James, and the Standing Committee chaired by Robin Bishop, and the purchase was concluded by the Director of Estates over a cup of tea. The purchase amounted to the 12.5-acre West Downs, which included the main, seriously dilapidated West Downs school building at risk of total collapse, and the adjacent 'Masters' Lodge', where the former school's teaching staff had lived, though it had long since been boarded up and was riddled with dry rot.

The reason for buying the school site was solely to build residences on its playing fields. The run-down listed buildings were not wanted, but planning permission was only granted on

condition they would be refurbished at some unspecified time in the future. Saving them cost the College much more than purchasing the site. The business plan was predicated on taking out sufficient long-term bank loans to buy the land and build the residences, with much future rental income being used to repay the loans. It was essential to open the first phase by September 1995, or the banks (NatWest and Allied Irish) could have foreclosed on the deal with the potential to bankrupt the

College. Planning permission was not granted until 6 January 1995, and building began in earnest three days later. Over the next two years the West Downs Student Village was created. Reception, a shop and a launderette were also added. In 1998 the student village was formally opened by His Royal Highness The Duke of Gloucester.

As in 1862, the celebrations of the opening encapsulated an element of great relief, for the builders had gone bankrupt towards the end of the project. Had it not been for a sharp-eyed site steward who noticed that (unpaid) subcontractors were removing copper tanks and plumbing, and so arranged for the drives to be blocked, delays would have been more significant. In the event, as at St Elizabeth's in the 1960s, irate parents delivering their children to a sea of mud were most unhappy, and having seen West Downs, they occupied a room on the campus in protest. In the end calm was restored and the students moved in. The benefits well justified these tense moments and risks, as it secured the College's future and its aspirations to grow

into a university. Notwithstanding the problems, the project had produced the first 200 study bedrooms in fewer than nine months, and therefore the essential income to fund the loan. The development designed by Feilden Clegg Architects won a National Housing Award, with the accolade that the main street with its balconies and external staircases was crying out for an open-air performance of *West Side Story*.

Also in 1994, St Grimbald's Court, then over 60 years old, was converted from residential to teaching accommodation, as the demands from the growing number of students increased. Extra accommodation for residential students was provided at Beech Glade Hall, which was built on the site of Beech Glade, the former Vice-Principal's house west of Medecroft. In 1995 Medecroft itself was extended by the addition of a new north-east wing comprising a series of new offices on the site of the former open pottery kilns, providing single studies for, among others, members of the Archaeology and History Departments which were consolidated at Medecroft from St James's.

Above: The Duke of Gloucester formally opened the West Downs Student Village (**left**) in 1998.

Right: A NATFHE staff union demonstration in Winchester High Street in support of a pay claim in 1998.

Bottom: New subjects such as Psychology took off.

A new and more predatory Vice-Chancellor, Howard Newby, in post at Southampton University from 1994, advocated amalgamation of King Alfred's into Southampton University. The government's transformation of the polytechnics into universities at that time and the possibility of merger and association with other institutions of Higher Education, described above, continued to swirl around Winchester. However, by 1995 King Alfred's superficially might have seemed safe, with burgeoning student numbers around 4,500, compared with under 1,000 in 1985, and with secure control of quality assurance and partnership in validation of courses in a widening variety of subject areas. It was the success of establishing these policies that enabled Principal John Dickinson to announce in 1995 that Winchester would aim for University Title in 2005. The institution was beginning to make its way in the wider field of Higher Education and the university sector. By 1995, when Vice-Principal Drey retired after ten years, there were significantly more students and opportunities than when he had arrived.

At this time a long-running struggle between senior managers and the governors and the Staff Conference came to an end. The Staff Conference had been in existence for many years, and even in the 1970s had operated in a hierarchical way with the Principal in the Chair. There were echoes of a school staff meeting which the head might dominate. However, in a period of stress and change there were challenges to the status quo. Before 1980 Principal Rose had been voted out of the chair and the Conference set a course of its own over a number of years. Another issue was the concurrent struggle with the union, the National Association of Teachers in Further and Higher Education (NATFHE). There were deep fears of a merger with Southampton University or elsewhere, which unsettled the staff, especially when rumours emerged of a secret meeting with representatives of The Southampton Institute of Higher Education in a local country hotel, Lainston House.

The year 1995 was a turning point. An application to establish a course in Business Studies failed that summer, but the upside of this was that with partnership in validation it was no longer in the hands of external people to prevent course development: Winchester could, and did, sort out the situation for itself. Relations with Southampton University reached a nadir when Winchester introduced an undergraduate course in Psychology, an area of study in which Southampton claimed regional hegemony. When Winchester persisted and the British Psychological Society (BPS) gave support, the programme went ahead, receiving the accreditation of the BPS in 1999.

There was, in addition, an underlying weakness in finance in the mid-1990s. As a college directly funded by central government, King Alfred's had long been organised on a 'break

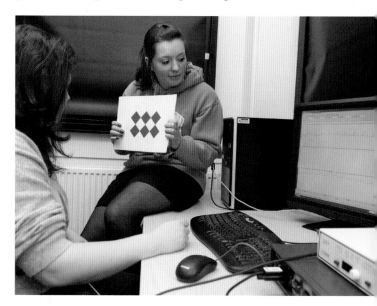

them. These changes were critical, but in a climate where colleges were again closing if they did not meet government requirements, they may have also been unavoidable. The whole BEd was threatened by a proactive leader of the Teacher Training Agency because of a deemed lack of quality in a single area, Design and Technology, and thus to save the Education degree the College was forced to sacrifice this department. By that time that department had evolved from a craft department, employing skilled wood carvers, a clock-maker and a silversmith, into a computer-drawing facility focusing on primary-school teaching. In the end disaster was avoided by such decisions, but it was a close-run thing, as La Sainte Union College in Southampton discovered when it lost its teacher training licence in 1997. Had this happened at Winchester, bankruptcy and closure could not have been avoided.

In the 1996 Research Assessment Exercise (RAE) areas of excellence were entered, and the first income was received in recognition of the quality of research – in Biology (largely that of Dr David Knight on collagen), in English and in History. In 1986 and 1989, when the College was not yet set on a research footing, there was no entry in the RAE, but the exercise showed the potential for another income stream, as it split teaching

even' principle, dating back to the long-standing era of the College Treasurer, with no financial reserves, which made it vulnerable to any unexpected shipwreck, such as a fall in recruitment (reputation) or an adverse report from an outside body such as the Teacher Training Agency. When the budget of 1995–6 was brought forward it showed a deficiency of nearly £1 million on finances of some £17.5 million, because HEFCE imposed a 7 per cent cut in grant to the institution – turnover at that time was approaching double that. This left a gap of £0.75 million in income from HEFCE and the Teacher Training Agency – which helped to focus minds – and a way forward involving lowering the staff salary bill was achieved in 1996. This was brought about by an unprecedented wave of 30 redundancies, of which almost half were compulsory. Fifteen 'Resignations/ Retirements' occurred on 31 July 1996 alone. Many were staff in Education, then under Head of School Bill Wardle; others were in areas such as Environmental Science and Philosophy that did not recruit strongly.

This painful step-change in the College's staffing had one positive effect, in that it opened the door to recruit staff in areas where students were plentiful and recruitment strong. Recruiters such as Business under Gerry Meek and Psychology under Tony Stone, who was appointed from South Bank University, replaced

Professor Dame Mary Fagan, DCVO, JP, previously Lord Lieutenant of Hampshire, became the University's first Chancellor.

from research money, offering rewards for peer-reviewed quality research. The RAE of 1992 most unfortunately also passed Winchester by as a result of poor external advice, ignorant of the College's academic strengths. However, by that time the College was quietly establishing a firm base in research.

Readerships were introduced via staff competition, enabling successful candidates to reduce their teaching of undergraduates, thus raising their personal research profile and also supervise fully funded research students. This contributed to the rapid development of research in the institution and was an essential first step on the road to University Title. Success in RAE 1996 showed that Winchester could compete in such national funding competitions, and with the next exercise delayed until 2001 there was time to prepare. In September 1999 the University held its first 'Research Day', organised by the Head of Research Roger Richardson, in which staff and postgraduate research students presented aspects of their research. These days have continued ever since – they are now known as Research and Engagement Week – and are well attended, showcasing the variety of work being undertaken.

Further encouragement for the College's plan was a strong endorsement of the quality of its teaching and systems in the final Higher Education Quality Council (HEQC) Quality Audit published in August 1996 (the organisation was re-formed as the Quality Assurance Agency (QAA) the following year). There was much to commend at Winchester, including better 'critical mass', the fundamental measure of viability through student numbers. The College's claim to be a 'community of scholars' was found by the auditors to be 'upheld', and they noted further that 'individual needs are not lost sight of' – a resounding outcome.

This vote of confidence contributed to the success of the College in a recruitment drive that began at that time, spearheaded by the governors to bring on board the great and the good of Hampshire county and businesses located and led from the county. Among those recruited to the cause was Mary Fagan, Lord Lieutenant (i.e. Her Majesty's Representative) of Hampshire since 1994, who was to become the first Chancellor of the University of Winchester ten years later. Dame Mary, patron of over 60 organisations in the county, provided a secure link with Hampshire, where she has taken an especial interest in education among charitable and many other causes. An assiduous attender at annual graduations, she finds time to talk personally to the many graduates as they receive their degrees.

Nonetheless, for all this progress, senior staff arriving in the institution in the 1990s still asserted that systems were old-fashioned, for example in record-keeping (carbon-backed 'flimsies' recording comments and marks for individual pieces of work by students); computing (the 'VAX' machine); a centralised management system that divorced power from responsibility for financial matters, still copied up into large leather-bound ledgers by Ken Heyes – only the second 'bursar' in office since the 1920s; and the historic policy of break-even budgets with no cash reserves. The reason for this was that prior to 1992 there was no incentive to generate surpluses due to the direct DES funding model. When Tommy Geddes arrived he found that he was personally provided each Wednesday with bundles of invoices to sign off, representing every single transaction of the institution, a laborious and time-consuming activity. For six months he undertook this task, by which time he had a firm grasp of the detail of the College accounts, and could move on to look more broadly at the financial situation and delegate that task to those who should have responsibility.

Such care with detail had undoubtedly contributed to the survival of the College through recent difficult decades. However, matters now had to accelerate, with a time-specific deadline of the aspiration for University Title in 2005. Senior managers now raised their eyes to more distant horizons, and planned ahead in the post-1992 world. Former members of the College who had gone elsewhere had moved their institutions forward rapidly. Most notable among these was (Dame) Janet Trotter, who had learnt her craft from Martial Rose before moving on via St Martin's, Lancaster, to Gloucestershire, where she cut through the restraints and combined the evangelical

Below: The Kenneth Kettle Building (former 1960s Chapel) in use as a computer centre in 2015.

Anglican teacher training colleges of St Paul and St Mary, together with other partners, to become the University of Gloucestershire in 2001. It was apparent that what was proposed at Winchester was not beyond reach.

When the new MP for Winchester made his maiden speech on 4 June 1997 after a disputed parliamentary election, he made a passing reference to the educational diversity and strength of his constituency, mentioning King Alfred's. A new and ebullient Vice-Principal, Christopher Turner, arrived in Winchester in 1996, honed by Janet Trotter in the dark arts of Human Resource management at Gloucestershire, and with a background in information science. Turner set about implementing his mantra that Winchester should 'punch above its weight'. The College soon responded, and has continued to do so ever since.

On campus by 1997, educational computing had outgrown its home in the Fred Wheeler Building. New accommodation was provided in the 1964 chapel, which was converted to an IT Centre and named the Kenneth Kettle Building, after a dedicated and long-serving governor who at his death in 1995 had served King Alfred's for 42 years. The 1881 chapel was comprehensively refurbished and restored to its original use in 1998. Communal worship on a Sunday had been replaced in 1993 by a service on Tuesday evenings, felt to be more accessible to a student and staff body that had no other formal College business at the weekend. Bishop Scott-Joynt described this return to the former chapel as 're-pitching the tent'. Further pressure for teaching space brought about the conversion in 1998 of The Cottage, which had been used as a staff residence, for academic use.

KENNETH KETTLE ....

Headmasters at Winchester College had supported 'the College on the hill' in many ways since its foundation in 1840, and continued to take an interest, serving as governors and advisers to successive Principals. Kenneth Kettle was not a headmaster, but provided the most sustained link between the colleges at the top and bottom of the hill during the second half of the twentieth century. Kettle's long and faithful service spanned huge changes at King Alfred's. As Secretary to the Governors, he was a signatory of the fateful letter of 22 December 1958, following Principal W. P. Dickinson's death, which announced that the College would 'become a mixed College of approximately 250 men and 150 women', and was still serving in 1994 when he signed the papers for the purchase of West Downs, with Principal J. P. Dickinson.

Following Kettle's death in 1995 Colin Badcock, a colleague at Winchester College, wrote of him that after his work at Winchester College (where he taught

for 47 years, was a housemaster, head of the Cadet Force and producer of plays at various times) and his family, King Alfred's came a strong third:

Sometimes Kenneth would blow in wearing a suit. No daughters or literature this time, for the suit meant he had come from a meeting at King Alfred's College, and this was the third of his greatest enthusiasms. He had been a governor there for years, I think since the 1950s, and as Vice-Chairman recently when the Chairman was the very busy Bishop, much business fell to him to handle. He was devoted to the College, watching with fascination its extraordinary growth, and intrigued by the complex changes now afoot in higher and tertiary education. He would love to have seen the completion of the student village at West Downs. Now King Alfred's College, up there on the hill, has lost a devoted and meticulous friend and governor.

This had been for many years used for staff and as the College Engineer's house.

Following a tendering process, Nursing and Midwifery degree courses were relocated to Southampton and Bournemouth universities in 1997, to intense disappointment at Winchester. This was a grave situation for the College's numbers. Meanwhile the students enrolled were allowed to complete their courses, from which they graduated in 1999. This made the role of those students who accompanied the Florence Nightingale lamp on its annual journey to Westminster Abbey in 1998 especially poignant. The loss of the contract left a very considerable hole in the College's finances, a reduction in income of nearly 25 per cent. Had these setbacks occurred earlier, while the West Downs project was being considered, the College might have drawn back from the investment.

Negotiations with the Winchester School of Art (WSA) had similarly blown hot and cold. At one point negotiations were apparently moving forward when the WSA suddenly announced in 1996 it was being taken over by Southampton University. Meanwhile back-up positions were investigated should King Alfred's College prove vulnerable on the grounds of its small

size. The School of Art had been one; another was La Sainte Union Training College (LSU) in Southampton, but there was too much overlap. LSU proved a vulnerable institution, and caused much anxiety when it was closed after it lost its teacher training licence in 1997, although on the credit side King Alfred's received 105 funded teacher training places from LSU, and a further couple of dozen from the Teacher Training Agency to sustain regional training of teachers. A third way was to talk to the Southampton Institute of Higher Education (now Southampton Solent University). This was a much larger institution, and many at Winchester saw that as a take-over, and a harbinger of inevitable loss of individuality. There were also talks with the Sparsholt College of Agriculture. None of these potential partners offered great benefits.

In these straitened times it was, surprisingly, the government, on the recommendation of Lord Dearing's report on Higher Education in 1997, which came to the financial rescue, through the introduction of tuition fees, initially at £1,000. His recommendation in this area (one of 93) was immediately accepted by the Labour government, and even by the National

Winchester Castle.

Union of Students (whose leaders loudly applauded his briefing on the subject). This provided further and essential funding for the University in the coming years.

Meanwhile building proceeded on the King Alfred's site. The Martial Rose Library received a major extension designed by Feilden Clegg Architects in 1999, which won an RIBA award. This set a new standard for academic buildings on the main campus, incorporating innovative environmental techniques and a three-storey stained-glass sculpture by Sasha Ward depicting a contemporary interpretation of the history of Winchester inspired by illustrations from the King Alfred jewel, now in the Ashmolean Museum, the Castle and the twelfth-century Winchester Bible.

This 1999 extension of the Library, opened on 18 May 2000, necessitated the removal of the remaining structure of the outdoor 'swimming pool', which had long ceased to be used for swimming, and had been filled in during 1993 as a health and safety hazard. It was originally built as a source of water in case of a fire at the south-west end of the campus. If it has a claim to fame it is because it was in this pool that Colin Firth, famous for his swimming scene as Mr Darcy in *Pride and Prejudice*, learnt to swim, along with other staff children.

THE COLLEGE AT THE TURN OF THE MILLENNIUM

When Principal Paul Light arrived in 2000, following resolution of various problems in the 1990s, there had been many positive achievements: a secure financial basis had been set, loans were being repaid, students were abundant, major building programmes had been completed. While the growth in student numbers was certainly due to the attractions of Winchester and the efforts made to present a welcoming, rigorous and interesting curriculum, the drive by successive governments to raise student numbers nationally was also highly significant at this time. The Annual Report of 1998–9 provides a snapshot at the end of the decade and on the eve of the Principal's arrival, asserting that the 10,000th student had 'graduated', and there were 5,000 students in the College in 19 disciplines.

A solid basis was in place not only in terms of student numbers, but also buildings and equipment, with the Library extension in progress and the provision of 700 desktop computers. Significant progress had also been made to ensure the staff was active in research as well as in teaching, with 30 per cent of staff research active and £1 million designated for research spending, according to the report. Now there was a secure platform from which University Title could be sought, although within a week

Above: The actor Colin Firth receiving an honorary degree.

Right: The long-demolished College 'swimming pool' where Firth and other staff children learnt to swim, taken c.1970.

Principals Cranmer, Dickinson and Light at an inaugural lecture in 2001. The appointment of professors was a significant indication of intent on the route to University Title.

proved problematic on the grounds of recruitment to shortage areas, expense, staffing, equipment and resources. The College was well placed, with a Post Graduate Certificate in Education in primary teaching, which recruited well, and had set up a secondary PGCE in Religious Education.

Top of the agenda after 2000 was re-application in 2001 for Taught Degree Awarding Powers (TDAP) for undergraduate degrees and Masters courses. The 1997 application had failed, which was a setback, especially as the College at Chichester was successful in TDAP in 1998. This re-application for TDAP succeeded in April 2004. For several years Quality Assurance Agency (QAA) grades for Winchester departments were good and improving: 1998 Japanese Studies (20/24), 1999 Psychology (21/24), 2001 Business Studies (22/24), and Archaeology and Education Studies both 24/24. Such reports were most encouraging.

In 2003 the QAA indicated that the College's 'standards and quality were fully commensurate with the university sector as a whole'. It was in this year also that the government declared an intention to increase cohort participation in Higher Education to 50 per cent by 2010, providing encouragement that recruitment would in such circumstances become more buoyant, particularly as Winchester was developing a strong track record in recruiting first-generation undergraduates from disadvantaged areas. This was to be accompanied by a 6 per cent rise in funding for the immediate future. TDAP brought a double benefit: first it began to break the link with Southampton University, which was

Light was reported in *The Times Higher Education Supplement* as saying that 'It is not realistic to have a university title by 2006', proclaiming his aim as the gaining of Taught Degree Awarding Powers. By this masterstroke he at once lowered expectations and enabled John Dickinson's plan to mature without distractions. Light, an academic psychologist, had worked previously both at Southampton University and at Bournemouth, and so knew how local university politics worked, and how matters could change rapidly and unexpectedly. However, circumstances were to change, and events were to move more rapidly than might have been foreseen in the year 2000.

As the new millennium opened the focus was increasingly on establishing elements of an independent course for the institution. First, the new mission statement included the necessity of raising the public profile of the College both in Winchester and further afield. Secondly, part of the plan was to join the Confederation of Church Colleges, a body that oversaw the Higher Education of some 44,000 full-time undergraduate students, to which the King Alfred's contribution would be around 6,000 by 2005–6. Thirdly, the Dearing report of 2001 called for the Church to 'move into' secondary teacher training, an oft-attempted path at Winchester, but one that had always

Progress by paper. The Business Studies Department provided over 100 boxes of evidence in support of their Quality Assurance Agency grading. Such a prodigious audit trail has been essential in all aspects of validation and quality assurance since the 1970s.

The Winchester Business School being opened in 2011 by Sir Mervyn King KG GBE FBA, then Governor of the Bank of England, with Professor Neil Marriott, Deputy Vice-Chancellor and the founding Dean of the Winchester Business School, Former Chair of Governors Roger Witcomb, Vice-Chancellor Professor Joy Carter and Dame Mary Fagan, Chancellor.

proving restrictive, not only because there were departments teaching the same subjects in both institutions – for example Education, English and History – but also because many of the areas taught at Winchester (Religious Studies, Drama, etc.) were not part of the curriculum at Southampton, and so caused administrative monitoring as well as assessment problems. Secondly, it released significant sums of money paid to the University of Southampton.

Also in 2001 was the outcome of a further 'Research Assessment Exercise'. Some 40 per cent of the staff submitted work to this national exercise, which in 1996 had produced a handsome £160,000 income. The outcome improved on 1996 and was highly encouraging, King Alfred's being the third most improved institution in the country, with a '4' grade in both History and Theology and Religious Studies (quality that equates to attainable levels of national excellence in virtually all of the research activity submitted, showing some evidence of international excellence), and some 3a citations not far behind in Archaeology and in Cultural Studies, along with a 3b in Education and Performing Arts.

High hopes of funding were dashed, however, as there was such a surge in performance nationally that funding fell back.

Despite the significant improvement, and notwithstanding a letter of complaint from Principal Light, the income received only amounted to £172,000, a disappointment but a benchmark for the future. Nonetheless in 2002 the College achieved a turnover of over £18 million. By 2006 it had an income of £31 million and was taking a profit of £1.8 million. The policies of developing parallel income streams had proved a resounding success, if not without anxieties and setbacks from time to time.

In 2002, for example, the Church asked for refunding of its loans in order to finance 'mission-related' projects. The Bishop and other clergy found much that was going on in the College and in wider society difficult for them, and yet the College for its part was bound by national legislation and policies. Thus to comply in matters relating to equal opportunities, for example, the College was required to offer students joint accommodation 'regardless of marital status'. The Vice-Principal on another occasion was dispatched to discuss the issue of civil partnerships with the Bishop who, although no longer Chairman (as then designated) of the Governors, remained a significant voice among the governing body, and was opposed to such unions.

I started work at the Graduate Centre in February 1999, when it was still King Alfred's College. We had about 60 research students, all at different stages of their research, and my job was to administer the documentation about their degrees. They were all doing MPhil or PhD. At that time there was no fee because the institution was trying to develop research degrees and encourage people to do them.

As we did not have Research Degree Awarding Powers back then, the degrees had to be accredited by the University of Southampton. We had to send off all the forms to the Colleges' Research Degrees Committee at Southampton for approval. Those who graduated had University of Southampton degrees.

How things have changed since then! King Alfred's College became University College Winchester and then the University of Winchester. In 2008 we eventually got Research Degree Awarding Powers, and now all our students graduate with University of Winchester degrees. We have increased our research student numbers to almost three times the number when I first started, and we now have over 160 students. However, most of them are still part time, and I still manage to know them all individually and try to give them a personal service.

I have seen a lot of staff come and go during my time at the University, although a surprising number have been there as long or longer than me. It seems to be a place that people enjoy working. And I am pleased to say that all the research students who were there when I first started have now finished.

Chrissie Ferngrove, 1999–

Chrissie Ferngrove, with a photo of her son, Carl Barât, receiving his honorary degree in the cathedral.

UNIVERSITY TITLE ACHIEVED 2005

After all these struggles and achievements, including myriad policy papers, in 2004 the College gained the accolade of the title University College, and on 30 June 2005 The Privy Council conferred the title 'The University of Winchester'. The only remaining hurdle was to gain Research Degree Awarding Powers (RDAP), which remained vested in Southampton University. This was a tough call, for although Winchester met the criteria for RDAP in terms of numbers of students graduating 'past the post' at Master and Doctor of Philosophy level, and there was a sufficient body of staff with the experience to carry this forward, objections were raised at Southampton and the process dragged on with the QAA over 18 months. Finally, RDAP was ratified by the Privy Council on 13 August 2008, 146 years after the new building on West Hill was opened, and the celebrations among those involved were no less joyous. The transformation from college to university was complete. Thus much was achieved under the leadership of Paul Light, who held successively the

titles of Principal King Alfred's College (2000), Principal of University College Winchester (2004) and Vice-Chancellor of the University of Winchester (2005).

One manifestation of the growing maturity, pressure on space and sheer size was increasing physical remoteness of the Principal's, and, more recently, the Vice-Chancellor's accommodation. This was a feature of institutional developments across the country. Thus Holm Lodge, which had been the Principal's residence since 1928, ceased to be used as such in 2000, before Professor Light was appointed. Since then Vice-Chancellors have lived elsewhere.

Plans were made for selling Holm Lodge, but it did not achieve the price hoped for. In 2005 its stables underwent major

The Holm Lodge allotments, a popular utilisation of a former private space.

The Interior of Holm Lodge.

refurbishment as tutor offices, and today Holm Lodge serves as teaching space and tutor offices for the Department of Law, part of the Faculty of Business, Law and Sport. The gardens provide organic allotments for staff and students. Vice-Principals had lived off-site since the retirement of Bob Breach in the mid 1980s, and the purpose-built house, Beech Glade, was long demolished. Adjustments such as these cleared space on the portfolio of sites for the main business: accommodating and teaching students. In parallel to the building works the realignment of faculty responsibilities occurred in 2001, when the six Schools of the early 1990s (praised in the HEQC report of 1996) became four Faculties: Community and Performing Arts, Cultural Studies, Education and Social Sciences.

Completion of student accommodation at West Downs was followed by work on the main former school building there, henceforward known as the West Downs Centre. This had been built in 1880 with extensions carried out between 1897 and 1910. Now in 2000/1 it underwent a major refurbishment designed by Feilden Clegg Architects to restore the listed Victorian school to its former glory first as a performing arts centre and now as the Winchester Business School, a project of Vice-Chancellor Carter, with further adjustments and changes of use in 2010 and 2011. At West Downs the extensive £6.5 million work on the former school building was funded by the sale of Chilbolton Court on Sarum Road and Chilbolton Avenue, with HEFCE support and cash reserves. It was completed by 2 May 2001, when it was opened as an Arts and Drama Centre by Lord Puttnam of Queensgate, the celebrated film-maker whose works included *Chariots of Fire* (1982), and who was the first Chair of the General Teaching Council. Completion of this major work enabled focus to turn in 2006 to the West Downs Masters' Lodge, built in 1904 and a Grade II (though derelict) Arts and Crafts building designed by John William Simpson, who later designed the Wembley Football Stadium towers. This was refurbished to a high standard and is now the Research and Knowledge Exchange Centre, part of the infrastructure underpinning the continuing expansion of postgraduate and community business support that contributed to success in RDAP in 2008. From the 1990s there was a conscious effort to embed the institution in the local community, both in business and in other aspects of community work. Christopher Turner took a lead in this after 1996 and was rewarded in 2000 with a splendid Millennium Egg at the Winchester Business Excellence Awards for his contribution to Winchester's economy.

The first major scheme of the new millennium following West Downs was to provide a new University Centre on the King Alfred campus. Following an architectural competition won by a Winchester firm, Design Engine, this major construction project,

Richard 'Tigger' Hoare OBE receiving his Honorary Doctorate from the University of Winchester in 2009, shown here with Deputy Vice-Chancellor Professor Neil Marriott. The Bulldog Trust, established by Richard Hoare in 1983, played an active role in the creation and development of the Winchester Business School and the University's Hoare Centre for Responsible Management.

planned and executed since 2002, resulted in an opening event in 2007. The large building, cut deeply into the hillside, occupies the site of the former Dining Room and kitchens (1962), and now includes the Student Union, Food Hall, Main Reception, Bookshop, Convenience Store and Wi-Fi-equipped Learning Café. The University Centre was commissioned to replace the outdated and inadequate Dining Room and Student Union buildings, combined with the creation of a sense of arrival with a more prominent and modern main entrance. The University Centre won an RIBA Design Award and has changed both the social experience for students and the perception of the University in the local community. On the sports front the new Bar End Sports Pavilion was opened, the original 1960s building having been destroyed by extensive vandalism and fire. In 2007 the Winchester Sports Stadium opened – an Olympic-standard athletics track and field facilities and an all-weather pitch – a joint venture with Winchester City Council, with additional support from Sports England, Hampshire County Council and Winchester and District Athletics Club.

The splendid new University Centre acted as a catalyst for the upgrading and redesignating of the post-war buildings nearby on the King Alfred campus and at Medecroft. In 2003 the Sports Hall and Movement Centre was converted and extended to form a Fitness Suite and a 'Black Box' flexible teaching/performance space for performing arts, which would subsequently release the John Stripe Theatre for restoration as the principal venue for large lectures by the removal of facilities for staging plays

Left: Principal Light initiating demolition of the Dining Room to make way for the creation of the University Centre.

Below: Outside the University Centre Food Hall.

The all-weather track and other sports facilities now at Bar End.

of Canterbury Rowan Williams. Enterprise Lectures also take place here, for example by Trevor Bayliss, the inventor of the clockwork radio, who has given his name to a 'Breakout', brain-storming and computer room in the Business School. The University of Winchester Writers' Festival has for over 30 years attracted a full house and speakers including Maureen Lipman, Sir Terry Pratchett, Sathnam Sanghera and Sebastian Faulks.

A NEW LEADERSHIP TEAM

and the refurbishment of seating. This work was carried out in 2006, when in addition the insertion of a steel frame through the existing structure added a first-floor extension, which provided a large new lecture room and a spacious gallery. Rebranded as 'The Stripe', this was the first time such a designated lecture theatre had existed on the campus, and it provided a suitable venue for the development of a series of public lectures to bring the institution closer to the wider community. This space accommodates a range of events and has hosted Foundation Lectures by luminaries such as Baroness the Rt Hon. Professor Shirley Williams and the leading theologian Dr Peter Vardy of Heythrop College, as well as, more recently, former Archbishop

In the autumn of 2005 Professor Joy Carter, a geo-chemist and coincidentally daughter of an alumnus (1946–8), was appointed Vice-Chancellor. She arrived in post in April 2006 with experience from the universities of Reading, Derby and Glamorgan: a double first, not only the first woman to lead the institution, but also the first *ab initio* appointment to that post. Her portfolio of previous achievement included strengths in key areas for her new post at Winchester in its new, fully fledged form. In the financial sphere she had raised several million pounds of research and contracts monies, had published several books and over 100 peer-reviewed articles, and had supervised two dozen doctoral candidates to completion of their studies. Her passion for the Christian foundation, for high-quality, values-driven Higher Education research and knowledge exchange

It is not what we say or think that defines us, but what we do"

Jane Austen
1775-1817

The Terrace Bar, University Centre.

Left: Vice-Chancellor Professor Joy Carter with Chancellor-elect of the University Alan Titchmarsh and Barbara Large, founder and former Director of the Winchester Writers' Conference.

Below: The welcoming Angel, part of a campus-wide series of art installations by Artist in Residence Amy Goodman.

underpinned a vision to define Winchester as a university whose staff, students and supporters are devoted to the common good locally, nationally and globally.

The old motto '*Qualis vita finis ita*' *(see p50)* may be translated in various ways, including 'As you live, so shall you die' – this may be read as a fire and brimstone warning to the male students about the dangers of going to hell. The new motto chosen after a process of consultation by Vice-Chancellor Carter to go with the grant of a coat of arms from the London College of Arms (Heralds) is '*Wisdom ond lar*', *lar* being the Old English word for 'learning', providing a contemporary link to the language of King Alfred, that patron of learning from whom the College took its name in 1928 and who is an inspiration for the proposed Winchester English Project Centre. Encouraged by the University, this centre proposes a celebration of the English language as a worldwide mode of communication.

There is no doubt that there is a vibrant agenda under the current leaders. The first line of the website flags 'delight in diversity', a reference to the inclusive nature of the University's mission: as a university should surely be, it is a place focused on learning and knowledge, but also open to those of diverse aspirations, orientations, origins and religions. When the Quality Council visited in 1996, they found no mention of religion in the institution's mission: in 2015 things are different. As First Deputy Vice-Chancellor Elizabeth Stuart puts it, the University today is 'self-assuredly values-driven'. It is unique in the United Kingdom in having 'Spirituality' as one of its values. The University highlights its Anglican foundation while welcoming those of all faiths and none. Together we aim to explore the mystery of life

and grow in wisdom and love. As a visible indication of this spirit a sculpture of an angel with arms open in welcome adorns the University entrance – an image appealing to those of all faiths and none. The University belongs to – and the Vice-Chancellor chaired until 2013 – the 16-strong University Cathedrals Group, which includes universities in Canterbury, York, Liverpool and elsewhere. The notion of 'Study in a Christian Context' is now a secure element in the University's recruitment agenda, and this, together with membership of the University Cathedrals Group, is highlighted in addresses to prospective parents by the Vice-Chancellor and First Deputy Vice-Chancellor Stuart.

On the retirement of Professor Christopher Turner in 2008, Professor Elizabeth Stuart, Professor of Christian Theology since 1997, stepped up to be Pro-Vice-Chancellor. Professor Stuart is an internationally renowned scholar in theology, with degrees

Professor Elizabeth Stuart, portrait by Ben Mousley.   **Below:** Chancellor Emeritus, Dame Mary Fagan in The Gambia.

from Oxford, and as Director of Research and Knowledge Exchange had led the triumphant acquisition, underwritten by the Privy Council in August of the same year, of crucial Research Degree Awarding Powers.

In 2006 the first Chancellor, Dame Mary Fagan, Lord-Lieutenant of Hampshire, was installed in a ceremony at Winchester Cathedral. As Chancellor she has been no distant figurehead, but has taken an active role in shaping the University's development, as instanced by her stalwart input to the acquisition of a coat of arms, in which cause she took a lead in the negotiations, the symbolism of the arms including the depiction of a book, unusual in modern heraldry. Thus with female Chancellor, Vice-Chancellor and Deputy Vice-Chancellor and president of the Student Union, the University in recent years has come to be run by women, a true reflection of the gender balance of the institution in recent decades and probably a first for an English university. In 2008, when the former Student Union underwent conversion to offices for the Faculty of Arts, the building was renamed the St Edburga Building, a step in the direction of redressing the balance on a campus occupied by buildings named after both sainted and more recent males. A window celebrating female saints is the most recent addition to the Chapel's stained glass, joining a group of male saints and martyrs from earlier times already represented in commemorative windows.

w and St Edburga in the Chapel.

EDBURGA AND ALPHEGE ....

Edburga (d. 960) was a daughter of Edward the Elder, son of King Alfred. She became a nun apparently at an early age (and possibly later abbess) of the Nunnaminster, the community of religious women east of the cathedral in Winchester. Nunnaminster, later St Mary's Abbey, was with Old Minster and New Minster one of three great religious foundations of Anglo-Saxon Winchester. After her death signs appeared that denoted her sanctity, and substantial shrines were successively created in her honour that attracted many pilgrims. A transect through the Nunnaminster/St Mary's church was excavated in the 1980s by archaeologists from the city and from King Alfred's, led on the College side by Annie Robinson. In the display of the site, recently refurbished and with new interpretation boards, the remains of the early structures associated with the cult and shrine of St Edburga's shrine may be seen marked out on the ground. Her feast day is 15 June.

St Alphege (or Ælfheah d. 1012) was Bishop of Winchester from 984 to 1006, when he was translated Archbishop of Canterbury. At Winchester he succeeded the energetic reformer Æthelwold, raising his tomb from the crypt to the choir of Old Minster. Alphege literally built on his predecessor's achievements: Æthelwold's tower over the high altar was raised to five stages surmounted by a gilded weathercock. The minster organ was 'stupendously' enlarged, making such a noise on festive occasions that 'men stop their ears with their hands ... and the melody of the pipes is heard all over the city.' Alphege not only negotiated peace with the pagan Olaf Tryggvason during a resurgence in Viking attacks, but also officiated at his Christian confirmation. He took Swithun's head with him to Canterbury and set it on the altar. Alphege was murdered by Vikings during a drunken feast, when the archbishop was 'pelted with bones and oxheads and one of them struck him on the head with the back of an axe, so that he sank down with the blow, and his holy blood fell on the ground', an end prefiguring that of Archbishop Becket in 1170, who commended himself to Alphege in his last moments. His feast day is 29 September.

To make way for another major development adjacent to the University Centre, the pre-war Great Hall (Arts Centre) and Gymnasium (Exam Hall) were demolished in 2010 to accommodate the St Alphege lecture theatre block, which came into use in September 2012. In 2010 part of the east wing of Alwyn Hall was converted from student residential to academic tutors' offices, and St Swithun's Lodge was also converted to offices currently occupied by the Estate Department and Campus and Conference Services. These changes further developed the core teaching and administration provision of the University on the King Alfred site, towards the periphery of which the Sports Hall and Movement Centre underwent small extensions in 2010. A large suite of dance and drama studios was also opened as the Performing Arts Building, built on the last remaining redundant tennis court south of Alwyn Hall.

Despite the modest budget, these studios won a National Civic Trust Award for the University and their local architects Design Engine. In 2011 the Movement Centre was renamed; the northern part of the building comprising the Dance Studio, 'Black Box' and Fitness Suite is now called the Bowers Building, after Doug Bowers, who served in the P.E. Department from the 1950s

Performing Arts students.

Left: Chute House, Basingstoke.

Bottom: Queens Road Student Village.

Road Student Village, west of Alwyn Hall, seven block halls of residence were built, creating 400 study bedrooms, many with spectacular southerly views down the valley and to the Isle of Wight on a fine day.

Yet closer still, immediately across the Burma Road from the Herbert Jarman Building, another recent project is a third student village. This was a joint venture with contractors Geoffrey Osborne to create some 500 study bedrooms, including seven with dedicated disabled facilities in five 'Pavilions'. The development also includes a state-of-the-art gymnasium and a laundry. The creation of these new residential blocks has involved working with a variety of funding sources. Teaching buildings on site, such as St Alphege, are funded by the University, which owns them.

The Dean and Chapter's site of 1862 thus continues to be expanded on to adjacent land. In strengthening historic Anglican links and traditions in recent years a Dean of Chapel, Peter Waddell, has been appointed, a theologian who participates in teaching duties. His office is located adjacent to the Chapel at the west end of the Main Building, in an area once the domain of Deputy Principals such as the Rev. Lockton. A weekly formal and solemn common worship Eucharist is held at 12.12 in the middle of each Wednesday during each semester, and attracts a wide congregational group of staff and students. The Dean, now supported by a Chaplain (Rev. Chris Day), in addition works in association with the diocese of Winchester in outreach projects with a social justice mission.

Volunteering both for staff and especially for students has risen up the agenda in recent years, to considerable acclaim from both participants and employers. Students may now gain

for some forty years, and the southern part, comprising the Sports Hall and the 1990s extension, is now called the Centre for Sport.

Nearby Medecroft, home to the Faculty of Humanities and Social Sciences, underwent extensive refurbishment and upgrading in 2011/12, with further facilities for Archaeology built on the site of the southern stores and remaining kilns not previously developed. The lease on the elegant Chute House, Basingstoke, built in 1773 and run as an outpost of the University from 2003, expired in July 2011, after providing accommodation for teaching as the second 'Basingstoke Outpost'. Links with Basingstoke are still flourishing: among current interfaces the University's History Department is piloting a new Victoria County History of Hampshire (to replace that completed in 1912), starting with the Basingstoke District. Music outreach led by Professor Boyce-Tillman occurs at the Anvil Centre, among many other projects.

As land became available on the adjacent hospital site the University took the opportunity alongside partners to build more high-quality, modern student accommodation. Thus in 2010, on land purchased from the Winchester Hospital Trust, Queens

Above: The Reverend Professor June Boyce-Tillman, the first Director of Foundation Music at the University of Winchester – an extra-curricular music department set up to enrich the student experience.

The St Alphege building.

establishment of a Student Academic Council, where students set the agenda and provide advice to management, for example on student-friendly ways of advertising scholarships. This system was pioneered at Roehampton University: at Winchester the council, which parallels the University's Senate, has a majority of student members.

In 2013 the new St Alphege teaching block was awarded 'excellent' and another King Alfred's Campus building 'very good' by the Building Research Establishment Environmental Assessment Method (BREEAM), part of a strong environmental agenda of sustainable development. Other achievements and awards have been legion in this area in recent years, with both South Coast and Winchester Eco Business of the year awards successes year on year, 1st class award in People and Planet Awards 2013, Gold Standard in Green Impact Student Unions Award three years running, and zero-waste to landfill sites since 1 April 2013. The presence of the Winchester Action Against Climate Change (WinACC) at the University further underlines the institution's determination to lead by example both locally and in the wider world in promoting CO_2 reduction. WinACC works to cut the carbon footprint of Winchester district, creating lower energy bills, healthier lifestyles and stronger communities. It comprises local residents, businesses and policy-makers, working together to tread more lightly on the planet. The Vice-Chancellor is its Patron.

academic credits for a volunteering module, which has proved very popular. It is to the great credit of all parties that many students continue volunteering after their official time is up. Examples include a Psychology student working with severely disabled motorcycle accident victims. Students often find this volunteering a 'life-changing' experience, and organisers of the scheme have found the positive feedback both touching and impressive. Staff throughout the institution also volunteer, both as individuals and in teams, and may take unlimited unpaid leave to volunteer according to demands of their contracts.

In addition to the welfare of staff, students have been given a louder voice beyond the Student Union with the

I volunteered for the Engage Project as an Honorary Assistant Psychologist. The project aims to decrease levels of anxiety and depression in over-65s in the hospital [Salisbury NHS Hospital] through various cognitive activities. My role involves going round the hospital chatting to patients, completing crosswords or taking part in other activities with them. Patients are always very pleased to speak to someone, as they often are quite bored and feel lonely.

During my volunteering I have improved my communication skills, talking essentially to strangers and those who could not communicate very well due to a stroke or neurological damage. Volunteering greatly increased my knowledge about injuries that patients were suffering with and generally how an NHS hospital works. The Clinical

Psychology team offered frequent training days on specific issues such as cancer, communication difficulties and anxiety. Additionally, I learnt more about how supervisions work, as the department held monthly supervisions with a Clinical Psychologist.

I would recommend this volunteering opportunity to anyone interested in a career in Clinical Psychology or someone who just wants his or her Psychology degree to be a more interactive experience.

The volunteering module has been one of the highlights of my degree so far!

Hannah Ear, Psychology student volunteer at Salisbury NHS Hospital, Engage Project, graduated 2014

"*I have been a volunteer with Hampshire Constabulary for 6 years and currently hold the rank of Special Inspector. I am responsible for the line management and supervision of three Special Sergeants and over 20 Special Constables across three police stations in the East Hampshire area. The role carries a minimum commitment of 16 hours a month, although I often far surpass this.*

Originally I joined the Special Constabulary as I was planning on joining the police as a full time officer. Although my desire to join the police full-time passed when I moved into my current career in Estates, my enjoyment and passion for policing stayed and so has my commitment to Hampshire Constabulary.

As a Special Constable you hold all the same legal powers as a regular officer, attend the same jobs and wear the same uniform, so the majority of the public do not realise any difference. The role is so varied with you being called to deal with a huge variety of incidents, occasionally volatile in nature, sometimes all just in one shift. Highlights in the role for me are working on the Olympic Torch Relay as well as achieving my promotion to Sergeant and now Inspector.

The University have been supportive to my role, with me taking advantage of the volunteering scheme in taking paid time off and matched leave to undertake training and assist with planned operations. During the riots the University also released me from work, and other Special Constables who work at the University (there are currently three of us), as we we received emergency calls for assistance to go in on duty.

Undertaking my role has not only increased my knowledge of criminal law but has also developed me personally. The role has increased my confidence, taught me to how remain calm with a clear head in difficult situations and given me opportunities to develop my leadership skills.

I find volunteering for Hampshire Constabulary a truly rewarding experience and would most certainly recommend volunteering, whether with the Special Constabulary or any other good cause, to anyone!"

Dave Mason, Staff volunteer from the Estates Department

Left: Dave Mason, staff, Volunteering as a Special Constable, 2015.

Below: The 'sheep' grazing on a wild flower meadow on the roof of The Stripe Theatre.

On a par with such environmental concerns, welfare of staff and students, animal welfare is another high priority in the green agenda, which is at the forefront of the University mission. The green and animal welfare agenda has resulted in a wide range of awards for successes in this area. All meat supplied in the University is free range, the Vice-Chancellor taking a personal interest in this aspect of provisioning. This novel focus on animals and nature more widely in all forms is visible around the campus. The introduction of a 'Puppy Room' where students can find relief from exam stress by stroking a dog is a first in an English university, and was welcomed by students and staff, and is a partnership with the charity Pets as Therapy. The reintroduction of a roof garden on the King Alfred site at The Stripe includes a sculpture of sheep grazing there.

Across the University's campus areas have been designated for various aspects of horticultural and nature conservation projects: on the King Alfred's site itself, long the beneficiary of careful and exotic plantings since the Second World War, pond conservation areas have been enhanced, and commemorative trees have been planted, while at Holm Lodge allotments have been established, echoing the former horticulture arrangements that existed on the site of St Elizabeth's Hall until the 1960s. At the West Downs Campus there is a butterfly habitat, and there is also – on the site of the former compost area – a Cosmic Walk, which contains sculpture and delights for children to share. There is also a long tradition of commemorative tree planting dating back to Jarman's days.

Apart from the green agenda the University's social justice and responsibility mission is visible for example in the education work with Ugandan girls (Rev. Dr Peter Waddell) and the increasing international profile of the Centre for Religions for Reconciliation and Peace (founded at Winchester in 2008), which has been working to relieve inter-communal tensions in Nepal among other projects.

'Dancers' by Lucy Unwin
at the University Centre.

WINCHESTER AT 175: AN ASSESSMENT

As the institution approaches 175 years since the foundation
in 1840, the University has come a very long way. Today it
is a leader in 'green' university catering and has a strategic
partnership with Compassion in World Farming. It is dedicated
to local produce and free-range meat and eggs and now also to
Fair Trade and environmental sustainability. The buildings of the
1950s to 1980s reflect the uncertainties of those times. In 1972
there were 160 colleges in the UK with some 111,000 students
in teacher training: in 1981 there were fewer than 70 ex-teacher
training and specialist colleges sharing 30,000 students, with
further reorganisation and closures in prospect. That Winchester
survived was due to much hard work and determination.

A snapshot of academic activity, achievements and reactions
to the Winchester offerings in 2014 reveals much, including
over 175 PhD, professional doctorate and MPhil completions.
In the 2008 Research Assessment Exercise 75 per cent of the
University's research submitted was considered internationally
recognised, with some research in History, Education, and Dance,
Drama and Performing Arts being of 'quality that is world-leading
in terms of originality, significance and rigour', achieving the
top grade (4*). In the 2014 Research Excellence Framework
the University entered eight units of assessment: Archaeology,
Communication, Cultural and Media Studies, Education, History,
Music, Drama, Dance and Performing Arts, Psychology, Sociology
and Theology and Religious Studies. The institution had 8% of
its research designated as world-leading and 82% of the research
judged to be of international standing, up from 75% in 2008. In
this, the first research excellence exercise to judge the impact of
research, Theology and Religious Studies, was judged to have
world-leading impact, scoring higher than departments in Oxford
and St Andrews on impact. Education, both in terms of Initial
Teacher Training and research, remains significant, achieving
recognition as 'outstanding' in England in the latest inspection
by the Office for Standards in Education, Children's Services and
Skills (Ofsted). In the 2015 National Student Survey the University
was ranked fourth in the country for student satisfaction, its
highest ever result with American Studies, Archaeology, Business
Management, Choreography and Dance, Digital Media Design,
Digital Media Development, Education Studies (Early Childhood),
Event Management, Health, Community and Social Care, History

and the Medieval World, History and the Modern World, Media
Production, Media Studies and Politics and Global Studies all
achieving 100 per cent overall satisfaction.

Winchester is ranked among the top 15 universities in
England in the following programmes: American Studies;
Childhood, Youth and Community Studies; Creative Writing;
Dance; Education Studies; Event Management; Initial Teacher
Education and Journalism. It is ranked among the top 30
universities in England, in terms of overall satisfaction expressed
by degree students from the University, in the following:
Accounting and Finance, Business Management, English,
Politics, Social Work, Sports, and Theology and Religious
Studies. Beyond the lecture room, overall satisfaction with the
Student Union is ranked first in the South East and in the top
ten among universities in England. *The Times* and *The Sunday
Times University Guide* 2014 acknowledged the University of
Winchester as rising 18 places from last year's ranking, the
second-biggest leap up the league table. Winchester is also
ranked equal seventh for the award of 'best modern university'.

In addition to the core areas reviewed above, new areas
are being added to the curriculum regularly, recent additions
including Ancient, Classical and Medieval Studies; Classical
Studies; Criminology; Digital Media; Fashion; Media and
Marketing; History, Civilisations and Beliefs; English Language;
Forensic Studies; Modern Liberal Arts; Philosophy, Religion
and Ethics; Street Arts; and Vocal and Choral Studies. Masters
programmes have recently been expanded from the Arts,
Business, Education and Social Sciences and Reconciliation and
Peace Building.

The University is also making a mark internationally. It
has embraced the Excellence Model of the Brussels-based
European Foundation for Quality Management (EFQM 2013).
In pursuing this challenging route the University of Winchester

Former Archbishop Rowan Williams, Master of Magdalene College, Cambridge, with Winchester Liberal Arts students, 2014.

has been awarded the five-star Recognition for Excellence accolade: the only university in the UK to be awarded five-star accreditation rating for the whole institution for overall organisational excellence by the British Quality Foundation, under its 'Recognised for Excellence' scheme, which uses the EFQM Excellence Model. Another proud achievement recently has been the 2011 International Faith and Spirit at Work Award for showing a strong commitment to nurturing the faith and spirituality of its students and staff. The award is given each year to a hand-picked group of companies throughout the world, chosen by a Selection Committee, who decide which organisations should be honoured for best practice.

Such an award strengthens the view that the original mission flourishes in a very changed world. The Christian foundation is exemplified by Foundation Music, which brings together staff and students in a common enterprise. On Holocaust Memorial Day, 27 January each year, a tradition is emerging in which the

Alasdair Spark and American Studies students exploring the Mojave Desert.

Right: University Centre, spring 2015.

Below: Rabbi and Imam singing in the cathedral on Holocaust Day.

University brings together representatives of various faiths in the city's cathedral, where graduations have been held since 1979. The event is named 'Space for Peace' and is the brainchild of Professor June Boyce-Tillman.

In 1978 a series of Winton Lectures was inaugurated by Principal Rose. These early lectures were miscellaneous in nature, on 'Victorian Things' (1978), on Education (1979), then in 1981 Christopher Fry, the 'Christian humanist' playwright and screenwriter of *Ben-Hur* (1959), gave a lecture focusing on his attempts to find 'language to express … wordless comprehension'. When the lectures were revived in the 1990s they were more overtly religious in character, all being given by senior clergy or Professors of Theology, and thereby emphasising the University's foundation. As for the January Holocaust Day commemorations in 2010, Christianity, Judaism and Islam were represented. Other projects reach out far beyond Winchester, such as the English Language Project, which aims to create a museum of world English in Winchester, the last resting place of King Alfred. The University is now firmly embedded locally, nationally and internationally: there are representatives of some 60 nationalities studying in Winchester University. In 175 years of the institution there have been significant – some would say unimaginable – changes at Winchester, but one thing remains the same: the commitment to faith-based world-leading values-driven Higher Education.

Epilogue: Valuing the Institution

The pleasure of studying and working at the University derives at least in part from its spectacular position and its views. This account of the history of the institution recognises the Christian foundation, values-driven Higher Education and the continuity of location and its buildings. University teaching and learning structures take full advantage of position and proximity to the heart of the campus. Very much has changed over the years in terms of curriculum, focus, mission and size. The campus, however, provides a continuing link for all alumni, staff, students and supporters.

In his 2006 article '"Things change but names remain the same": Higher Education Historiography 1975–2000', Harold Silver, whose College of Education at Bulmershe has been obliterated, reflected on the survival of names and changes in function. The development of the single campus in Winchester at King Alfred's and West Downs, and acquisitions of land between the two, have enabled the University to expand its offerings. The disposal of the old hostels in the city, now private houses, has meant that residence in these buildings is now preserved in memories and occasional written accounts. There

THOMAS HARDY AND THE TRAINING COLLEGES ....

In its author's own words 'a story of the deadly war waged between flesh and spirit', *Jude the Obscure* (1895) is set perhaps in the 1860s, 20 years or so after the establishment of the Diocesan Training Colleges for Salisbury and Winchester, when Salisbury

(Melchester) Cathedral was being repaired and Jude was working on the site. Hardy draws first on the Salisbury Training School, where the iconoclastic and wilful Susanna Bridehead (who regarded the railway station more highly than the cathedral as the 'centre of the town's life') is 'immured'. Hardy's sisters Mary and Katherine were students there. The Salisbury Training School, 'an ancient edifice, once a palace' (today the Salisbury Museum), faced the west end of the cathedral, and we are provided with information on the restricted diet, the 'cubicles' in which the girls slept and the long gas-lit days of study, and a brief introduction to the student body:

> *The seventy young women, of ages varying in the main from nineteen to twenty one, though some were older, who at this date filled the species of nunnery known as the Training School at Melchester formed a very mixed community, which included the daughters of mechanics, curates, surgeons, shop-keepers, farmers, dairymen, soldiers, sailors and villagers.*

This could have been a description of the background of its twin institution for men in Wintoncaster (Winchester). Phillotson, the

The entrance to St Michael's College, Salisbury, with students, c. 1890.

Left: Reception in the University Centre, with Alice Kettle's stitched textile wall hanging of 2008 depicting the history and values of the institution.

Below: Title page of *Jude the Obscure* (1895).

are myriad memories among thousands of alumni: in 1852, after 12 years, 115 students had gone out into the world; in 1999, nearly 150 years later, the 10,000th student is recorded as having successfully completed at Winchester.

From its earliest days Winchester engendered lasting affection among its members, not only for the institution but also for fellow students and staff. Such a friendship is illustrated from an early date in the fictional relationship of the former schoolmates Richard Phillotson and George Gillingham, who had both subsequently attended the thinly disguised 'Wintoncaster Training College' in Thomas Hardy's *Jude the Obscure* (1895).

This fictional long-standing friendship and mutual support was exemplified in reality initially by the foundation of the Re-union Club, which first met – and whose founder-members were photographed – in August 1874 at the Old Market Inn in The Square near the cathedral *(see p38)*. Here they indulged in time-honoured student activities: drinking, feasting, reminiscing, singing together and proposing toasts to the Principal and their 'Masters', among others. Students wrote both music and lyrics, such as 'A Song for Winton' by Edward Gale (1896–8), music by Reginald Mussell (1895–7). Former Principal Martial Rose recalls his astonishment at the 1966 Winton Reunion Lunch to find very aged former students from '1888 and 1895' still coming to the reunion: 'One of the old boys from way back in the nineteenth century was carried in on a stretcher by two other Wintonians. By his side walked a nurse in full uniform with flowing headdress, and behind her came a wheelchair, into which the ancient one was placed at the start of the Grace.'

greying schoolmaster, in agonies over his relationship with his young wife, turns to his old College friend in his despair, for they had proceeded together from school 'many years before this time' to the Wintoncaster Training College. The chronology suggests that the middle-aged Phillotson and Gillingham would have been at Wintoncaster in the 1840s, and therefore have been among its earliest students.

> *[Phillotson] discovered his friend putting away some books from which he had been giving evening classes. The light of the paraffin lamp fell on Phillotson's face – pale and wretched by contrast with his friend's, who had a cool, practical, look. They had been schoolmates in boyhood, and fellow-students at Wintoncaster Training College, many years before this time... Though well-trained and even proficient masters, they occasionally used a dialect-word of their boyhood to each other in private...*

The tenor of the book, with its attacks not only on Oxford men but also on the Church itself, and the unfortunate relationships of the protagonists, caused the Bishop of Wakefield, a fierce opponent of 'indecent and irreligious literature', such shock and horror at what he read, that he threw his copy in the fire! For his part, Hardy was so despondent at its reception that he never wrote another novel in the remaining 33 years of his life.

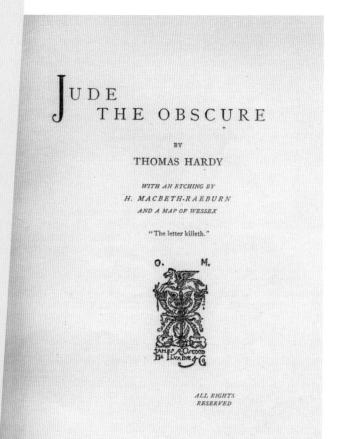

Early edition of *The Christian Mind*, by Harry Blamires.

Below: Students relaxing in the Kettle Building refreshment area, 2015.

In 1811, at the foundation of the National Society for Promoting the Education of the Poor in the Principles of the Established Church in England and Wales, it was stated that 'the National Religion should be made the foundation of National Education', which was in time to lead to the foundation of teacher training institutions as well as schools. The strong ecclesiastical, diocesan influence at the beginning of the planning and founding of the College has remained a strong thread. For over a century Principals were clergymen; the Governing Body, when it emerged before the Second World War, was similarly composed of clergy, and chaired by successive bishops of Winchester, until the mid-1990s. Compulsory chapel continued until 1934. The appointment of a layman as Principal after the Second World War was no doubt part of a trend towards secularisation in educational leadership.

Winchester College, always a close friend in the first 150 years of the life of the 'college on the hill', chose a similar lay leadership route at the same time. Among Principal William Dickinson's papers are records he made of declining numbers attending chapel services, a worrying issue for him, for which he sought answers. Elsewhere in the College in his time the tradition of Christian philosophy and literary studies, so prominent in the early days when Trench was lecturing and Samuel Wilberforce was preaching, re-emerged under Harry Blamires. Blamires toured America as a lecturer and published works on Christianity and vocation while at Winchester and for many years after retirement, as well as novels and literary criticism on the works of James Joyce and T. S. Eliot.

Separation of Principal and Chaplain in the 1950s was not, because of personalities, initially a success. Chaplains (and Principals until 1958) continued to teach Divinity, with some success. The Rev. H. Paul Kingdon taught the students with the mantra 'Watch the board while I go through it.' From 1970 chaplains, licensed by the bishop, were freed from teaching responsibilities. However, chapel congregations did not recover,

although less formal groups, such as the Student Christian Movement, held well-attended meetings elsewhere on the campus. There are currently about 70 members of the Christian Union who meet in the Chapel at 7pm on a Monday night, led largely by students studying primary education, and so tracing a direct line back to the foundation and its 'missionary in the classroom' ethos. However, in the mid-1990s there was not much that was visibly Anglican about the institution. Some senior staff were not asked at interview whether they were communicant members of the Church of England, while other staff had no recollection of such a question in appointments since William Dickinson's days. The demise of La Sainte Union College in 1997 led to the transfer of Theology staff and the establishment of a professorial chair of Christian Theology at Winchester. Today a recent appointment to the post of Dean of Chapel, held by the Rev. Dr Peter Waddell, former chaplain of Sidney Sussex College, Cambridge, is a move which restores the tradition of the 1960s and earlier chaplains' dual pastoral and teaching roles in the College, with the Chapel as a musical and artistic as well as ecclesiastical setting. He is now supported by a chaplain.

Below: St Luke the Evangelist window in the west wall of the chapel. He holds a book. The University was successful in persuading the College of Arms to allow a book in its coat of arms.

In 2011 the National Society for Promoting Religious Education celebrated its 200th anniversary. This was preceded in 2001 by a report by Lord Dearing on Anglican education. His report noted the continuing significance of Church schools, mainly primary, to a lesser extent secondary, but with no presence in Further Education. He devoted a chapter to the Church Colleges – by then moving towards University Title – considering them a limited resource in Higher Education beyond the 'Church Colleges Certificate'. One element of the University's current mission addresses this lacuna by stressing the Anglican Foundation. In common with the Dearing and subsequent reports, the University of Winchester emphasises inclusiveness and plurality. Such continuity as there has been since 1840 at Winchester has certainly been in teacher education, although increasingly the educationists combine basic 'training' with more intellectual and theoretical approaches to their subject.

Beyond the Christian ethos and the Chapel, with its fluctuating attendance, efforts were made over the years to create a feeling of belonging, collegiality and togetherness in a variety of ways. The original models for Winchester were Oxbridge colleges, with their small, personalised teaching styles, boarding, communal dining and worship in designated chapels. Principal Martin's introduction of team sports and his support of the military volunteers were examples of this muscular Christianity in the late nineteenth century. The Re-union Winton Club began to publish accounts of its activities, student achievements, obituaries of those who died and other materials,

THE COLLEGE AND THE CHURCH

Relationships with the Church have not always been easy. The debates over the training provided to teachers in the Church colleges came under vigorous attack in the early 1930s. Principal White regretted this, and in 1937 recorded sadly that there had been no Religious Knowledge inspection of the College for over 20 years, although he noted that the majority of primary teachers were then trained in Church colleges. Most Church college teachers went out into state schools, some no doubt down to the present fulfilling the Victorian founders' wish that they should be missionaries in the classroom.

Since, and in part no doubt because of, the two world wars, faith has declined. After diversification and social change since the 1960s and 1970s the nature of the College changed yet further. By the mid-1990s the retiring Bishop, having sat through discussions about the placing of contraceptive machines in the Student Union (an issue of discussion for over 30 years by then) among many other issues, recorded that it was not apparent to him that the College was doing anything Anglican at all. His successor faced thorny issues on equal opportunities, on civil partnerships and other issues of the day with which College and then University had to comply while holding to its Anglican foundation.

For its part the institution felt abandoned by the Church. In a report to the governors in 2002, it was noted that 'The College feels disowned by the Church … they are not supportive towards us'. That was the year the Church asked for the return of its loans in order to put them into 'mission projects'. The College authorities felt then that the ecclesiastical authorities did not understand how things had changed, with a majority of students on diverse courses other than teacher training, but that the Church representatives still believed that King Alfred's was solely a Church college, involved purely in initial teacher training for primary school teachers. This had not been the case for over 25 years. Today (2015) the University celebrates its Christian Foundation. It is an inclusive and liberal institution welcoming those of all faiths and none. Together, as the values statement says, the university community aims to explore the mystery of life through wisdom and love.

again similar in style to magazines such as Winchester College's *The Trusty Servant*. The earliest survivors of these publications were edited by George Sampson (1892–4), who went on to edit the *Concise Cambridge History of English Literature* (1941, in print 2009). *The Wintonian* magazine further kept former students in touch. Since the 1970s alumnus status appeared of less importance to College and students alike. In the 1990s, Principal John Dickinson established an alumni association parallel to the Winton Club, so diverse did the two groups appear to him. Happily these organisations are now reunited.

The foundation of the London Masonic Lodge for Wintonians from 1904 provided another avenue for students and staff to keep in touch, and has proved durable. This grew in part out of the camaraderie of the Volunteer corps, which had developed a College Company by 1875, as is demonstrated by early members' backgrounds and the choice of the senior mason, Sir Edward Letchworth, who was deeply involved with the Volunteer movement, at the 'consecration' in July 1904.

War service throughout the twentieth century, which claimed the life of Lionel Martin, the Principal's son, in 1905, and continued to claim lives in both the First and Second World Wars and in Korea, bound students together in a sense of shared experience and a desire to commemorate fallen comrades. One legacy of wartime experience, preserved in today's nomenclature, is the name 'Burma Road' for the right of way that passes north of the College, bordering the hospital. This became known as the 'Burma Road', according to William Dickinson's Secretary, who commented recently, 'because some of those that came back in '46 and beyond had been Japanese prisoners of war, and had been on the famous railway and that was a long straight road at the time and so it was called the Burma Road, and I noticed the name is still there'.

Teacher education and training have always had a place within the institution and its curriculum. In mono-technic days from 1840 to 1976, supported by subject studies, this was the primary function of all who entered the institution as staff or students. The approach has changed from the 'training' of the old monitorial and pupil teacher eras to more intellectual and theoretical teacher education. Notwithstanding the ecclesiastical and diocesan impetus which started the College, and which has sustained it through more than a century and a half, successive government policies have long determined the path that was taken. The Timeline in this book *(see p10)* lists some key

developments. It is a truism that we are ruled by law, but there is no doubt that ever since the Revised Code of 1862 affected funding for teacher training, almost every major change in the institution has been prompted by, or has resulted from, national legislation and political ideology.

Government policy is one thing, demography another. The rising birth rate, especially in the 1950s, had inevitable consequences for teacher education, as more primary teachers were suddenly required and later, when the rate fell back, too many teachers were being trained for primary work, and sharp cuts ensued. These fluctuations convinced successive Principals and governors that new income streams were necessary, especially as income for many colleges simply ceased when letters arrived from the Ministry ending teacher training recruitment. Attending euphemistically named 'commemoration' services at Bristol and Salisbury on successive days in June 1978 no doubt focused Principal Rose's mind on accelerating the process of 'diversification' of the curriculum, which had begun in 1976 and developed from the old support departments for training.

At Winchester government demands, which had to be implemented by the College management if the institution was to survive, were tough, involving the changing of traditions – for example in admitting women – and the re-evaluation of skills, away from mono-technic teacher training towards a broader Higher Education curriculum catering for students who were not aiming to become teachers. A way out was found for many staff through the government 'Crombie' redundancy scheme from 1975. Some of those who remained felt abandoned and isolated. In November 1978 the first CNAA graduation was held, a step on the ladder to national standing in areas beyond teacher education. Demography in the form of the baby boomers and their successors contributed to a pool of students aspiring to Higher Education. What the College had to do was to develop courses that would attract these people in sufficient numbers to achieve 'critical mass'. For many staff the traditions of the College as a training institution were undermined by the rise of new areas, among which were Nursing, and later Business, Law and Sport. Other training institutions were forcibly closed, or chose closure rather than travelling on such a new trajectory.

This task of making a viable curriculum diversified from a mono-technic training college model was addressed in the 1980s and 1990s, and not without a good deal of pain, as staff changes

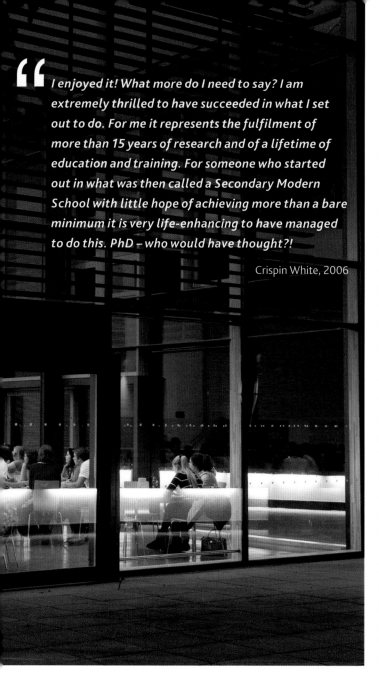

> *I enjoyed it! What more do I need to say? I am extremely thrilled to have succeeded in what I set out to do. For me it represents the fulfilment of more than 15 years of research and of a lifetime of education and training. For someone who started out in what was then called a Secondary Modern School with little hope of achieving more than a bare minimum it is very life-enhancing to have managed to do this. PhD – who would have thought?!*
>
> Crispin White, 2006

University Centre Food Hall.

Close links with successive Headmasters of Winchester College survived until the 1980s; although thereafter Headmasters continued to attend the Governing Body they were less prominent in decision making. Individual teachers at Winchester College, such as Kenneth Kettle, continued the link. Since the appointment of laymen as leaders at Winchester and King Alfred's colleges in the 1950s, and with the exponential growth in numbers and the changed mission of 'the College on the hill', links have slackened. The reversal of the gender balance from an entirely male to a largely female institution was also a divergence from the experience at Winchester College. The University is now more than ten times the size of Winchester College, and has a larger local footprint and employs more people in Winchester – although there any comparison of resources ends. In mission and curriculum as well, the colleges have diverged, with a diminution of focus on school education and training and the development of university courses, based not on Oxbridge but on the curricula of the new universities of the 1960s, initially with 'Main' and 'Associated' subject combined honours degrees, single honours courses coming later. The development of non-school subjects degrees, for example the recent Journalism and Modern Liberal Arts degrees, and development beyond teacher-training into additional 'vocational' subjects such as Business, Performing Arts and Law are other areas of divergence.

Despite all these changes, hopes and fears, continuity can be discerned not only in the buildings but also in the staff and the traditions. Values-driven Higher Education now underpins the institution. Anyone who has been a part of the College, now the University, on the hill will recall for the rest of their lives their experiences in and around that Gothic building with the panoramic views. The academic dress adopted by the university today incorporates elements of previous validating institutions, the London gown (Southampton), the Aberdeen-shaped hood (CNAA), but proudly bears colours drawn from the university's own history in drawing upon 'St Aidan purple' for the BA hood, a colour echoing the King Alfred's palette of former days. Undergraduates, graduates and postgraduates all go forth, whatever their academic discipline, on a life's mission to contribute to society, realising the University's mission: 'To educate, to advance knowledge and to serve the common good.'

were required and spaces were again needed to staff new areas of study. Fierce battles over these changes developed involving governors, staff and students. The 'modular' programme that enabled small departments to grow if they could recruit students, coupled with imaginative schemes for funding the extra student places in time, established a basis for the future. As well as increasing the breadth of the curriculum offered, the student base also grew exponentially at this time, from 1,000 in the mid-1980s to about 4,500 ten years on. Today there are over 7,000 students studying at Winchester. The University is often described as 'punching above its weight': one aspect of this is seen in the outcome of the 2008 Research Assessment Exercise, when 75 per cent of the material submitted by Winchester staff was judged to be of international standing (two- and three-star) and some was judged to be world-leading (four-star).

Appendix 1:
Principals, Vice-Chancellors, Bishops and Chairs of Governors

1841–6 Rev. David Waugh, Trinity College, Dublin, d. 1846.

1846–58 Rev. John Smith, Magdalen College, Oxford, retired 1858 to parish work, but retained interest in the College.

1859–79 Rev. Canon Charles Collier, MA Trinity College, Dublin, 1850 *ad eund* MA Oxon 1854. Ordained priest 1854. Curate of Kimberworth, Yorks., 1853–6, formerly second master of Sheffield Royal Free Grammar School, assistant curate at Sheffield parish church. Fellow of the Society of Antiquaries. Honorary Chaplain to St John's Hospital, Winchester, and to the Hampshire Volunteer Rifle Corps. Oversaw the creation of the new buildings on West Hill in 1862. Vicar of Andover, Hampshire, 1878–89, of Chilbolton 1889–90, where he died and is buried. Excavated a Roman villa at Itchen Abbas, 1878 with son Ernest. Published lectures on Wolvesey Palace and St Swithun.

1879–1912 Rev. Canon Henry Martin, St Edmund Hall, Oxford, BA 1872, MA 1876. Classical Master Elizabeth College, Guernsey, 1872–3. Deacon Winchester diocese 1873. Vice-Principal St Paul's Cheltenham 1873–8, Christ Church Cheltenham 1876–8. Honorary Canon of Winchester Cathedral 1898. Introduced sport and encouraged music. Raised the number of students significantly. Enthusiast for the alumni club, which he reformed also for the Volunteers. The longest-serving and a most highly regarded Principal.

1912–33 Rev. Canon Ernest George Wainwright, University of London 1893, Trinity College, Dublin, BA (Resp) 1899, MA 1902. Lichfield Theological College 1901. Assistant Chaplain and Lecturer St John's College, Battersea 1901–3. Diocesan Inspector in Chief of Religious Knowledge Lincoln Diocese 1905–12. Vice-Principal and Assistant Chaplain, DCT, Winchester 1903–5. Honorary Canon of Winchester Cathedral 1927. Chaplain of St Cross Chapel, Winchester 1933–6.

1933–46 Rev. Richard Clement White, Exeter College, Oxford, BA 1926 (Modern History), MA 1931. Elector of the University. Deacon 1927, Coventry and Lichfield Diocese in Warwickshire, before becoming a lecturer at St Luke's College, Exeter. Warden of Stephenson Hall and Lecturer, University of Sheffield and Examining Chaplain to Bishop of Sheffield, 1931–3, whence he was appointed to Winchester. Retired to parish work after the Second World War, Hardingstone 1946–51, Great with Little Packington, 1951–4.

1946–58 William Parker Dickinson, MA Corpus Christi College, Oxford. Headmaster of Ormskirk Grammar School before coming to King Alfred's as the first non-ordained Principal. Worked hard to re-establish the College after the war and to rebuild a collegiate ethos.

1958–67 John Arthur Stripe, MA Oriel College, Oxford after war service in the RAF was Deputy Principal St Luke's College, Exeter, Chevalier de l'Ordre des Palmes Académiques, coming to Winchester as Principal in 1959. Presided over significant expansion and the admission of women.

1967–84 Martial Rose, MA King's College, Cambridge, was a schoolmaster at Leyton County High School for Boys, then at Bretton Hall College of Education, Yorkshire, before coming to Winchester as Deputy Vice-Principal in 1965 and then following Stripe as Principal in 1967. An expert on medieval drama, his version of the Wakefield Mystery Cycle ran at the Mermaid Theatre in London in 1961 and 1963. He published *A History of King Alfred's College* in 1981, later updated to 1990. Presided over diversification from a mono-technic into new areas of study.

1984–92 John Abery Cranmer, Cert. Ed, MPhil (Southampton) followed his training at King Alfred's College into school teaching in Hampshire and then at colleges of education at Gloucester, at Sittingbourne and at Christ Church Canterbury, where he was Head of Education before returning to Winchester, where he was the only alumnus Principal in the College's history. In retirement he became a priest in the Winchester Diocese and Chairman of the Historic Churches Trust.

1992–2000 John Dickinson, MA Downing College, Cambridge, MSc and PhD (Leeds), taught in the universities of Lancaster, Western Australia and Dundee, was Professor of Accounting at Stirling before becoming a Professor and Dean of Business and Law at Glasgow whence he moved to Winchester. Declared the aim in 1995 that Winchester could be a university in 2005.

2000–6 Paul Light, MA St John's College, Cambridge, PhD (Cantab.), held a Chair in Education at the Open University then of Psychology at Southampton before becoming a Pro-Vice-Chancellor at Bournemouth prior to coming to Winchester as Principal in 2000, subsequently Principal of University College Winchester 2004, Vice-Chancellor University of Winchester 2005. Realised Dickinson's vision of University Title.

2006– Joy Carter, BSc (Dunelm), PhD (Lancaster), CGeol, FGS, a geochemist. She was formerly a Reader in Environmental Geochemistry and Health at the University of Reading, before moving to the University of Derby where she became Dean of Science. She was then Pro-Vice-Chancellor (Academic) at the University of Glamorgan before taking on the role of Vice-Chancellor at Winchester in 2006. She has held a number of national roles, including Chair of GuildHE, Chair of the University Vocational Awards Council and Chair of the Cathedrals Group of Universities. She became a Deputy Lieutenant of Hampshire in 2013.

BISHOPS OF WINCHESTER AND CHAIRS OF THE GOVERNING BODY

The lead in establishing the Diocesan Training School was taken by Bishop Sumner. Successive Bishops of Winchester followed Sumner and oversaw the Governing Body until Bishop Scott-Joynt on his appointment as Bishop of Winchester in 1995 declined to take the Chair, but remained a governor.

BISHOPS

Charles Richard Sumner 1827–69
Samuel Wilberforce 1869–73
Edward Harold Browne 1873–91
Anthony Wilson Thorold 1891–95
Randall Thomas Davidson 1895–1903
Herbert Edward Ryle 1903–11
Edward Stuart Talbot 1911–23
Frank Theodore Woods 1923–32
Cyril Forster Garbett 1932–42
Mervyn George Haigh 1942–52
Alwyn Terrell Petre Williams 1952–61
Sherard Falkner Allison 1961–74
John Vernon Taylor 1975–85
Colin Clement Walter James 1985–95

CHAIRS SINCE 1995

Canon Dennis Ernest Hale 1995–2001
Daniel Hodson 2001–6
Roger Witcomb 2006–11
Richard Wilkinson 2011–

Appendix 2:

Select Bibliography

PRIMARY SOURCES

The Hampshire Archives, Sussex Street, Winchester, records used include:

Hampshire Chronicle

The King Alfred's College/University of Winchester Archive

20M65/94/ I – VIII Winchester, Diocesan Training School (later named King Alfred's College and in June 2004 renamed University College, Winchester) Colour plans by Colson 1860

215M85/49 Volume, entitled 'Winchester Scraps' 18th–20th century

The National Archive (TNA), Public Record Office (PRO), Kew, records used include:

Home Office (HO) and Registrar General (RG) census records 1841–1911

War Office Records (WO): 1916 WO 98/8 Victoria Cross Citation, T. E. Adlam

University of Winchester documents

Principals' Annual Reports to the Governors, Various from 1948–1990 (PRGB). *Winchester Training College Club Report and Balance Sheet 1913–14 and College Year Book 1840–1914* (Winchester: Warren and Son Ltd)

Minutes of Governors, Academic Board meetings, etc.

EMS 2010/11, RJWEstate Management Statistics, Richard J. Webster (RJW)

SECONDARY SOURCES

Mark Allen and Tom Beaumont James, *The 1871 Census for Winchester* (Winchester: Wessex Historical Databases, 2006)

Alexander Anderson, *Hartleyana: Henry Robinson Hartley, eccentric scholar and naturalist* (Edinburgh: Scottish Academic Press; Southampton: University Press. Supplementary volume in the Southampton Records Series, 1987)

Albert E. Attwood, *In the Running* (Ilfracombe: Stockwell Ltd, 1977), with additional sheet at HRO 47M91W/Q4/6/1

Gloria Atkinson-Carter (ed), *In Being. The Winton Lectures 1979–2000* (Winchester: King Alfred's College, 2001)

Jennifer Bone, *Our Call to Fulfil. Westminster College and the Changing Face of Teacher Education 1951–2001* (Bristol: Westminster College Oxford Trust, 2003)

R. W. Breach, 'Winchester: the community on the eve of the General Strike 1926', *Proceedings of the Hampshire Field Club and Archaeological Society*, vol. 39 (1983), pp. 213–22

R. W. Breach, 'Winchester in 1926 – the Labour movement and the General Strike', *Proceedings of the Hampshire Field Club and Archaeological Society*, vol. 40 (1984), pp. 115–26

Asa Briggs, *Secret Days: Code-Breaking in Bletchley Park* (London: Frontline Books, 2011)

L. W. B. Brockliss (ed), *Magdalen College, Oxford. 1458–2008* (Oxford: Magdalen College)

http://www.cheshire.mmu.ac.uk/aboutus/history.php

http://www.culham.ac.uk/sg/remembered/lamb.php

Harold C. Dent, *The Training of Teachers in England and Wales 1800–1975* (London: Hodder & Stoughton, 1977)

Geoffrey D. C. Doherty, *A Case Study of the amalgamation of Crewe and Alsager Colleges of Education* (Crewe and Alsager College of Higher Education, 1981)

Clarissa Ellis, *The ATS in Winchester* (c.1982)

William Evans, *University of the West of England Bristol: a family history* (Bristol: Redcliffe Press, 2009)

Matthew Feldwick, 'Angels in the Chapel', booklet (2005)

Robin Freeman, *The Art and Architecture of Owen Browne Carter (1806–1859)* (Winchester: Hampshire Papers 1, 1991)

Derek Gillard, *Education In England: a brief history* (2011), http://www.educationengland.org.uk/history/index.html

Thomas Hardy, *Jude the Obscure* (London and Basingstoke: Macmillan, 1895, rp 1973)

Mark Hichens, *West Downs. A Portrait of an English Prep School* (Edinburgh, Cambridge, Durham: the Pentland Press, 1992)

Patricia Hooper, *The story of William Whiting and the Quiristers of Winchester College* (Southampton: Paul Cave Publications, 1978)

Andrea Jacobs and Camilla Leach, '"No Women please": Co-education and Expansion, Crisis and Change at King Alfred's College, Winchester, in the Mid-Twentieth Century' in eds. Michael Gohlich, Caroline Hopf and Daniel Trohler, *Persistence and Disappearance: Educational Organizations in their Historical Contexts*, VS Verlag für Sozialwissenschaften 2008

Andrea Jacobs and Camilla Leach, 'Teacher Training and the public good: the University of Winchester Alumni Project', *History of Education Journal* 40:2 2011, pp. 213–228

Tom Beaumont James, *Winchester: a Pictorial History* (Chichester and London: Phillimore, 1993)

Tom Beaumont James, *Winchester, from Prehistory to the Present* (Stroud: Tempus, 2007, rp 2010)

Tom James and Martin Doughty, *King Alfred's College: A Pictorial Record* (Stroud: Alan Sutton, 1991)

David Kent, *Popular Radicalism and the Swing Riots in Central Hampshire* (Hampshire Papers 11, 1997)

Alan Matterson, *Polytechnics and Colleges* (London and New York: Longman, 1981)

Gary McCulloch, 'Historical Insider Research in Education', *Researching Education from the Inside: Investigations from Within* ed. Pat Sikes and Anthony Potts (London: Routledge, 2008), pp. 51–63

Rebecca Oakes, 'Adolescent Mortality at Winchester College 1393–1540: new evidence for medieval mortality and methodological considerations for historical demography', *Local Population Studies*, 88 (Spring 2012)

Oxford Dictionary of National Biography (Society of Antiquaries)

Nikolaus Pevsner and David Lloyd, *The Buildings of England. Hampshire and the Isle of Wight* (Harmondsworth: Penguin, 1967)

A. Cecil Piper (ed), *Winchester War Service Register. A record of the service of Winchester men in the Great War 1914–1918* (Winchester, Warren and Son, 1921)

Brenda Poole, *John Colson: a Hampshire Architect of the Victorian Age* (Winchester: Hampshire Papers 20, 2000)

http://www.rae.ac.uk/1996/index.html

Martial Rose, *A History of King Alfred's College, Winchester 1840–1980* (Chichester and London: Phillimore, 1981)

Martial Rose, 'Wolvesey Palace 1847–1862: The Home of the Winchester Diocesan Training College', *The Hatcher Review*, vol. 3, no 24, Autumn 1987

Martial Rose, *1980–1990 King Alfred's College, Winchester: A Decade of Change* (Winchester: King Alfred's College, 1990)

Pat Sikes and Anthony Potts (eds), *Researching Education from the Inside: Investigations from Within* (London: Routledge, 2008), pp. 51–63.

Harold Silver, 'Higher Education and Social Change: Purpose in Pursuit?', *History of Education Journal* 36 (4–5), 2007, 537

Harold Silver, Things change but names remain the same: Higher Education Historiography 1975–2000', *History of Education Journal*, 35(1) (2006)

John Simons, 'R. C. Trench and the Development of English at King Alfred's College', *Winchester. History and Literature*. Ed. Simon Barker and Colin Haydon (Winchester: King Alfred's College, 1991), pp 90–107

Stephanie Spencer, Andrea Jacobs, Camilla Leach and Tom Beaumont James, *Alumni Voices: The Changing Experience of Higher Education* (Winchester: Winchester University Press, 2015)

Tim Tatton-Brown and John Crook, *Salisbury Cathedral: the Making of a Medieval Masterpiece* (London: Scala Publishers, 2009)

Brian Tippett, 'Diversifying the Colleges' in Trevor Brighton (ed), *150 Years: The Church Colleges in Higher Education* (Chichester: West Sussex Institute of Higher Education, 1989)

Brian Tippett, 'The in-between years: King Alfred's College in the 1980s and 1990s' (unpublished typescript, May 2011)

David Watson, 'Reinventing Liberal Higher Education: Profile of the University of Winchester' in David Watson, Robert M. Hollister, Susan E. Stroud and Elizabeth Babcock, *The Engaged University. International Perspectives on Civic Engagement* (London: Routledge, 2011)

R. G. Wing, *A Short History of King Alfred's College 1840–1949* (Portsmouth: A. G. Searle and Sons, Winchester Training College Club, c.1949)

The Wintonian, various dates

NB: Footnotes have been removed in the interest of design and space. A footnoted text has been deposited with the University.

Index

Acknowledgements

Martial Rose has provided a sure-footed account. Additional materials for the period since 1990 were collected in an unpublished memoir by Principal John Dickinson (1992–2000) and Principal and Vice-Chancellor Paul Light (2000–6), and these have been made available to the author. Other senior staff have contributed from their knowledge of developments from college to university both orally and in writing.

Beyond these management perspectives, much has been learnt from the testimony of former students and staff to be found in the Hampshire Archives and the University archives. Members of the Winton Club, especially Howard Horstead and John Hartley, who has researched those who lost their lives in the First World War, have been especially generous. Interviews given by former students and staff recorded and transcribed for the Alumni Project are dealt with in a separate book, compiled by Stephanie Spencer, Andrea Jacobs, Camilla Leach and Tom Beaumont James and entitled *Alumni Voices: The Changing Experience of Higher Education* (2015). Dr Jacobs has also kindly commented on the text and has contributed to the timeline found at the end of this work. Staff and former colleagues and students have shared their memories and have provided interviews, written accounts and images of their time at Winchester. I would especially like to thank Pro-Vice-Chancellor Martin Doughty (University of Worcester), my co-author of *King Alfred's College Winchester: A Pictorial Record* (1991); former Vice-Principal Tim Drey; former Deputy Vice-Chancellor Tommy Geddes, who has kindly read and commented on the latter sections; and former Dean Professor Brian Tippett. Many other current and former members of the College and University have made generous contributions. These have included Mark Allen, Ian Bailey, Chloe Battle, Jen Best, Ian Denness, Roy Faithful, Howard Horstead, Liz Larby (formerly Jones), Roger Lowman, Corinne Mackenzie, Philip Ray, Geoff Ridden, Edward Roberts, John Shannon, Richard Webster, current and former Library staff and many others who in diverse ways have contributed time and expertise to this project and have thereby cast much new light. Staff at the Hampshire Archives, especially Gill Rushton, have likewise readily provided assistance and saved me from errors, as has Suzanne Foster, Archivist at Winchester College.

The Jubilee Exhibition based on the Vice-Chancellor's idea to showcase the 'estate and outreach' was mounted at West Downs in June 2012. It was researched and mounted by Chris Higgins (formerly Director of Estates) and myself, with Tim Griffiths and the able assistance of Louise Fairbrother. It could not have taken place without the support of the University and Trish Kernan, the Link Gallery administrator.

The Directors and staff at Third Millennium have been models of support, enthusiasm, kindness and patience, especially Joel Burden in initiating work, Neil Titman, Matthew Wilson and Patrick Taylor. George Ramsay worked wonders on an unpromising winter day with his camera.

Picture Credits

We would like to thank all of those who supplied images for the book, in particular Chloe Battle who manages the University of Winchester Asset Bank and the Third Millennium photographer George Ramsay.

The copyright for the majority of images is held by the University of Winchester. We are especially grateful to Peter Jacobs who prepared most of the images found in Martial Rose's *A History of King Alfred's College 1840–1980* (1981); and also Tom James and Martin Doughty, *King Alfred's College Winchester: A Pictorial Record* (1991). For preparation of the images used in 'The University of Winchester: sixty years of development and community outreach. An exhibition to mark Her Majesty the Queen's Diamond Jubilee 1952–2012' and sponsored by the architects Design Engine of Winchester, who provided a selection of images from their own archive, we would like to thank Tim Griffiths, who has answered many queries, and also staff in the alumni and marketing offices of the University.

Other picture credits include (page and location: B – Bottom; C – Centre; L – Left; R – Right): 113T **Dick Attwood**; 65TL **Courtesy of the Auckland Castle Trust © Auckland Castle Trust**; 38, 42T **Author's collection**; 155BL, 160BL **Angus Beaton**; 99T, 102B, 104TR **Pat Brockway**; 86–7 **Harry Burden**; 26BL **University of Chichester** *MS no BO 004* **(Janet Carter)**; 41R **Frank Chippindale**; 51B **Chronicle/Alamy**; 115 **Crewe and Alsager College**; 52 **John Crook/Winchester Cathedral**; 2–3, 20TL, 20B, 42–3, 134L **Design Engine/Keith Collie**; 106BR, 107TR, 110T **Roy Faithful**; 100T **Farrows Creative LLP/Annie McKean**; 11B **© Fitzwilliam Museum Enterprises Ltd**; 132T **Christopher Gerrard**; 123B **Tim Griffiths/University of Winchester**; 32T, 72–3 **Chris Grover**; 94L, 140–1, 145B *Hampshire Chronicle*; 4, 9BR, 12BL, 25B, 28T, 29B, 39R, 40BL, 45TL, 49, 50T, 54–5, 58B, 59, 60, 64TL, 106T **Hampshire Record Office and Local Studies** (photography by Matthew Wilson); 41B, 47TL **Hampshire Record Office and Local Studies**; 146B **Mike Hart**; 74–5 **Reproduced by permission of Historic England**; 51T, 64TR, 84T, 89BR, 90B, 113B **Howard Horstead**; 109B **Jonathan Howell/Alamy**; 116 **Peter Jacobs/University of Winchester**; 87BR **Richard James**; 141BR **David Knight**; 8, 120, 120–1, 121 **Liz Larby**; 104–5, 118–9, 122B, 123T **Tony Lee**; 12TR **Jim Linwood**; 73R **Corinne Mackenzie**; 157T **Dave Mason**; 115B **Carol Miles**; 89L, 96B **Ministry of Education/University of Winchester Archive**; 9T, 33T **The National Archives**; 27L **© Courtesy of the Warden and Scholars of New College, Oxford/Bridgeman Images**; 80T **Clifford Nolloth**; 37TL **PA Images**; 7BR, 10T, 11TR, 12TL, 16TL, 16TR, 17T, 18BL, 24L, 24–5, 27R, 32–3B, 37R, 43T, 44, 44–5, 48B, 54, 57R & inset, 61T, 62, 81L, 105BR, 118L, 130B, 148T, 149T & R, 153BR, 159BR, 164B, 165 **George Ramsay**; 83R **Douglas Randlesome Collection**; 122TR **Geoff Ridden**; 32B **© Royal College of Music/ArenaPAL**; 107B, 108 **Martial Rose**; 162 **Salisbury Museum**; 111B **Jean Sawyerr/University of Winchester**; 28–9 **Martin Smith**; 159B **Alasdair Spark**; 153TL, 159T **Elizabeth Stuart**; 37B **Andrea Tallett**; 80B, 90T **D. Tatters/University of Winchester**; back cover TR & BL **Peter Thatcher**; 92–3 **Carole Thompson**; 130TR **Brian Tippett**; 129T **Ann Tramaseur**; 30T **UK City Images/Alamy**; 30R **courtesy of Wandsworth Heritage Service**; 29L, 31, 81BL & R, 86TL, 94BL, 144 **Winchester College Archives (by kind permission of Richard Shorter)**; 11TL, 104TL **Winchester City Council/Hampshire Cultural Trust**; 40–1 **Winchester Museum Service** (image 2642).

Every effort has been made to trace copyright holders and to credit pictures correctly. In the case of an error or inadvertent omission, please contact the publisher. We would also like to thank all those who sent in photos or memories that we were unable to include.